MISADVENTURES OF A TEENAGE GUNRUNNER

Joseph Johnson

Dedicated to D.A. White, whom we lost entirely too early. We miss you, buddy.

When this book first came into thought, the idea of it terrified me. I immediately pushed it from my mind, for several years. With much encouragement from my wife Denise as well as my children and friends, I decided to attempt it. It was a rocky start at best. Denise has lifted me up and gotten me started again more times than I can count. Many people, including her have made the statement that I was her "Knight in Shining Armor." It was actually the other way around. She and the kids saved me.

The people that have helped me along the way I owe a huge debt of gratitude towards. Including Tammy Adams, Celene Wilson, Jay Gold, Jeff Sheets and Sheryn Smith who is a writer and recognized just how inept I was and provided me with the knowledge to carry forward. James Horne, who saved my files and everything else more than once. Last but not least my cousin Hiram Smith.

To all of you, I thank you from the bottom of my heart.

I had never intended to be a writer, and still do not consider myself one. I am just a guy with a story to tell.

This book is based on some true events, however, parts have been fictionalized and all persons appearing in this work are fictitious. Any resemblance to real people, living or dead, is entirely coincidental.

CONTENTS

1

WANTED: DEAD OR ALIVE

Adrenalin surged through my body, followed by the fear that was building in side of me uncontrollably .My heart beat so rapidly I thought it would give me away, surely they will hear it, I thought. *This was not good!*

The three Sandinistas were less than 30 feet away, talking to the old woman who had fed me earlier that day. My conscious brain was trying hard to override my subconscious to keep me from puking up the food and warm goat milk. The "fight or flight" reflexes were kicking in with the fear coursing through my body.

I had given her a twenty dollar bill for the food earlier, (which she had left with and returned two and half hours later), and I let her keep the change of about seventeen dollars. Then and there, twenty dollars went a long way. Apparently it went far enough for her to risk her life for me. She had nothing to drink except goats milk from a pail that was covered by a piece of plywood, that had been sitting in the shade. It was horrible, but the only thing wet there was to be had. No water even close by that I was aware of. I could not understand how people lived this way, even though I did realize, they had no choice. It was survival. Period. Nothing else mattered much and I was beginning to understand this concept due to my present situation. In fact, I downright appreciated this whole survival concept!

The Sandinistas were looking for me. Well us, actually. They probably had no idea that we were separated. I was on my own.

The cold plastic of the H&K G3 assault rifle was wet from my sweat, or maybe it was tears? I don't really know now. The Sandinistas had their M-16s slung on their shoulders, giving me a little edge. Two were on the left of the old woman, one on the right. Could I get them all? I wasn't so sure. Would I hit the old woman? Did I care if I hit her? It would seem simple enough to shoot all three, before they could get me, but could I? Things like that work well in movies, but in reality, I had no damned idea. Pulling the trigger could mean me dying. Top of my list of things not to do today. Die! Screw that, dying sucked! *"DO NOT DIE!"* I thought. To this day, that thought crosses my mind on a fairly regular basis. All of these questions and a hundred more spun through my mind at once. I needed to answer the important ones. *"Be cool."* I told myself. Yeah, right! I was way out of my league and I knew it. This was a "Big Zero" as my pot head friend Brad would have said.

Lying on the cool dirt floor, I wondered how many times it had been swept, so many it was almost, well, it was almost clean. It felt clean. And cold. It had been swept so much the floor was probably five inches below the outside ground surrounding the little two room shanty. Pine and juniper branches stuck out of the ground and were being used to hold cardboard up against the limbs with bailing wire. Bread ties or anything else that would help form the walls up and provide protection from the elements had been used. I asked myself why these stupid details were running through my head, not really understanding the effects fear had on a person's mind at that time in my life. Too young to comprehend, but old enough to appreciate the fact I was in real trouble. The events that had led me here were a blur and muddled, it didn't matter anyway, I had to deal with this, this here, now. Besides my pistol, I had one, twenty round magazine lying next to my hand in the dirt, one in the gun, one on my belt. The one on my belt was mostly empty. I would not have time to reload anyway.....it would be over before I got that far, I was pretty sure of that.

2

A BOY NAMED SUE

I was born on the 5th of July. One day after Independence Day. People told my folks, they were lucky I wasn't a "firecracker" Mom always told them, "He's the aftermath. Lots of destruction."

My parents were hardworking country folks. Mom's dad had been a section gang foreman on the Southern Pacific railroad. She was raised in a house made of boxcars set off the railroad track.

Dad's family was Mormon and consisted of one brother and five sisters. He walked four miles to school, and since Grandpa owned a .22 rifle, my Dad did the hunting for seven families with it, during The Great Depression.

Dad grew up tough. He was 5'9" tall and 225 pounds. Most of it was in his shoulders and arms. He never lifted weights that I knew of, but he was what we called "country tough."

He dropped out of high school at 15, lied about his age and hired out as a truck driver, hauling coal and dynamite at a local mine. At that time a diploma wasn't really needed. He could read and write very well but making a living was just more important.

Mom and Dad first had two girls, then my brother. They figured that was enough so Dad had what he called a "Vee sectomy." Ten years later I came along. Mom denied anything, and Dad went into town and started whipping some asses looking for answers. The ass whippings were dished out but no answers came forth.

While in court on the fighting charges, Dad was ordered by the Judge to go see a Doctor. The Doctor informed Dad that his "Vee sectomy" had grown back together and he would give Dad another one, this one on the house, if Dad promised not to whip his ass.

I didn't find out about this until I was well into my thirties. I thank my Aunt for the story.

Mom had a name picked out for me. Two syllables, one word, no middle name. The Doctor told her she had to have a middle name for the birth certificate. She said fine, put down Joseph Kerry.

My oldest sister, who I have thanked for this, more than once, figured that was just too much. She intervened and relayed the instructions as Joseph Calvin. It didn't matter anyway, but it was something. I would be called by what my Mother wanted me to be called until I was an adult.

My name is Josey. I am proud of it. But I've taken a lot of shit over it. I whole heartedly identified with the song "A boy named Sue."

I was wild as a West Texas wind, twice as loud and left handed to boot. Just like my Dad. I remember Dad telling me a teacher smacked him with a ruler one time for writing left handed. Dad stood up, took the ruler and broke it in two. No attempts were ever made to make him use his right hand again.

I distinctly remember hearing someone talking about me mention "The right hand of the Lord, and the left of the devil." I didn't like that, it seemed judgmental to me. What the hell did they know about me anyway?

One thing is for certain though; I did have a mean streak in me. I think it was brought on by my environment, but who knows? Mean streak or not, I can honestly say, throughout my life, I've always known what was right and what was wrong. I may not have always chosen the right course when I came to those forks in the road of life, but I knew the difference when I made my choices, even if I didn't know the outcome. I feel fortunate to know that. I was probably an adult before I realized some people really don't know the difference between right and wrong.

Every bad choice I've made, I can honestly say, I did it for pretty much one reason and one reason only. Fun.

I thought for quite awhile in my life, that lots of people had backgrounds like I did. I just started opening up the secret parts, the parts of your life that a lot of people don't talk about, but that a lot of us have.

Boy was I mistaken. I would tell a story from my childhood or "other activities" and people would laugh and say "Man, you should write a book."

I heard that for fifteen years, and then one day I thought why the hell not? Worst that could happen is I land a prison sentence or take a bullet. Both are pretty damned bad in my book, (no pun intended) so I kept putting it off. I finally decided to change some names, (to protect the innocent) and change a few facts to keep my butt out of jail.

Most of these stories are mine. One from my teen years, was a great story that had to be told. I thank my old Sergeant ("Body Count") Dave for it. A couple from my preteen years are borrowed from my brother but assigned to me for lack of embarrassment within the family. After all, they already know I'm a fuck up. If Mom and Dad were still alive, I probably wouldn't even write it. Then again, I might be surprised at what they did know. Parents are like that sometimes.

As a kid I was full of questions, about anything and everything. Up at daylight, and at full throttle, that's how I liked to live. I could talk a dog off a meat wagon.

Mom asked me one time, when I was about eight years old, why I was, the way I was. I don't remember what I told her, but I do know what I thought at the time and pretty much how I feel now.

I've always felt that life was a gift, a gift to be enjoyed. As far as I know, we only have one life on this earth. It truly is a gift. Live it. Experience it. Love it. Ride it. Enjoy it. Revel in it. Even the bad.

Growing up I wanted to be an astronaut, a cowboy, fighter pilot, soldier, fireman, cop, cycle jumper (Evel Knievel was *my* childhood hero, and I really didn't give a damn who yours was) or anything else that was fun or exciting. Dad discouraged me from truck driving. He always told me, "It's a good job, but I don't think you'd like it."

Dad's wisdom still amazes me to this day. He's been gone for over nine years now, and I try hard to think back to things he told me. I wished I could have his guidance again. The older I got, the smarter Dad got.

My eyes sucked. I had a lazy eye and to top it off I couldn't see shit either. I didn't know my vision was bad. I just knew I had a hard time seeing things until they were pointed out to me. Scratch the fighter pilot/astronaut career. The weird thing was, when it came to guns, if I could see it, I could hit it!

I set out early to have a fun, exciting life. I had to hurry to try and get it all in; you never know when it might end. It was time to get started, while I still could.

I mean, what if you planned for something half your life and then something else happened to prevent it? I didn't want to plan, plan and plan. I needed to hurry in case I ran out of time.

After all, no sense taking any chances.

3

THE FIRE

I don't remember the fire that burned my Mother & me very well. I suppose God has a way of taking care of small children and keeping them from being mentally scarred. The way it happened (or so I was told later) was my Dad had been filling up our pickup with propane from a propane trailer, on our farm. The pop off valve, which is supposed to push air out of the propane tank until full, releases propane into the atmosphere when the tank is full, which it did. Dad climbed up onto the trailer tank to shut it off. The wind was blowing that day and as our camper filled with propane fumes from the campers tank, it swirled around, blew into the driver's side open window and hit an ignition point. I was sitting in the middle of the seat, my Mom next to me on the passenger side. We were engulfed in flame.

My memories of the hospital are few and bittersweet. One powerful memory is of my Dad rocking me in a rocking chair, on more than one occasion, and one I treasure. Another was of the nurse who "changed my feet." She was the only one who had the stomach to unwrap the bandages from my feet and to peel away the dead skin from a child screaming in pain, only to wrap them back up to prevent infection and do it again the next day. I would dream about this for years, but as dreams and bad memories can go, I remember it as her taking my feet off and putting them back on. She would never look me in the eye. To this woman, I feel I owe a debt that can never be repaid. No one else apparently had the guts to do this. I think this was the basis for a very important life lesson as I grew up.

You do some things because you have too, not for yourself.

My older brother (Colter) by ten years, has told me stories of his friends and him racing me up and down the hospital hallways in a wheelchair, and of the Christmas that I spent there. The small town we lived in of 3500 people, was located a few miles north of the Mexican border had pulled out all the stops for the little boy that wasn't expected to make it. They had set up a tree in the lobby with all my presents, which were quite a few. I got two pedal tractors and one pedal car that I remember! Colter said I just sat in my wheelchair and looked at the presents and Christmas tree set up in the hospital lobby, just for me. I don't remember it and apparently I could not have cared less. He pushed me over to the window so I could see out front and it was snowing, a rare occasion for the high desert we lived in, a White Christmas. Old Doc Baker (who really wasn't an M.D. and was responsible for bringing me into this world and saving my ass thus far) walked over and for the first time, since the fire, saw me smile, and told my brother "He's going to make it." For whatever reason, in my two year old mind, life was good again, and worth living.

Ol Doc was quite a scoundrel himself, as I found out later. Maybe all this exposure to these people when I was young had something to do with the way I turned out. Doc, who was a great Doctor by the townspeople standards and expectations, had a nurse that worked for him for years. She was ugly enough to haunt houses but apparently she must have been pretty good in the sack and was not being satisfied at home. So Doc, told the nurse to send her husband in and he would help him out.

Doc put him on Saltpeter. For those of you that are not familiar with Saltpeter effects, it will kill the libido of a 16 year old going through puberty. Erections are next to impossible. Doc wound up with the nurse and they stayed together to their deaths.

After Doc had gotten our own hospital, he brought in two more Doctors to help with the work load and they found out our Doc was not an MD. They didn't like the fact that he was running a hospital, delivering babies, performing surgeries, saving burned little boys, etc. and raised hell.

We ran them out of town. We kept Doc Baker.

The scars were bad, my Mom and I both had the top of one ear melted over. I was burned from the waist up and from the knees down. Saved the important parts! Thank God! Most times when I met people, they always asked what happened to me because the scars were that prominent.

The town's people and my family felt so sorry for me that I was spoiled rotten. If I wanted it, I got it. Period. My first horse was given to me at five years old, as well as my first BB gun, but I had to wait until seven for my .22. That was rough! I felt I was ready before that but no one agreed! The horse I had until I was about 15 and I am pretty sure its sole purpose of existence was to kill me and finish off what the fire did not. I still don't care for horses. They have always been more trouble, grief and pain than they ever seemed worth in my observation. I think the Indians had it right, ride'em, then eat'em.

I had also been taking cussing lessons from Colter and his friends but they were not apt to coach me, they just said I could say whatever I wanted. Which always brought a great laugh. My Mother while very much a lady was prone to speak her mind also. A family friend told me a story many years later of his wife, himself and my Mom, witnessing me watch a spider climb up the side of a pickup, (I was not aware of anyone else around.) the spider was not going fast enough for me, so I decided to encourage it.

"Hurry up, you fuckin asshole dick, sonofabitch."

My mother was aghast, she said "I wonder where he learned to talk like that?" Meanwhile the couple the couple were trying hard not to laugh.

The neighbor replied "Yeah, I wonder."

My use of profanity may not have been clear and concise at that age but it was there and it was to be used! Made me feel older. All little boys want to be like their older brother, I was no different.

I was wearing cowboy boots by the time I was three. Mom had to have them made for me. I wouldn't wear anything else and didn't until I was in junior high school where I had to have tennis shoes for gym class. Mom had the first pair bronzed and made into bookends when I outgrew them. I still have them.

Around 4 or 5 years of age, my brother and his cowboy buddies, were at our house one day, and I distinctly remember a conversation they were having about me, as if I weren't there. It went something to the effect of:

"He sure is little for his age." Red said.

"Yeah, he'll be a runt, got his growth stunted." Ben or Zeb, (I can't remember which, and neither one of them will take credit, therefore they can both be blamed) "Ya know, my Dad saved a runt out of a litter one time just to see if he could, that little fucker was mean! He had too be to survive against them bigger dogs."

Colter said "Yeah, but Mom and Dad spoil him too much, they won't toughen him up."

Silence.

This was not good; something told me, that my little ass should be moving on.

Red said it first. "Guess it's up to us to toughen him up."

They all agreed, and the beatings, ropings, and wrestling matches, started from that day on. I was never allowed to win, if I got a good lick in on one of them, it was only because they were drunk or I had pretended to give up and when they least expected it, let fly with a boot or fist to their nose. This always brought on a flourish of beatings but the blood I drew was like a badge of honor to me. True to their word, they tried their damndest to "toughen me up."

The ropings were the most brutal. If Colter & Zeb had ropes in their hands and started shaking out loops, it was time to run. On some prearranged agreement one of them was the "header" and one was the "heeler." If the header got me first the heeler would then pull my feet from underneath me and drop me on my ass. But if the header missed and the heeler got me, it dropped me on my head. I learned quickly to run for grassy areas. Cement hurt. One day, I simply decided not to run. This not "playing along" by yours truly was not appreciated by the high school ropers, but what the hell; they wouldn't dare hit me with a cattle prod, would they? They didn't, I was hit with the rope which hurt like hell and I bolted, the header missed.......sometimes your lot in life must be accepted. Lessons can be learned and plans of revenge can be made though!

The "calf roping" practice was somewhat more fun for me. One and only one would rope me and throw me down and using a pigging string would tie both my hands and one foot. When calves are roped they tie both hind legs and one front. They went in reverse order for me because I had learned to strike out quickly with any free hand. They all agreed that I was much harder to throw and tie than any calf, which made the actual calf roping easier. While it still wasn't great fun for me, it did allow me to get in the occasional blow and draw blood from my antagonists. Another lesson. Sometimes victories have to be taken in small doses....

At six or seven years old, I was quite a handful and could drive anybody crazy, I constantly asked questions and talked about anything and everything. Today I suppose they would have put me on Ritalin or some such shit, but back then, they just told you to shut up or get your ass kicked.

Around this time I also started drinking, I loved beer!! Coors beer to be exact. Usually, only because I was thirsty and too busy to actually stop long enough for a drink, I would just grab a quick gulp of someone's beer. It was always cold and much less hassle than getting something to drink myself. I also learned that if I drank out of the same beer too much, I drew attention, not the kind I wanted though. If someone set their beer down...well that was different. I could usually wipe out half the can and they would not notice. When they finished it, I was usually sent to fetch them another one and like a good little boy, I opened it for them. The first swig out of the can was the best anyway. Brother and friends also thought that when the parents were not around it was pretty fun to get the little foul mouthed kid drunk. But not too drunk. This soon became a negotiable tool for them and me. If they wanted something done, I did it. For a beer. Later on about the ripe old age of 12 and spending the summers with my brother, (who had moved out by then), it was Coke & Whiskeys in exchange for doing dishes or vacuuming etc. If they wanted me to keep my mouth shut about something they had done, I was paid in booze. If they wanted me to do something outrageous, like walk up to a good looking girl and grab her ass, I was also paid in booze. They had the system down. They picked the girl and pointed her out to me, I quickly got her attention in some outrageous way. They "rescued" her from the evil little brother and usually wound up fucking her and a friend, now that they had met. And I went and had my beer. It worked fairly well for all. There was the occasional unseen boyfriend or brother of the intended target that would want to whip my little rude ass, but this usually worked in our favor too, simply because the girl couldn't get too mad at the little boy who obviously had no manners but such great taste in women

Mom and Dad needed a break, especially after one two week period that I set two fires, (they were accidents, but one was in the house) and I got my ass whipped for accidentally hitting the neighbor girl with a BB gun. She lied, I didn't hit her, but it was fired in the general direction of our horses. That alone was reason enough to get a whuppin, and lose the BB gun for a while. I was pissed! I told my Mom I was going to run away. This didn't go over anything like I thought it should. Mom packed my suitcase so quick it made my head spin and I was saying my goodbyes. Only place I could get too was next door. This also happened to be the house of the little girl that I had "shot." They wouldn't take me!

I had to go back home and tell Mom I was sorry.

The fires I blame on Colter, I had been given an electric train that ran around in a circle, and one day Colter showed me that by putting a little drop of oil in the smoke stack it would smoke, just like a real train. This was neat!

I was an apt pupil when it came to anything my brother and his friends did. Hadn't I watched them take a firecracker and snap it half and light it? They called it a "fusee," I think.

If I took a fire cracker and broke it in two, poured it down the smokestack of my train and then squirted the oil in it, I would get a lot of smoke, wouldn't I? The train set was in the living room and after acquiring all the items needed, put my plan into action. It didn't work. I went to get Mom, because she could help me get it to work right. When we returned the carpet was on fire! Mom sprinted for the kitchen! I was shocked. No one had told me Mom could run. This was simply fucking amazing! As Mom ran back and forth from the sink to the fire, I shouted out orders and questions. "CALL THE FIRE DEPARTMENT! MOM, DON'T RUN, YOU'LL HURT YOURSELF! MOM DID YOU HANG UP ON GRANDMA?" "DO YOU WANT

ME TO CALL HER BACK?" "DID YOU USED TO RUN WHEN YOU WERE A LITTLE GIRL, MOM?" The train set disappeared, I didn't care. It was kind of a pain in the ass anyway

The second fire was Colter's fault too, as far as I was concerned. Colter and his friends had taken too shooting ping pong balls out of a tube using lighter fluid. I asked Colter for the ping pong balls. He had to know what I wanted them for. He did, and made me promise not to try and shoot them like him and Red did. I agreed, but it was ok as long as I didn't get caught right? I mean, he gave them to me, so it was ok. He had to know I was going to try it. I just couldn't get caught, or if I did, leave his name out of it. This was standard operating procedure. I found a tube in the yard, lighter fluid, and had to sneak the matches. The matches didn't work too well, and I ran out of them before I could get a launch, maybe the tube was too big. So I went to get Mom, to help me. When we came back outside, the grass in the ditch next to our house was on fire.

What the hell was this all about? Every time I left my fire making equipment alone for just a little bit, it worked!

I got to see Mom run again; she was always a lean woman and could really pick them up and lay them down. Her speed surprised me. The water hose got the fire out.

Yes, Mom and Dad definitely needed a break.

It came in the form of my brothers and two sisters. As soon as they realized that they were going to have to help care for the fucking little monster I had become, they went to plan "b." The oldest sister simply got married and moved out, the younger one was too young to move out, so she got pregnant, then got married and moved out. This left my older brother. Perfect! I liked hanging out with him anyway!

On weekends, the conversation would start with my brother being told by my folks that they "had plans" and that he would be watching me. He would throw a fit, "Mom, I've got a date tonight."

"Fine, take him with you." Mom would say. Or he would be going out of town to a rodeo or dance. Mom simply told him, "Take your little brother, he'll keep you from getting into trouble." This just meant negotiation time! I loved dances, rodeos too. There were always beer and fights at dances and rodeos, and I liked both. Life didn't get much better.

Dad was driving a truck for a living and a good living at that, and was usually only gone eight hours a day, Mom was a CPA and kept a garden, as well as the farm my Dad ran and worked on the side with my brother's help. Food was never in short supply.

I had to confirm this later in life, after I had a couple of incidents of attacking people that reached for food on my plate. All family members agreed that nothing had been done to me that would have provoked me going after someone over a French fry. I was thrown out of school for three days in junior high for smashing a tray across a kid's head that reached for a French fry. A co-worker reaching for a shrimp resulted in me blacking out and then coming to the realization that my hands were on his throat as he was passing out while pinned against the wall. I also attempted to stab my fiancé in the hand with a fork, after I was done eating. The bad thing about these occurrences is that I do not remember them very well. It was weird.

After one of the above mentioned incidents, I asked all my siblings what they had done to me that caused this reaction in me. Both sisters denied anything. Colter said;

"The rude sunsabitches, shouldn't reach for *your* food."

THAT'S WHAT I TOLD'EM! I'm still suspicious though, they did something.

Ben and Zeb's parents both had ranches outside of town, and I think Red's grandparents did too.

Ben was raised on his parent's ranch. He was a good cowboy. Lean, and baby faced, every bit the gentleman. The ladies loved him. Ben was a good bronc rider.

Zeb stood tall and rangy. He didn't talk much, and when he did he was somewhat quiet. He was smart, even as a teenager. He grew up on his Dad's ranch, and he grew up tough.

Red, on the other hand, was loud, obnoxious, and loved to fight. At a little under six foot tall, Red packed a lot of muscle. He too had grown up cowboying. Rodeoing and drinking was more his style. The drunker he got the more fights he seemed to start, but it was always Colter that seemed to have to bail him out. When the movie Cowboy Way came out with Kiefer Sutherland and Woody Harrelson cast as Sonny & Pepper, we all laughed at the similarities between Red and Colter.

Colter was the bull rider of the bunch as I recall but all of them probably did it at one time or another.

Spring was always spent rounding up cattle and spending time on the back of the evil death horse, as it came up with new ways to maim and destroy me. I really wished they would have just given the fucking horse to Paco, our wetback. He could work more than me anyway. But I wanted to be a cowboy, like everyone else in my family. Hell, I could already shoot pretty good, (just ask me.) My Mom was always telling me to "Watch the sights, *squeeze* the trigger" no matter if I had a toy gun or a BB gun. Seems like I couldn't pick up anything that resembled a gun without being told that by someone. "Ok, ok, I got it already." I felt like saying.

I really liked this whole hats, spurs, early morning breakfasts, branding cattle thing. I loved branding because when we untied the calves I would straddle them and practice my "bull riding," staying on the calf as long as I could until being dumped in the dirt. This would always get a laugh, then it was back to work, no crying allowed. I was well on my way to being a cowboy, except for those fucking horses. I hated horses. Too tall, too unpredictable and I couldn't get on them by myself. They bucked when you didn't want them too and bit and kicked if you weren't paying attention and sometimes did all that crap if you were paying attention. There was one other little thing that bothered me too. Deep down inside, I wondered if I was tough enough to be a cowboy. Colter and his friends worked *hard*. I didn't look at the fact that I was ten years younger, all I knew is I couldn't throw a bale of hay, and I ran out of steam long before they did. I was also highly allergic to alfalfa. Every damn time I went to a barn, I got sick! What kind of cowboy was that? John Wayne never got a snotty nose and runny eyes. In the meantime, life carried on, and I kept trying to "cowboy up." Other plans had to be made though. I just wasn't sure what I should do with my life. I figured at five or six years old though, I might have a *little* time to figure it out. Maybe that was if a damned horse didn't kick my skull in or buck me off on top of a rattlesnake.

I also got my first girlfriend while in the 1st grade. She asked me to be her boyfriend.

"Sure." I told her. I had no damned idea that made it ok for her to kiss me in the coat room at school. I ran this by Colter and Zeb, so I could see what else was expected of me. They had a good laugh about it and told me a few weird things that I didn't quite understand. Like why the hell would I try and put my tongue in her mouth? A couple days later, before I had the chance to try the tongue thing, she broke up with me. It didn't matter to me. I was running late for recess.

Sometime after this it was back to the ranch for work that needed to be done. The evil death horse had been out at Zeb's parents place and needed to be ridden anyway. Freaking yay. I could hardly wait. We left one weekend night, and packed plenty of beer and ice in the rope cans. One rope can could hold all our ropes. No sense letting the others go to waste. Colter and Zeb may have been old enough to drink by then, as the legal age was eighteen. Drinking and driving was still illegal though, but tolerated much more than now. Driving down the highway, I was quiet. When I was quiet, it scared people. I didn't know that, back then. I had seen the cattle prod in the back of the truck, (We called them Hotshots) and was somewhat worried about retribution from any previous incident. I had never been hit with a Hotshot, but if it could make a 400 pound calf bawl, I didn't want to know what it could do to me. Ring of Fire was playing on the radio, I knew all about fire.

Colter asked Zeb if he was ready for a beer. Zeb said "Yep."

"How about you, you mean little fucker, you want a beer too?" Colter asked me with a grin.

"Sure." I replied. I climbed over Zeb's lap, and out the window at 65 miles per hour, with Zeb half ass hanging onto me until I safely made the pickup bed. I fetched out 3 beers and handed them to Zeb and climbed back in the open window of the truck. I had done this so many times for them, it was hardly even exciting anymore. It saved time, I was told. Apparently any previous incident was forgotten, at least temporarily, which was fine by me. I kept an eye, throughout the weekend on the location of that Hotshot though. No sense taking any chances.

At the ranch, the next day, Zeb's Mom, (whom I adored) Martha, got us up bright and early and fed us fresh eggs, homemade biscuits, and steak.

Martha, at one time had been a nurse in a nearby town. Silver City, I believe. This put her in charge of all things medical. Animals to humans. If you needed stitched up, Martha did it. If you got a fever, Martha nursed you. Vets and Doctors were saved for more serious things. Like life and death.

Zeb's Dad, as far as I know, was a rancher all his life. The ranch he had inherited which was quite large, had actually been divided four ways amongst his brothers and sisters. This meant there was always work to be done somewhere. With his knowledge of the country and a strapping young son in Zeb, who ran with a first rate cowboy like Colter, there was plenty to do.

After breakfast and getting saddled up, we were on our way under the New Mexico sun. This had been the border land of the Mescalero and Chiricahua Apache. Before that it was the land of the Anasazi. Evidence was abundant of their passing and of their lifestyle. If you looked.

My grandfather, on my Dad' side, had fed a renegade Indian, called The Apache Kid, who had refused to go to a reservation, less than 30 miles from here. This was the land of Geronimo, Mangus Colorado, Cochise, Billy the Kid. At six years old, I was already aware of these facts. I loved my home. I was proud of it. I was part of it, and it was part of me.

My horse apparently felt like running and decided to bolt with me on his back that day. It galloped across the flats, heading towards the canyon I knew to be ahead, I screamed at the top of my lungs and held onto the saddle horn for dear life. I do remember thinking it was a pretty smooth ride compared to when he trotted, but still, this was too damned fast. I swear in the middle of the run, I saw a snake too! Zeb yelled at me. "Quit fucking around, you'll wear that horse out!"

Colter pitched in too, "Ride that sumbitch!"

When I finally got the evil death horse slowed down, I was ready to go back to the ranch house. Zeb & Colter wouldn't let me. I was glad I didn't, when later in the day I saw Colter and Zeb get about as excited as I had ever seen either one of them.

Colter was pushing about a dozen cows and calves along a ridge and a couple strayed out and topped over the ridge. Colter told me to go get them. I had been sticking pretty close since the evil death horse might start fucking up again and I would need some help. I topped over the ridge and got on the outside of the cattle and started to push them back. One of the ranch dogs started barking from where Colter was, just on the other side of the ridge. The evil death horse's ears perked up and the cattle stopped and stared. Something was up.

The next thing I saw was a coyote come barreling over the ridge. Colter was right behind it, his horse on a dead run and Colter was swinging a loop! He was going to try and rope the coyote! Colter's loop settled on the coyote's neck and shit started happening fast! The coyote, who did not want to be roped and could not continue east with a rope around his neck, turned west and went back up the rope! Colter's horse didn't care much for that and decided a wild vicious animal coming at him was plenty of reason to retreat. Colter screamed at me. "HEEL'EM, DAMMIT HEEL'EM!"

I looked around quickly. Surely he wasn't talking to me! I had been practicing roping for a couple of years, but I had never actually roped off a horse. Hell, the only reason I carried mine on the horse was because everyone else did, and I sure as hell wasn't going to try my first time off the evil death horse on a snarling, pissed off coyote. Was Colter, fucking crazy? He was on his own, as far as I was concerned. I wondered if the coyote got Colter if I could have his room. The coyote was halfway up the rope now. This was not going to be good.

I yelled back, "LET'EM GO COLTER! LET'EM GO!"

By this time, Colter was out of options. The ranch dog that had been with us, and barking at the coyote was now joined by the two hounds that had been with Zeb, as he came riding over the hill to see what all the ruckus was about. Zeb took in the scene, in an instant, and also looked pretty excited. His best friend had roped a coyote! This was something! Now that all three of the cow dogs were together, they tore into the coyote, with Colter, still trying to keep the slack out of the rope.

I yelled at Zeb. "HEEL'EM ZEB, HEEL'EM!"

It seemed liked good advice, after all, hadn't Colter just told me to do the same thing? Zeb actually shook out a loop and attempted to heel it, but the dogs were in a big ass melee of dust, hair, and teeth. About the second or third attempt, Zeb got a loop on the coyote's hind legs, and as

Zeb and Colter stretched out the coyote between them, the dogs finished off the coyote who was pretty much all done in, anyhow.

Colter, Zeb and I were all yelling at each other.

Zeb says to Colter, "Are you fucking nuts?"

"Did you see that shit? Fucking wow!" I exclaimed.

"Why the hell didn't you heel him, when I told you too?"

"What? Are you fucking crazy? Why did you rope him anyway? You gonna brand him?" I asked.

By now, the three of us were laughing so hard, we had the giggles. The adrenalin dump from the excitement had no place to vent and as we recounted the incident to each other from our own perspectives, over and over, it started to subside. There was still work to be done, but now we had something else to think about.

Later on at the ranch house I barreled into the door at top speed and announced to Zeb's Mom, Dad and sister about the boys roping a coyote. Zeb's Mom gave the boys a proper ass chewing for being foolhardy and exposing me to extreme danger.

Zeb's Dad, whose name was Ralph, laughed and said we were lucky, we didn't get handed our asses by that coyote. Which was true.

That night there was a dance somewhere, and me, Zeb and Colter, were going. I couldn't wait.

After getting cleaned up, and putting on cologne, (no actual need to shave at six) and my best clothes, we were all ready and climbed into Colter's pick up and away we went. Roger Miller sang "Chug a lug chug a lug" on the eight track.

Zeb's Mom was a good Baptist and after hearing the usual admonishments and warnings from Zeb and Colter, about not mentioning any drinking, a bottle of whiskey was pulled from behind the seat, and I was given a can of Coke with some whiskey poured into it. They were stingy with the whiskey, so I watched carefully to see where it was stashed. I would have to hit it later on my own. Colter asked me if I wanted a chew. Of course I did! I took the Copenhagen and after sticking a little in my lip and being called a pussy, by both of them, for taking so little, I sat back to enjoy the dizzy sensation I knew the snuff would bring on. It always made me dizzy. I asked what a pussy really was. This drew a good laugh, and no clear answer that I remember. This was filed for future reference, so I could in fact find out what the hell it meant. It wasn't the first time I had heard it. I just didn't know what it could possibly mean.

The dance was fun. I got in one fight with a kid a little older than me, and held my own pretty well. I asked Colter for the keys to the truck so I could go lay down. Colter chewed me out for getting my clothes dirty and asked if I had started the fight. Of course not. I never started anything. I really don't know why he even asked.

Colter gave me the keys and I made my way to the pickup. I got a Coke and dumped out half, and filled it back up from the whiskey bottle. After a few minutes I took Colter his keys back and told him I wasn't tired anymore. I went and found my new friend, (the guy I had gotten in the fight with) and shared my Coke & Whiskey with him. The band had started playing the bunny hop which was always the last song, and we loaded up to head back to the ranch.

Driving down the two lane, Zeb asked me if I got any pussy. This drew a laugh, and as I started to ask what pussy was, Colter said "Snake!"

Sure enough, a big rattler was stretched out on the highway. Zeb produced a .22 pistol that I had never seen before and he and Colter took turns shooting at the snake. I had never seen them shoot a pistol, and had also never seen either one of them miss so much! Both of them were excellent shots, and were always teaching me to shoot. It had always been with rifles though. I couldn't see how this made any difference. I had actually fired Dad's .38 pistol once before and informed Zeb and Colter of this and the fact that I already knew to *squeeze the trigger*. After informing them a couple dozen more times that I could shoot it, Zeb told Colter, "Hell let him try."

I took the pistol and shot the snake in the middle of its body. The snake was rattling like all get out and flopping around on the pavement. Colter took the gun away from me with a dirty look and Zeb finished it off with a shovel. I pulled out a pocket knife and Colter cut the rattles off for me and we were back on our way. We hadn't even got back up to speed when Zeb said, "There's another one."

We stopped again and I had already asked to shoot it at least five times before we even got out. A shovel was produced and this one was killed also. Why didn't they use the gun? I asked this after getting the rattles from this one and climbing back in the truck. I don't remember what they told me, but I'm sure it was bullshit. Barely two miles went by and another snake was seen. It was one of those New Mexico nights that the snakes were out and on the pavement.

This one was a bull snake and after picking it up and moving it off the road so it wouldn't get hit, we were on our way home again. If I remember right we killed five rattlesnakes that night before turning off the pavement for the ranch.

The next morning I was up bright and early, as soon as I heard Zeb's Mom starting breakfast. Colter and Zeb were out cold. Dressing quickly, I hurried out into the kitchen. Ralph was drinking coffee as Martha went about the daily chores.

"We killed five snakes last night on the way home." I told them. They listened, and then Ralph explained to me that sometimes the highway was warmer and that snakes would be on it, just like when they would sun themselves on a rock.

Zeb's Mom asked me if I had a good time at the dance.

"Yep, had a blast, got in a fight though, but its ok, he's a friend now." I informed her.

"Were the boys drinking?" she asked.

Time to switch gears. Lying wasn't right.

As Ralph started to sip his coffee I looked at Martha and replied,

"What's a pussy?"

Ralph choked on his coffee, and quickly wiped a smile off his face. Martha turned *real* red. Uh oh, I may have messed up. She looked pissed.

"Where did you hear that word?" she asked with anger just dripping from her voice. "Did you hear that from Zeb and Colter? Answer me!"

"Well yeah, that's what they called me, but I'm not mad about it, I just didn't know what it means, is all, I don't want to get them into trouble, I don't mind, Martha." I quietly replied.

Ralph suddenly thought of something he needed to do and left the kitchen. I was being left to the She Wolf, and I knew it.

"Go get the boys up." she ordered,

"Uh, they're still asleep." I informed her, as if this were new information to her.

"Get them up, *now!*" Martha ordered.

I knew they would be furious for me waking them up, and didn't want to do it. Maybe I could still get out of this.

"Uh, ok, but what is a pussy? Is it bad?"

I was scared, not realizing this was probably one of the stupidest questions I had asked thus far, this morning, and that was saying a lot!

Martha stormed past me into Zeb's room, snatching a fly swatter off the wall on her way by me. Uh oh! I heard Ralph make a noise in the living room. I hurried into the living room with Ralph.

"Do you need help with the chores, Ralph?"

Martha was yelling at the boys, "Get up, get up *RIGHT NOW!*"

"Mom, we were sleeping…" Zeb sounded groggy.

"I said to get your butts out of bed now, and I mean it!" Martha yelled.

WHACK!

"Ow, Mom, what the hell?"

"DON'T YOU DARE CURSE AT ME, ZEBIDAIH, I DON'T CARE HOW OLD OR BIG YOU ARE, I WILL TAKE A BELT TO YOU ANYTIME YOU NEED IT AND YOU'RE LIVING UNDER THIS ROOF, YOU UNDERSTAND ME?"

Colter started screaming, "MY EAR, LET GO MARTHA, WHAT DID I DO?"

WHACK!

"Son of a bitch, that hurt!" Colter yelled.

WHACK, WHACK, WHACK!

Ralph said "Let's go." to me and I followed him out the front door, which was unusual, since we normally used the kitchen door. We took a long time doing the chores that morning and checked on the generator, (which was fine) and checked the oil in all the pickups and even Martha's car. We could still hear an occasional yell from the house, and I picked up a couple of words about "Church" and "drinking" from time to time. Ralph decided to check out the pond and make sure the pump was ok, even though it wasn't running. I followed dutifully. I thought about asking Ralph about the pussy thing, since it was out in the open now and decided against it and asked if we could go fishing instead. Ralph said no because we probably had a lot of work to do that day and Zeb had found a huge bass in the pond and he didn't want anyone else to catch it, except him. Maybe tomorrow or the next day, though.

When we returned, to the house, Zeb and Colter were eating breakfast, and just positively glaring at me. Martha left the kitchen to do something and Zeb told me,

"Your ass is fucking grass."

"I'm never taking you anywhere again." Colter said.

I was pissed now, "Fuck you, I asked you what a pussy was, you should have told me."

"Watch your mouth!" Zeb said. What? Now all of a sudden they were going to be adults. Bullshit, I wouldn't stand for it.

Martha walked back in. We all shut up. No sense taking any chances.

I was sent to fill up a ten gallon water can in the back of the pickup, which was cool, because I had to move the pickup to do it. Any time a six year old gets to drive, it's cool, at least in his mind. I knew Ralph was watching and was careful not to pop the clutch or stall it, and moved Zeb's pickup nearer the yard so I could fill up the can. Using the water hose, I filled it up. Colter came out, looked inside of it, and told me to dump it and rinse it out, and not be so lazy. I did as I was told.

Zeb grabbed a couple of post hole diggers, shovels, and some other tools and threw them in the truck also. As Colter, Zeb and I climbed into the pickup, Ralph gave the boys instructions about where the fences needed mending and we left the ranch house. The ride out was quiet.

"Anyone got a chew?" I asked

"You're too young to chew." Colter answered.

"I wasn't too young last night." I hated when they did this.

"Shut Up!" the both yelled in unison.

They were grumpy. I had yet to learn about hangovers. I looked out the front of the window, they looked out the side windows and across the ranch we went.

One part of the fence we needed to work on was not really all the bad. The boys dug up the old post, cleaned the hole out a little bit, with me using a shovel to some-what help. Colter hollered at me a couple of times and told me to watch out after almost hitting him with the shovel handle a couple of times. He was standing too close. We put in a new post, buried it, and started stringing a couple new strands of barbwire.

"Maybe we ought to let him, pull the wire." Colter said to Zeb.

"Yeah, maybe."

"What do I have to do?" I asked. I was generally eager to help, or at least learn about it. If it sucked, well, that was a different story.

Colter hooked a strand of barbwire with a claw hammer, pulled it around the post and Zeb nailed it down.

"If you fuck up, you'll cut your throat, or lose an arm, you want to do it?" Colter said.

Zeb chipped in. "Yeah, when that wire snaps, it moves so fast, you can't even see it. Flies back, wraps around ya, and you're just covered in blood before you even know it. No time to get ya to the hospital…"

"You want to try it?" Colter prodded.

"Sure." I answered. They were trying to scare me. I wasn't sure why. Colter hooked a strand for me, put it around the post, and I leaned back, putting all the weight I could into it.

"Tighter." one of them said.

"I'm…. trying."

Colter took the rest of the tension up that was needed and Zeb nailed it down.

This continued for awhile without me, until some problem came up. Colter put some tension on a strand and I held it as he went over to help Zeb. As they worked together, they would tell me to loosen or tighten the tension as needed.

"If I let this go, will it cut your throats?" I asked.

Zeb stood up quickly and stepped backwards.

"Don't let it go!" he said

"Keep pulling on it dammit." Colter said

"I am." I assured them.

"So, would it *really* cut your throat?"

"Just hold onto it." Colter told me.

They *did* seem a little concerned. I started to get the giggles as I thought about them being scared of me.

"Don't you fucking dare let that go!" ordered Colter.

"Quit fucking around." Zeb hollered

I leaned back some more, and they finished nailing it down.

I got up to get a drink of water, as Zeb and Colter strung another strand. I was kneeling in front of the water cooler that was sitting on the back of the tail gate. It was hot out. Colter pulled a strand tight, Zeb leaned over to nail it. *ZINGGGG*, went the wire, I saw the barb wire whip through the air, curling as it went. Zeb threw an arm up, and ducked. The wire passed over his head.

"YOU OK?" Colter yelled at Zeb.

"That was close!" He answered.

"You ok, Zeb?" I asked.

"Yeah, fine."

"You're lucky it didn't cut your arm off, huh Zeb?" I asked.

They restrung it, warning me to stay out of the way the whole time, which was fine by me. When they were done, I asked if either one had ever been hit by a busted strand. Zeb showed me a scar on his arm, where a strand had wrapped around his wrist as it went by. It had scarred good. I wondered why Martha had not stitched it up. Probably easier to let it scar than to get it sewn. Sure would have been less painful.

"Don't look like it could have cut your arm off." I said.

Zeb popped me in the head with his glove. I grinned and tried to punch him in the balls. Colter grabbed me from behind, threw me down and pinned me, laughing, while Zeb took his snuff out of his lip and stuck it in my ear. Again.

After lunch at the ranch, we went out to check water holes and windmills. As we were leaving a windmill, Zeb and I got into it about something. I reached over, snatched his cowboy hat off his head, and flung it out the window of the pickup. Mine followed it. Colter slammed on the brakes and said "Go get it."

"No, Zeb can go get it."

"I said go get it."

"Fuck you, you son-of-a-bitch." I told Colter as I crossed my arms.

"Fine, walk home then, you little bastard." Zeb answered as he grabbed me.

I looped my arms through the steering wheel as Colter pried my fingers off, and Zeb tried to keep from getting kicked in the face as he pulled me loose and pushed me out the window of the truck, dumping me on my ass in the dirt. Zeb locked the door as I scrambled up for the handle and smacked my fingers as I reached for the lock, rolling up the window part way so I couldn't reach the lock again.

"Get my hat."

"You're an asshole, Zeb!"

"Get his hat." Colter told me.

"Fuck you! Your both assholes, I'm telling Martha, when we get back."

"I'm telling Martha, I'm telling Martha." Colter mimicked back to me.

"Might be awhile, you know which way the ranch house is?" Colter asked.

Uh oh, this was reason for concern, but for once, I did know. I pointed north.

"Nope, you're fucked, it's over there." Colter pointed North East.

"See ya." Zeb said as Colter eased the truck forward.

"All right, I'll get your hat." and walked back to where Zeb's hat was, picking mine up on the way.

I walked over to the pickup door.

"Gimme the hat." Zeb told me.

"Let me in, first." I wasn't stupid. I knew how this would turn out, if I weren't careful.

"Give me my hat, and I'll let you in."

"No, let me in and I'll give you the hat." I said, as I reached for the door.

Zeb reached out, knocking my hat off my head. As I reached for it, he snatched his hat out of my hands. The pickup roared forward with Colter at the wheel. They were laughing their asses off.

The pickup stopped 15 yards away, I calmly walked up to the door.

"Let me in, Zeb, or I'm telling." I was barely holding back the tears.

The pickup moved forward again. I could see them talking and laughing.

Twice the distance this time, Colter stopped the pickup again. As I walked up to the door, Zeb said, "You can ride in the back."

As the pickup moved forward and I reached for the bed, Colter punched it. I sprinted. The pickup was barely ahead of me and gaining speed, as it got farther away, I started to slow down, then Colter slowed the pickup too. I got a little closer, and really turned it on. I dove for the tailgate. My fingertips touched it, barely, then my hands slapped the bumper as I fell face first into the middle of the dirt two track, skinning my nose and bloodying my lips as I got a mouthful of New Mexico dirt. I lay there crying, and not moving. I was hoping they would think I was hurt and come back. The boys kept driving, just laughing as hard as they could. They both said for years, it was one of the funniest damn things they ever saw.

After I picked myself up, I decided to stay on the road going east instead of trying for the ranch house to the North. As I walked down the road my face was covered in tears, dirt, blood and snot. The bastards had left me! I was scared but not surprised in the least. Less than five minutes went by when Colter & Zeb came roaring back up.

They took one look at me and burst into laughter again. Zeb was always pretty quiet and solemn, but he was about to piss himself laughing so hard. I tried hard not to laugh, as I continued crying but eventually gave in and let out a couple of chuckles between sobs as I climbed back into the truck. As we got calmed down and Colter gave me a handkerchief to clean my face up, I formed a plan. I reached across my body with my right hand, giving the handkerchief back to Colter. As he took it, I let go and swung backhand as hard as I could. The back of my hand caught Zeb square in the nose. His mouth dropped open, he blinked, then blood started gushing out of his nose onto his shirt and lap. YES! I had connected, and good.

Colter slammed on the brakes. "YOU LITTLE FUCKER!!" He yelled.

"No, no, I'm alwight." Zeb spoke through the blood.

Colter grabbed me by the collar, "I'll kick your fucking little ass, right here and now, you understand me? Knock it off!"

Zeb came to my defense! "Naw, hell, it's ok Colter, I had it coming. Little Fucker got me good though." as he pinched his upper lip and tried to stop the blood. Zeb looked at me.

"You're not gonna twy and hit me again, are ya?"

"No trying about it, I done hit your big ass." I smarted off to him.

"*You won't twy and hit me again, will you?*" Zeb had spoken very slowly. He sounded serious, even if he was talking funny.

"No, we're even, now." I replied.

"Good, shake on it." Zeb said as he stuck his hand out. Was this another trick? I slowly put my hand out, watching Zeb's nose as I did. Zeb reached out and as he started to take my hand tells me "Don't you fucking twy and hit me again."Quickly grabbing my hand, we shook on it.

Zeb relaxed a little.

"Me and Colter ain't even though." I explained to anyone that needed to know.

"I'll kick your little ass, if you try it" Colter said harshly. "You need to apologize to Zeb. I'm sorry he hit you Zeb."

"It's ok, weally."

I giggled a little bit. Zeb winced, but I was looking at Colter.

Colter eyes were slitted as he glanced at me.

"*Don't you fucking dare try it!*" Colter warned.

I can wait, I thought. No sense taking any chances.

The next morning, Martha told me to get the boys up. I couldn't wait. I went to Colter's bed first. He was lying on his belly, with his hands underneath his pillow, he was sleeping good. I saw the hair in his armpit and just couldn't control the idea that was spinning through my head. I almost started giggling but stopped myself as I looked over my shoulder, checking the floor for any obstacles between me and the kitchen.

I reached out with my left hand and grabbed Colter's underarm hair, and yanked hard, as I started running for safety.

"YEOWWWWWW, WHA TH FU!" screamed Colter as I bolted across the room.

I was laughing so hard I felt like I could barely move. I was less than one step from being out of the bedroom and into the kitchen, with Martha to protect me. I remember seeing a flash, in my eyes, and hearing a dull thud as something struck my shoulder on its way down. What would be falling down from above me? And why were my legs not working anymore? I was almost safe, I had thought, as

I hit the floor next to Colter's boot. His boots had been next to the bed, I was sure of it. I had checked my escape route. They *were* next to the bed. I was crying, and a little confused as Martha picked me up off the floor. My head hurt, real bad.

"How come my head hurts, Martha?" I asked. I didn't want her to see me cry.

"I'd say cause Colter's boot hit ya in the back of the head. Look at me." she said. I looked at her, although I had no clue why. She seemed to have a serious expression.

"You'll be ok. Them boys are a little big for you to be rough housing with. You should stick with kids your own size."

"There ain't any." I informed her. Which was true. I was small for my age. Everybody was bigger than me. I got used to it early. If I ever had "little man syndrome" I am pretty sure it got beaten out of me early.

Later that day, I drifted out to the stock pond. My head still hurt a little bit. I threw in a line and sat down to wait. I caught a couple of catfish, and had put them on stringers, until Colter could help me clean them. I still didn't have cleaning fish down real good and sometimes the fish looked like it had been through a meat grinder when I was done. I got my line hung up for at least the fifth time that morning and hollered at Colter to help me. He was in the corral next to the stock pond, shoeing horses with Zeb. As I turned around to holler for help, the pole fell out of my hands and shot into the pond. I was stunned! I saw the pole laying on the edge of the water and went after it. I yelled at Colter.

"I got a big one Colter, he's got a be a big ol cat!" Colter didn't seem much interested and was digging away at a horse's hoof. The reel spun out a little.

"Zeb, this is a big cat!" I tried to get his attention. Zeb looked up casually and nodded at me. About that time the water exploded in the middle of the pond and a big gleaming fish shot out of the water, straight up into the air, turned around and crashed back down with a big splash. Zeb and Colter stopped what they were doing and stared. When the fish broke water again, they both dropped anything they had in their hands and started running towards me. By the time they had gone through the fence and came around to me, I had the fish, just a foot or so from the edge of the water. I was sweating.

"Would you look at the size of that sumbitch!" Exclaimed Colter.

"I see it." Zeb said quietly

"I've never caught a fish this big, what is it?" I was pretty excited.

"It's a bass." Zeb answered.

"A big fucking bass!" Colter said.

"It ain't that big." Zeb coolly stated.

After getting the hook out of its mouth, we put the fish on a stringer. Colter told me to bring it in. After huffing and puffing with it all the way to the house, and Zeb telling me at least three times to be careful with it, I got it in the front door. Ralph and Martha congratulated me and someone filled up the big cast iron bath tub for it to swim around in. I announced that I would clean it for supper, myself.

Zeb asked, "You sure you want too?"

Martha grinned.

"Huh? You want to help me clean it Zeb?"

"No, I don't." he replied

Ralph had a huge grin on his face. I thought that was pretty neat that Ralph and Martha both were so happy for me.

Zeb told me, "If you put it back, it will make a lot more bass for us to catch."

"Well there's more in there now or I wouldn't caught this one." That drew a laugh.

All of a sudden, it occurred to me! This might be Zeb's trophy bass!

"Is this your trophy bass, Zeb?" I asked excitedly.

"I don't think so, besides, I think she's pregnant." he said, still not looking at me.

"How can you tell it's a girl, how do you know it's pregnant?" I wanted to know.

Ralph chuckled and asked "Yeah, how do you tell that, Zeb?"

Zeb threw his Dad a sharp look, and went back to staring at the fish that was not his trophy bass as it swam around the tub.

"Well, see how *her* belly is kinda low?" Zeb said to me.

"It's a fat fish." I said.

Martha burst out laughing, "It sure is."

Now I was really unsure of what to think or do. Zeb didn't want us to eat this fish.

"So there's baby fish in it" I inquired

"Eggs. Fish have eggs." Zeb stated.

This had to be bullshit, I looked at Ralph and Martha. Martha came to the rescue.

"Not eggs like you're thinking bout." she explained. "Little, like the bait you use, them Fireballs, those are actually fish eggs."

"Really? Yuck."

Zeb continued to stare at the fish that wasn't his trophy bass.

"Well, ok Zeb, we can put her back I guess." I said kind of sadly, I think. "You'll catch bigger fish." Zeb informed me.

I haven't.

I saw Ralph and Martha when I was in my late thirties, they were both in their seventies by that time. I had pretty much forgotten about the incident, until Martha reminded me of it. She laughed, exactly as she had laughed standing behind me at the ranch house, watching that fish in her bath tub. Telling me, "I'll never forget the time you caught Zeb's bass, he was so danged mad, he couldn't talk, never would let anybody fish the stock pond no more, after that. Oh was he mad!"

Rodeos were good times too. The thing that always puzzled me, was that it seemed that sometimes Colter and Red would leave without enough money to get there and back. I don't know that this was actually the case but I could not figure out why we always did what we did.

We would leave for a rodeo somewhere and within a few hours we would stop at a bar. In New Mexico, at the time, anyone under eighteen could be in a bar with a parent or guardian. The child couldn't sit at the bar, and only the parent or guardian could serve him. Yep, you read that right. Kids could drink, as long as they were in the company of a guardian. It was not unusual to see two or three kids in a bar. Playing pool, dancing, or on the pinball machines.

Red and Colter would always start a game of pool. After hogging the table and buying some drinks an offer would be made to play someone else at five dollars a stick. After losing a couple of games, Red or Colter would drunkenly suggest twenty dollars a stick! They would not lose the next couple of games.

I played a minor part in this also. It was my job to be in the way, make noise when the opposition was getting ready to shoot and just generally be a distractive little pain in the ass. I was good at it.

I would also, on some prearranged cue from Colter, ask for the truck keys, so I could go "lay down." My job was to get the pickup doors unlocked and maybe started. I never actually got to be the getaway driver, but I always wanted too.

Red and Colter seemed to pick the most fucked up places for these little money making operations. An Indian bar in the middle of an Apache reservation for example.

C'mon guys, you had to know how this was going to turn out, for fucks sake. I think they were trying to get all of us killed. No other explanation.

One time in particular we left town, heading for a rodeo. I climbed out the window and fetched the beers. Jeannie C. Riley sang "Harper Valley PTA" on the eight track. After an hour or so, (and a few more beers) I started getting a lecture.

We were going to stop at a bar.

"Big deal, what's new about that?" I thought.

I was not to tell Mom & Dad.

"Yeah, I knew that already."

And if I did tell Mom & Dad, I would get my ass kicked and never be allowed to go again.

Right, just like always.

We'll give you a drink, and you can even mix it yourself if you promise to keep your mouth shut.

Sounded good to me. Break out the Coke & Whiskey.

We pulled into the parking lot, it was actually paved, no signs either that I remember. I didn't remember this particular bar, but that didn't make any damned difference, I probably hadn't been to every bar in the state. Hell, I wasn't even seven years old yet, there had to be a lot of bars I hadn't seen.

Walking in, after being warned and threatened at least five more times, I noticed a few things. This really wasn't my kind of bar. They had carpet on the floor. Shag carpet to be exact. There were no pool tables, and no juke box. What the hell was I supposed to do here? Where did

anybody dance? Maybe it was one of them restaurant/
bars, where you could get a steak and a drink, like down
in Animas.

They did have some little round bar tables, and couches. A few couches. Hmmm? This must be some high class
place, I remember thinking. I didn't see how this was going to be much fun for me. This would definitely cost the
boys another drink.

I found a place to sit, on one of the couches. A girl
walked up and sat down next to me. She was wearing pajamas! What the? Another girl appeared on my other side.
Damn! She was in her pajamas too! Just what in the hell
was going on around here?

This had to be absolutely the strangest fucking bar I
had ever been in.

The smell was nice though. The girls all smelled pretty
and kept talking to me and laughing. I was having fun, I
didn't even notice where the boys went. Who cared? Not
me. Far as I was concerned, they were missing out.

Pretty soon the boys showed back up, and told me it
was time to leave. That was fine by me, wasn't a whole lot
for me to do anyway. Time to go rodeo.

I got another Coke & Whiskey when we got back into
the pickup, just to keep my mouth shut. No sense them
taking any chances.

4

THE DRIVE

After I was sprung from 1st grade, probably the summer of 71, I found out we were moving. Dad's company had a change of operations. Whatever the hell that meant. Later on I found out that it had affected lots of truck drivers, because damn near everyone we knew moved also. We only moved about 150 miles east of where we had been, and still along the Mexican border. Right outside of El Paso Texas. I am sure I didn't want to move, but most kids don't. My first day of school, I put on my best cowboy hat, boots, and went to meet the new kids. My old school had been largely Hispanic. So was this one. Nothing new there. I went from ranch country to border farming country. The first kid I saw snatched my hat off my head. The fight was on. By the first week of school I had been in so many fights over my damned hat, I quit wearing it. This place sucked! I went home and informed

Mom & Dad we had to move back. No dice. Fine, I would go live with my oldest sister. I told Mom & Dad. This didn't go either.

On the second week of school, I noticed the kid next to me, who was pretty nice, but I couldn't say his name, he signed his paper Jesus. I had been to church several times against my will and even a couple of times when I wanted to. This was not Jesus. I told him, "You're not Jesus."

He says "My name is Hay sous."

"What?"

"Hay sous, man, my name is Hay sous."

"Fine, then don't' write your name down as Jesus, it ain't right, take it off your paper."

Hay sous, was tougher then he looked, it was bad enough getting in all these damned fights, but this one I lost! Talk about adding insult to injury. This place just sucked all the way around.

When I got home, Mom & Dad were still at work and Colter wasn't home from school yet either. It had been a bad day, I went to the fridge and opened a beer. Just let someone try and stop me. The little half cans of beer were in vogue then, so it wasn't like I was drinking a whole one. It was cold and good. I finished it, opened another and went and sat on the front porch and told my dog Blue Boy about my day. Colter pulled into the driveway, I started to hide the beer and then thought "What the hell."

Colter got out the truck and walked over to me. "Who said you could have a beer?"

I looked him in the eye squinted and said "Me."

Colter tells me, "You mouthed off to one of them Mexican kids didn't ya?" I wondered how he knew. Maybe the black eye, gave it away. He took the beer and drank most of it, till I took it back and told him to get his own. I told him what had happened and tried to talk him into just me and him moving back. Or Australia, so we could have a cattle ranch there. He wouldn't go either. I did not understand why all of a sudden I wasn't getting what I wanted. I was getting pissed all the way around, why wouldn't anyone listen to me? Sometime after that, Mom and Dad explained it all to me. I still didn't like it, but now I understood. It was about making a living. Some things, you just have to do. That made sense to me.

Mom and Dad also told me to stay out of the beer. How did they know? Surely Colter didn't say anything, he wouldn't fucking dare. Would he?

Several days later I asked him about it, and this turned into a wrestling match. After pinning me down and being cussed out by me, Colter took his Copenhagen out of his lip and put it in my ear. I was livid. This was not the first time that it had happened or the last. Another "trick" that I wouldn't fall for anymore was them handing me a "Coke" that was actually their spittoons. This was pretty damn disgusting by anyone's standards. The chew in the ear thing had to stop though. Zeb, and Red often took part in this too. I was getting tired of it. Time for plans to be laid and put into action.........they would pay! My chance came the very next weekend. Zeb came down and him and Colter went partying without me.

Another reason to be pissed, they had left me behind. I got up bright and early on Saturday morning. Colter and Zeb were still crashed. They obviously had been out drinking. We shared a bathroom that opened on each end. One side into my bedroom, one into Colter's. Colter's room also had two more doors, one into the living room and one into a short hallway that went into the kitchen. Lots of escape routes!

Colter had two twin beds in his room, separated by a lamp table. I snuck into his room, and checked them out. The boys were out hard. I looked up at the bookcase and had my plan. I went out of the room and opened all the doors that I would have to pass through and placed my bicycle at the front steps. I had learned by now, escape was essential to survival.

Slipping back into Colter's room I saw his boots and knew they would be better suited for my purposes. I picked them up and slowly, as quietly as I could, climbed up to the top of the bookcase, carrying his boots. Upon reaching the top, I slipped Colter's boots on, over my tennis shoes. I looked down. It was a long way. I touched the ceiling, while crouching and launched myself out, kicking my feet out, aiming for Colter's crotch.

I screamed, "FUCKERS!" as I landed on Colter's balls with both feet and my fists in his face, then launched myself over onto Zeb's bed. Zeb was on his belly and rolling over as I landed on his side and drove one knee into his crotch with a quick left jab to his nose. I was up and running for the front door, kicking off the boots as I went. All hell was breaking loose behind me. Colter was in a lot of pain and screaming obscenities.

"I'LL KILL YOU, YOU LITTLE BASTARD!"

Zeb apparently was not damaged as much and was coming after me. I heard a loud crash in Colter's room from one of them crashing into something, or the book case I had launched myself from had come down.

"OW! YOU ROTTEN LITTLE BASTARD!" I made the bike and started pushing, someone was coming out right behind me. *Go, go, go* I told myself, I couldn't get the pedals moving. Zeb had me! About the time Zeb grabbed me and I hit the dirt on my back here came Colter with Mom right behind him. Good Ol Mom!

"What in the HELL IS GOING ON HERE?" Mom screamed.

Colter was still coming at me and man was he pissed! Before he could reach me, wearing nothing but his underwear, Mom had gotten hold of him and was yelling at him to stop it. It was all the break I needed. I was on my bike and moving. Mom yelled at me to "Get back here." I wouldn't dare go against Mom, but I kept the bike moving while I circled at a safe enough distance that Zeb or Colter couldn't get me. They were standing in a gravel driveway in their underwear. I was pretty sure I could get away. Colter and Zeb both were telling Mom what I had done.

"They started it." I said. Zeb's nose was bleeding a little bit and Colter had obviously been racked pretty good. This was cool! Mom told them to go inside and asked me what I was doing. I asked her if I could go ride my bike.

She gave me the ok, and Zeb gave me a dirty look and said I would never go anywhere with him again.

Colter, said "I'm gonna beat your ass."

"MOM." I yelled. She stepped back outside and told Colter to come inside. I flipped Colter a finger and rode off quickly. Colter was mad enough to chase me down barefooted in his underwear.

No sense taking any chances.

I went to Billy's house. He lived about a mile away from me.

I had met Billy the first day of the 2nd grade. He was in junior high.

He was listening to a transistor radio, the song playing was "Drift Away." It was the first rock and roll song I had ever heard. I'm not saying I had been sheltered, but where I came from I thought we had both kinds of music. Country *and* Western.

That first day, I met him he asked me if I liked rock & roll.

"What is it?

"Music, you know, rock & roll, like Jimi Hendrix, Elvis Presley."

"Oh music, yeah, I like music, I know the words to all the Johnny Cash songs, and Charlie Pride, and most of Jerry Reeds too."

This friendship took some work to get off the ground.

Billy also had long hair, clear to his shoulders in fact. I had never seen a boy with hair that long and had only heard about hippies.

Zeb and Colter had only seen him from a distance and thought he was a girl. Both asked me if I had gotten any pussy yet.

Colter and I had been watching Kung Fu and the Wild Wild West on T.V. and one day informed me that he knew Karate. This was news to me. I didn't believe him and told him so. He said he would show me a couple of moves. I declined figuring this would hurt. He promised me he wouldn't hurt me and had me stand up straight. I didn't see his foot slide in front of mine. He hit me in the back of the neck (karate chop) and drove me nose first into the floor. When I came to, I was crying and had a bloody nose.

Colter, who was working as well as being in his senior year of high school, bought a Honda 350 motorcycle. Mom and Dad were mad. Real mad. Dad called them "murder cycles."

I thought it was pretty cool though. Colter would get home from school, strap down a case of beer on the back rack behind the seat, put me in front of him and away we went. Colter handled the shifting and stopping for me, but let me take care of the throttle and steering. I drove, Colter got drunk. This is one of my favorite memories of Colter and I.

The house we had moved into was in the middle of a farm. It had a big horseshoe shaped drive way that went from a ditch road, into our property and around the house. As you turned off of the ditch road, another ditch had to be crossed. It had a culvert but there was a hump in the road right where you made the turn. Apparently Colter thought it was an easy place to wreck the bike and would always make me stop and get off, before he crossed it. I didn't see the big deal. We drove cars and pickups through there all the time. Colter insisted it was a "bad place." This one time, Colter stops and makes me get off, (again) to pull it in. He was lit up pretty good, it had been a long ride and Colter had been drinking a lot. As he started the turn, he flops over right in the ditch! I was dying laughing. After getting out from underneath the motorcycle, and righting it, he started chewing my ass about it, which just made me laugh harder. I told him, he was too drunk to ride it, and he should have let me do it.

I never told Colter this, but five years later, I dumped my motorcycle in the exact same spot.

Ok Colter, I agree, it was a "bad place."

One of my earliest memories of my Dad was standing in front of him learning to drive a John Deere tractor, on our farm before we moved. Although I had driven pick-ups and tractors out on the ranch, it was here that I really learned to drive.

Dad had an old Willy's Jeep. He had bought it military surplus sometime shortly after the Second World War. Olive drab green and still had the white star on the hood. He pretty much used it for hunting and that was about it. He had owned it for twenty six years. When I was eight, he took it to El Paso and brought back a brand spanking new, ca-nary yellow, CJ-5. Mom and I were waiting for him when he drove in to the driveway, Mom and I looked at each other. We both thought the same thing. "Yellow!" What the hell?

Dad put me in the driver's seat, put the jeep in low range, and said, "Have fun."

I tore all over that farm in that jeep. I never did wreck it but I did make Colter bail out once, when I ran over something. He didn't trust me like Dad did.

I survived the second grade, (barely) and was paroled for the summer. I couldn't wait to get the hell out of this place, even if for a little while.

Zeb came down and Colter and I were supposed to go back to the ranch with him. We left the night before we were actually due there and went to a dance on the way.

The dancing and drinking was going pretty good and Zeb & Colter both had picked up a couple of girls. Being too drunk to drive or more accurately trying to get laid they got a motel room after the dance. They made sure I got well liquored up so they would not have me pestering them all night.

The next morning, we stopped at a restaurant. The boys were pretty hung over. The girls had left around daylight. I felt pretty good. I climbed into a booth with Zeb on my right and Colter on my left.

The waitress came over and asked for our orders. Zeb claimed he was hurting pretty bad and ordered 7-Up. I did the same. Colter asked for tomato juice.

When the waitress came back with our drinks, we still hadn't figured out what we were going to have. I wanted Chorizo and eggs but couldn't remember what they were called. Colter really wasn't in the mood to try and figure it out. She said she would come back.

"My head is killing me." Zeb said.

"This tomato juice tastes like cunt juice" Colter said, as Zeb half assed chuckled. Cunt juice? What the hell was that? A juice, I wondered. Maybe a dirty word? I quickly ran all the dirty words I knew through my head, which were quite a few. Shit, piss, motherfucker, fuck, damn, asshole, bitch, son of a bitch, bastard and pussy. Nope, it's not a dirty word. Must be something else, like pomegranate. The waitress was coming back.

"Can I take your orders now?"

"What's cunt juice?" I asked Colter.

Zeb sprayed half a mouth full of 7-Up across the table. Uh oh, was he going to be sick? Colter looked white, but the waitress was the one that had my attention. She was holding her order pad in one hand, and her pen poised above it with the other. Flushes of red like waves were going up her neck to her face. Her eyes were darting around real quick to Colter, me and Zeb and back again. Her mouth was slightly open and moving up and down trying to find words.

"Whawawhat did y-you s-say?"

I looked up and answering her as I asked again.

"What's cunt juice?"

Colter back handed me. Hard. I was thrown against Zeb as Colter told me to shut up. I was stunned, and pissed as well as hurt. And to top it all off Zeb was laughing! I honestly thought at the time he was laughing at me for getting hit by Colter. I exploded! First into tears and then fists. I didn't care if I won or lost, they were going to pay.

I tried to punch Colter and kick Zeb as he grabbed me by the neck and Colter hit me again, this time in the stomach knocking the wind out of me as I went after him.

With the wind knocked out of me, and unable to yell or scream, Colter took me outside. Zeb came too.

"You can't being saying that kind of shit!" Colter yelled at me.

"He didn't know it was bad, Colter, but you can't say that, Josey"

"You said it, fuck face" I barely managed to get out as I was trying to get my breath back.

"Yeah I said it, but not in front of the damned wait-ress." Colter was poking me in the chest with his finger.

"How was I supposed to know? I don't even know what the fuck it is!" I cried.

"It's pussy."

"You bastard motherfuckers, you won't tell me what pussy is either!"

"We'll tell you right after breakfast, I promise ya, won't we Colter?"

"Yeah, we will. Let's go eat. You ok?"

As soon as we hit the highway, I was informed of what "pussy" was. Big fucking deal. I was a boy, I would never have a baby, I could care less. That's what all the hell rais-ing was about? Where babies come from? I didn't under-stand. I knew about birth, I was raised around a ranch for crying out loud. Yeah, but it's a dirty way of saying it, I was told. Oh, ok. Fine, I won't say it except around them. Didn't seem like much of a reason to take an ass kicking.

In the third grade, I joined cub scouts. I was immediately disappointed that we were not camping every weekend and there were no guns. What kind of shit was this? How could you learn Daniel Boone stuff without a gun and the outdoors? This wasn't going to last too long.

One day, I was picked up at Cub Scouts, after school, by Colter and Zeb in the jeep. They had their girlfriends with them. They were all dressed in shorts, tennis shoes and t-shirts. I scrambled in and sat down on the plastic console in between the two front seats. Everyone was very quiet. Something was up.

I had to know. "What's going on?"

All four of them raised beers, pointed them at me and cracked them open. They had been shaken up. I was drenched in beer from four directions wearing my Cub Scout uniform. The party was on!

We headed out in the desert towards the Mexican border. We took off cross country just four wheeling, drinking beer and having a good time. I was getting drunk and trying to kiss Zeb's girlfriend. This was not pleasing Zeb! The girls, however thought an eight year old trying to kiss one of them was quite funny. They wanted to know where I learned about the tongue thing.

Colter went over a sand dune, getting the jeep off the ground and into the air, just a little bit. When it came down, we were high centered on a big mesquite bush. We tried to back up, tried to go forward and tried to dig it out by hand. It wasn't coming. We were stuck. We had the girls get out and Zeb stood on the rear bumper and Colter on the front to try and get some traction. I was to try and back it out. Colter was standing on the front bumper yelling at me. He had stripped down to just his cut offs and tennis shoes and had to crawl over the hood to avoid the mesquite to get to the bumper. He kept yelling at me. This wasn't exactly my fault. Fuck him, as I popped the clutch out, I reached up and beeped the horn. The horn was just enough to startle him. He rose up, standing straight above the bumper and threw his arms out to try and catch himself. He waved his arms back and forth like a tightrope walker trying to get his balance. He must have stood there at least three seconds before gravity and beer took over. He went over backwards into the mesquite, wearing only his cut offs.

"YEOWWW! YOU LITTLE BASTARRRDD!!!!!!!"

Zeb looked at me, "You shouldn't have done that! He's gonna kick your ass for that, but *damn*, it was funny."

Colter came scrambling out of the mesquite, across the hood, and heading for me.

I headed for his girlfriend. Colter was covered in red blood polka dots. The girlfriend saved me from the wrath of Colter and probably smoothed him down with some sympathy.

The decision was made that Colter and his girlfriend would walk into the nearest town and call Dad. Town was probably five miles back down dirt roads and it was hot out. We were out of options, Dad would be pissed. After giving them what beer they could carry, they set out.

After arriving in the small town, Colter was spotted by three Mexican kids from school. He was obviously not at his best, and they sensed that now would be a good time to fuck with him, while he had his girlfriend with him. It wasn't.

Colter may have been tired, drunk, and worn out, but years of cowboying had left him anything but weak. By the girlfriend's account, the fight didn't last long. Two tried to grab Colter, and one hit him. He tore away and knocked the one out that hit him. He was grabbed again from behind and spun and knocked him out. The third one didn't think his chances were all that great with his two buddies out of the fight and left.

Colter told me he caught up with the last one, the next week at school, and settled up. Just so he wouldn't get any stupid ideas in his head. This turned out to be an important lesson for me later on. Don't let enemies think you won't attack. They see it as a sign of weakness.

Colter, Dad and girlfriend showed up about three hours after leaving. Dad was fit to be tied and madder than hell. The jeep was dug out, and we headed back to where Mom and Dad had been, at some friends house barbecuing. The girls were taken home, but I was forced to stay behind with Mom and Dad. I was bummed. I had just about worked up the nerve to try and kiss Colter's girlfriend.

I have memories of driving my Mom and Dad around in that old jeep, as well as my sisters. Most of my nephews and nieces learned to drive in it, so did my three daughters. The first deer I ever killed was brought out of the hills in that jeep. It's still in the family. I inherited it after Dad passed.

It has two bullet holes in it. One from my nephew in the right hand floor board and one from my partner, years and years later. It's centered in the right hand mirror, from a Glock 40. I'll let him tell you how that one happened. Lots of dents and bruises on it, from many hunts and drunks. You just can't let that go very easy.

Life was good. But, as I would soon find out, life changes, whether you want it too or not......

5

REALITY CHECK

I came home from school one day (third grade) and Mom and Dad told me they wanted to talk to me. I figured it was pretty much about all the stupid stunts I had been trying on my bike. Evel Knievel was my hero, and I did need to start somewhere, and had been trying lots of stunts and jumps. Not too successfully either, I might add.

Mom told me she hadn't been feeling well and had gone to a Doctor.

She had cancer.

I, like any kid, wanted to know if she were going to die. She said there were treatments for it and didn't think so. I believed it.

Over the next few months, as she went under treatment and experimental radiation therapy I watched her get skinnier and sicker. She would climb onto her bed, on her hands and knees, kicking and screaming in pain. At eight years old, this scared the shit out of me!

Everyone promised me everything would be ok, and I shouldn't worry. I worried anyway, but figured, it would be ok.

Thanksgiving, 4th of July, and Christmas, were always spent in Texas. My great grandparents, grandmother, and cousins, on Mom's side lived there and we were a pretty close knit family.

In October, my great grandfather, or "Granddaddy" as he was called, died. Granddaddy and I were pretty close. He still mowed his own yard at eighty three, and got around pretty good.

The family packed up and we went to the funeral.

We were going to come back on a Saturday, but on Friday night, Dad told me Mom was having a bad spell and would stay behind.

She had been pretty sick, but with her mom and grandmother there, it seemed like a wise choice.

Back at home we continued to work and go to school and carry on with life. I was encouraged to stay in Cub Scouts even though I had wanted to quit. These guys were lame. Not so much the Cub Scouts as an organization but the troops themselves. Let's clean up our community, whoo hoo! Fuck that, let's go camping, hunting, trapping, fishing, anything fun, but not picking up litter on the side of the highway. That sucked.

One day, I'm at a Cub Scout meeting, at someone's house. There is a knock at the door and my oldest sister is asking for me. My oldest sister lived 150 miles away. I walked outside, and got in the car. My brother-in-law was driving. She turned around, smiled at me and asked if I wanted to go to Texas. I started crying and asked her if it finally happened. She said "Yes." I was pissed off and said something to the effect of, "I thought it was all going to be okay?"

My brother-in-law informed me, "You knew it wouldn't."

Mom had died. Colter had been with her.

I have never been pissed at any one adult, in this whole thing. Not my Dad, not my Mom, Colter or my Sisters. One thing I did realize though, probably not until my mid-thirties, I believed them and their promises that everything would be alright. It wasn't. At forty, I was still pissed about it. I never did deal with it very well.

I kept hoping it was a bad dream, and would cry myself to sleep at night, years later.

How bad it affected me I will never know. I had a psychologist once tell me that I had reinvested the love of my mother into myself, and that it is not uncommon to do that. I still have no fucking idea what that means, other than, I'm stingy.

Another life lesson here. Don't lie to kids. It fucks 'em up.

It wasn't like anyone in my family had a lot of experience dealing with this situation, so I don't blame them, they tried to make the best of a bad situation. My Mom's illness had taken eighteen months from start to finish.

You ever want to see me get pissed to this day though, lie to a child in front of me. It doesn't matter whether I know them or not. If you're blowing smoke up the kid's ass about something important, I'm coming uncorked and I *will* un-ass you, and someone *will* tell that kid the truth, whether it's you or me. I won't and can't stand for it. When it comes to lying to kids, I'm telling you from experience. *It's wrong!*

Mom was buried three weeks before Christmas. She had died on December 5th and was buried on December 7th to be exact.

I'm not superstitious by nature, but this has been a piss poor day for me. Not all the time, but enough. Twenty years later on this date, (while I was thinking about Mom) I walked into the bloodiest damn close quarter's gun fight I had ever been in or ever hope to be in again.

Dad, Colter and I moved into a smaller place, a little closer to town. We just didn't need a big, three bedroom house for just us. Colter was in his last year of high school anyway, and was already working.

Dad was still driving trucks, but didn't have weekends off anymore. With Colter busy and Dad working the weekends, my future rodeo career died fast. I didn't have any way of getting to them.

Colter moved out within a year and Dad and I tried to lick our wounds from Mom dying. I don't think Dad ever got over my Mom dying any more than I did. He just handled it better.

Mom made my Dad promise to her that he would do his best to raise me right, and that I was taken care of. He lived the rest of his life around that promise.

She made Colter promise to take care of the youngest sister. She was on marriage number three, kid number three and needed taken care of.

Colter has recently become pissed about this. Especially since it appears that I may have turned out ok. Maybe, we're still not *positive*. Colter may not feel the same way after he reads this. I think there may be a few things he was unaware of. Colter says when Dad died his obligation was done with me, but he still has to take care of my sister. I think it's funnier than hell. I'll give him this though, he's held to his promise for over thirty years.

Colter, all I can tell ya, is you've done right by Mom and by Sis. Better you than me Pard.

I made it through 5th grade and I think it was around this time, or a year or so later, that I finally talked Dad into buying me a dirt bike. A Yamaha YZ 80. Billy had been riding for awhile and had an older brother who raced. Billy ate, slept and breathed motocross racing. We went riding together all the time, even though I was not very good and never got much better. I wrecked a lot. A whole lot.

I spent a lot of time on that bike riding up down the dirt roads and ditch banks of the Rio Grande Valley, thinking about Mom and what I would do with my life. No answers were coming, but I still tried to enjoy it. I had watched Mom die slowly, and there was no way it would be right to be miserable with the life that God gave me, even if I was miserable. Mom wouldn't have wanted me to be miserable and sad forever, so I was determined to try and be happy. I guess, looking back, sometimes I was happy, sometimes I wasn't.

Mom and Dad had joined the local country club, prior to Mom dying. Colter was quite the golfer. I tried it, starting when I was six. The club had a swimming pool that was much more fun for me. Everyone knew the little foul mouthed kid with the burn scars on the motorcycle, and a few even liked me. But my mouth did prevent me from making a few friends. I spent the summers in the pool and got so dark, people would routinely speak to me in Spanish, before they realized I was a gringo. Dad would get some questions about my heritage too. He never cared, he'd just say, "He's dark, spends all his time outside."

I was at the pool one day, and me and the lifeguard's brother, Donny, were playing around. Donny would let me stand on his shoulders and throw me as high and as far as he could. He was in his early twenties and a pretty good sized guy, so he could really launch me. His sister, Kim was just barely out of high school, and I thought she was quite pretty. I had known her for a few years. Kim had been our lifeguard at the pool every summer since I had been there. Donny says "Try a flip, Josey." As he launched me I curled up and managed to hit the water on my back. As I sunk into the water at the shallow end I realized I would hit the bottom if I didn't put my hands out or straighten up. In an instant, I formed my plan. I barely touched the bottom with the back of my head, and I just relaxed. Danny came through the water at top speed and picked me up out of the water, I was limp in his arms. "KIMBERLY, HE HIT HIS HEAD KIM!" As Danny laid me on the edge of the pool, Kim ran over and knelt down next to me and put her cheek next to my mouth. I quit breathing, just for a couple of seconds. As Kim tilted my head back and opened her mouth to place it over mine, I wrapped my arms around her neck and stuck out my tongue!

Kim went nuts. "Josey, you scared the shit out of me. Are you Ok?"

"I am just fine. I think I'm in love." I told her.

Donny's eyes were wide, then he started busting out laughing. "Hey Kim, did he just tongue you? Wait till Mom & Dad hear about this. This is great!"

"Shut up, Donny! You scared me, Josey, you're out of here, no more swimming for you today."

That was the only time I got kicked out of the pool.

I had finally talked Mom and Dad into a .22 before Mom died and spent quite a bit of time hunting rabbits and other small game. Mom had left me her 30-30 Winchester (I still have it) and was getting pretty proficient with the guns, at least I thought so. I also would spend dove season with a 20 gauge single shot, wondering why I couldn't hit them. I'm still not very good with a shotgun, but I think I'm getting better.

Dad had an old cotton trailer that we had just never gotten rid of, we did use it from time to time but mainly it just set out behind the house. One morning, when I was about eleven, I got up, put my pants on, and walked into the bathroom to piss, and looked out the bathroom window to see our cotton trailer pulling out of the back yard. Dad had gone to work the night before and I was by myself. I ran to the front door just in time to see an unfamiliar pick up pulling out of our driveway pulling the cotton trailer. I grabbed the 30-30, flung open the garage door, started my motorcycle and took off down the highway. I had no idea what the hell I was going to do if I found it, but I just couldn't watch somebody steal it. If it was in fact being stolen. I just didn't know.

Barely a mile down the road and across the river was an International Harvester House. Basically they were tractor part stores and garages. The pickup and cotton trailer were parked out front.

I pulled in, put down the kick stand and walked up to the front door. I wasn't sure what to do, so I set the rifle just outside the door where it couldn't be seen and opened the door before I went walking in. There were two people standing behind the counter but three standing in front of it.

They all turned to look at me. The look on their faces said they had no idea why the hell a kid was walking into a tractor parts store. I stood there and looked at all of them trying to figure out if I knew any of them or which one had taken our trailer. Finally one of the employees behind the counter asked if he could help me. I told him, I was looking for the person that was driving the pickup parked out front.

One of the customers, a large Mexican man, asks "Why do you want to know?"

I reached for the 30-30 and brought it into view. "That's my Dad's cotton trailer, I don't know you."

"Oh! You're, uh, you're, you're, I know your Dad, I forgot your name, your Dad told me about you, Colter right? Your Dad's G.A, he said I could borrow the trailer. I'm George." He didn't know who was who, but he obviously knew Dad.

I breathed a sigh of relief.

"What were you going to do? Shoot me?" he laughed.

The man behind the counter said, "That's a pretty real looking gun, can I see it?"

"Sure, let me unload it." I said as I racked the shells out and handed it to him. Everyone was quiet.

"What is this?"

"It's a 30-30 Winchester, it was my Mom's. Now it's mine."

He handed it back, "Do you know how to shoot that?" he asked. George had quit laughing. Everyone was still very quiet.

The danger seemed to be over and I didn't think riding back home with a loaded gun seemed wise if I wasn't going to need it, so I stuffed all the shells into my pocket.

"Yeah, it kicks a little, not as much as my Dad's 30-06, but I can handle it."

I knew I might be in a little trouble for this, so it seemed like the best thing to do was just leave. I said goodbye and got back on my motorcycle and went home.

Dad got home about two hours later, and I told him what happened, all of it. I was kind of shocked when he replied; "Oh yeah, I forgot to tell you about that."

Dad never mentioned it again, which was fine by me. I'm still not sure how the hell I didn't get in trouble over it. I wasn't about to bring it up. No sense taking any chances.

The next day, I decided to go for a ride. I wanted to take a gun but thought after the previous day's events, it might not be a good idea. When I did go hunting rabbits or dove, it was always close to the house down on the Rio Grande and Dad always knew where I was. This day, I decided to go for a long ride. I headed up the river and started cutting through alfalfa field roads and across ditches until I got to the town of Chamberino. I stopped and bought a Coke at a little store that was run out of the front room of a house. An old Mexican couple ran it and had a daughter in my class. After talking to them for a bit, I started south out of Chamberino and into the sand hills. As I rode over a dirt dike, I saw a group of wetbacks coming towards me, walking slowly. There were 4 or 5 men, a couple of women, and one baby. These people had to be way off track.

Wetbacks were nothing new around here. They used to stop by the house all the time and ask for water or where they were. Occasionally we would feed them sandwiches or what not. They were always very polite people and just trying to escape their oppressive, poor country for a better life. Dad never turned them away and if for no other reason than Dad's example, neither did I.

This day though, as I started to turn around, the woman carrying the baby waved for me to come over. I dropped off the dike and rode down to them. One of the men asked "Dond`e esta Santa Teresa?" ("Where is Santa Teresa?")

Santa Teresa was a small upscale golf community started by Lee Trevino, just north of the U.S/Mexican border. They were at least twenty miles west of it. They had apparently missed it by a couple of miles but continued walking north. I pointed behind me and said "Chamberino." They seemed puzzled. The woman with the baby walked over to me and showed me her baby. Its mouth was open and his lips were dry and cracked. They were all carrying water jugs but they were empty. The baby didn't look real good. One of the wetbacks was a little younger and smaller than the rest. I motioned for him to get on and bring his water jug. We rode back towards Chamberino and stopped in the back of the first house we came too. I pointed to a water hose. As the man filled up his jug from the hose a Mexican man stepped out the back door of the house to see why a motorcycle had ridden up to the back of his house. He spoke Spanish to the guy I had given a ride too. The homeowner, told me to leave him there and go get the woman with the baby if I could. I headed back to where I had left them and gave them the jug of water I had brought back and pointed in the direction of where I had taken their friend and motioned for the woman and the baby to get on the motorcycle with me. After dropping her and the baby off, and two more trips, the rest of the wetbacks could see where we were going and walked the rest of the way in. They were sitting in the shade of a tree in the home owner's back yard, drinking water while the woman of the house dished out frijoles (beans) for them. Someone gave me five dollars and I headed home.

Riding back, I realized I had just stumbled onto a way to make a little extra money, if I wanted. Taking money from them seemed wrong. I would discuss it with Dad when I got home, I decided. I probably should have thought about that a little more before I discussed it with Dad though, as I came to find out.

When I told Dad about my day, "he had a cow" as we used to say at the time. He was mad, and not a little bit either.

Dad told me, "You're no match for three or four wet-backs! They could knock you in the head, and take that motorcycle and be miles away before anyone knew what happened."

I had not really considered that. I really hadn't sensed any danger, but there was no use arguing with him. Dad had a point.

I needed to start looking out for myself a little better, when I was on my own, I supposed. Perhaps start carrying a weapon too. I liked that idea, even if I really didn't need it. My hunting knife went on my belt the next day. Dad had always insisted we had folding hunting knives. It was pretty common, and no one seemed to notice. I couldn't carry it at school, only pocket knives were allowed then, which was fine by me. I also bought a belt buckle knife. It cost me 30.00, which was a good deal of money back then, especially for a belt buckle or a knife. It didn't look like a knife and was quite a nice buckle. It saved my ass though, one time, so it was worth the money to me. I still have it.

That winter, (I was either eleven or twelve) was my 3rd year deer hunting. I had not even had a shot yet but looked forward to going every year. Someone always killed at least a couple and our freezers always had venison in them. It was and is still my favorite meat. On the first morning of the hunt, Dad and I walked away from the jeep, along a ridge and then crested over the top. Dad had much better eyes than me so I usually stayed pretty close to him, plus I seemed to get turned around a lot. This morning though as he topped out, I noticed a big rock pile on the top of the ridge we were on, to our right. It blocked the view of the entire canyon from us upward. I swung right so I could see the rest of the canyon. As I looked down, into the canyon, I spotted three deer. Two were does and not legal to take, the other one had its head behind a bush. They were about 250 yards away. I looked around, no Dad to be seen. I ran back around the rock pile and got Dad's attention. He looked at me and lit his pipe. Finally he recognized that I was excited and casually strolled over. I told him what I had seen and we went around the rock pile and I got ready while Dad watched through his binoculars. Still two does to the left, one unknown with its head behind a bush on the right. I sighted on it, and waited.

"Shoot the third one from the left" Dad said. BOOM. I levered another cartridge in. "Low." Dad said. I aimed at the top of his back. BOOM. I levered another round into the chamber. "Just over his back." Dad said. What in the hell, how long was this animal going to continue to let me shoot at him? Why am I missing? Maybe I jerked the first shot, (it did go low) and then the 2nd shot was good, but since I had aimed over it, it went high. I aimed again right at it, holding a little further back behind its heart but still in its lungs. I was getting frustrated and my confidence was starting to go. After all, when it came to shooting, *I was good*. Right? Right. I told myself. I squeezed the trigger, BOOM. THWACK. I heard the bullet impact and the deer dropped. "YEAH!!" I yelled, "I GOT HIS ASS!" Dad looked at me kinda funny, so I calmed down a little bit and went down the canyon. I wanted to gut it myself but Dad wanted to hurry and get it done. I think we may have compromised on that, and I helped a little. Dad insisted on driving the jeep to it. (I wanted to pack it out on my back) I got another lesson before the day was out. Jeeps can go a lot of places, I didn't think they could. Dad scared the hell out of me going after that deer. The deer wasn't very big, but I didn't care. It was my first deer and I would get to eat a lot of it. To this day, I'm still a meat hunter. I would like to have a nice big buck to hang on the wall, and if I ever get a chance I would take a bigger one. But when I see deer, my mouth starts to water, and I take the first one I see. Dad had the horns mounted, since it was my first deer, which was pretty cool. I am grateful for the memory and the gift.

In my mind I had taken a step towards becoming a man. I could hunt, kill, clean, cut and wrap food for myself and my family. I could survive off the land now. Well as long as I had a rifle, ammo, supplies and shelter anyway. That sort of bothered me, there was a lot involved with this whole "survival" thing. I started to appreciate the mountain men of the old west a little more. These guys had to have balls so big, it was a wonder they could walk.

I spent at least two summers in Deep East Texas, with my Aunt, Uncle, and three cousins. This probably went a long way towards helping me heal from Mom's death. My Uncle (my Mother's brother) had moved from Lubbock Texas to East Texas a few years before. We were pretty close and saw them every Christmas and 4th of July. My Uncle was a stern man, and raised three good boys, one whom was my age. My Aunt cared for me deeply and during these summers with them, I was subjected to the same rules and discipline they were, including having to go to church on Sunday. The Southern hospitality stays with me to this day.

I know I caused them some grief during those summers, but they did put up with me. I was in a couple of fights, including taking my first real ass whipping. I had come out on the short end of the stick in a fight before, but I still got my licks in. Not this time. When the kid hit me, I was knocked on my ass. I got up. I was knocked on my ass again. I got up slower and more cautiously, trying to put some distance between him and I. On my feet and watching him, I closed in, now I felt I had a chance. I closed with my fists up and ready. I was knocked on my butt *again*. This was pissing me off, I jumped up, intending to tackle him. I had to get him to the ground. I never saw it coming, I was back on my butt. FINE! I would just stay here, let him come to me. He wouldn't.

I came home with a black eye and a fat lip. My Uncle looked at me and not so much as asked but stated. "You sassed off to one of them boys, didn't you?"

"Yes Sur." I answered.

"Maybe you'll learn now." he told me.

My Uncle didn't know me as well as I thought. Or maybe he just hoped I wasn't that hard headed and stubborn. But I did watch what I said to folks a little more after that. People can say what they want about rudeness and criminal behavior and all that, but I'm convinced that sometimes violence *is* an option, and a damned good one at that.

6

THE GREAT QUEST

Several things happened my 13th year of living. One, I got my driver's license. Dad had gotten me a Yamaha 125 on/off road bike that was street legal, and decided I needed a license. In New Mexico at the time you could get a driver's license at 15. But Dad said since Mom had died, and Colter had moved out and he worked out of town, the local judge would issue a "hardship license." I didn't think life was that hard for us, but what the hell, I wasn't about to turn down a chance to be mobile. The license would only be good for me to go to school and to and from town. But, I could get a motorcycle license for 125cc and under and go where I wanted, when I wanted! I liked that. So we went down to the DMV, I took the test, and was issued a driver's license. I was now mobile. Cool! I couldn't believe it. No more riding up and down the ditch banks and looking for cops before I crossed a paved road. I was legal!

Also about this time, something else happened. Later on I found out it was called puberty. I could have cared less what it was called, I could care less about the hair and having to shave my face. What I did care about was the raging hard ons I had day in and day out. I couldn't masturbate enough to calm myself down. I thought life had been hard before. Now it was a living hell that I thought was great! I had to be the horniest little dude on the planet. To make things even worse I wasn't even cool at school. All my friends had lost their virginity by 11 or 12, or so they said. I was behind the curve, and "hurtin for certain." This just had to be addressed. I had a slim head start in the knowledge department from Colter, Zeb and Company, but damn! I couldn't get laid! I mean where the hell were the willing girls? They would talk about different girls at school being "whores" or "sluts." Any time I tried anything with them I was lucky to get to kiss them. Try moving a hand where it didn't belong and all hell would break loose. I didn't want to get pushy, but something had to give.

I finally figured out what I would do. I got some money together and talked to Billy. We could take a Greyhound into El Paso, round trip for seven dollars. It was less than an hour ride, and dropped us exactly one block from the Mexican border. I had been to Juarez plenty of times with my parents and knew the routine and also knew it could be a dangerous place. Billy was to be my back up. In case there were trouble or problems I was going to rely on the world's biggest chicken shit. Billy had never been in a fight in his life, to save me. As soon as I had this part planned out, I figured out a life lesson here. "Pussy, (or lack of) makes men stupid." And sometimes, it makes us stupid enough that we don't care that we are being stupid.

I figured me and Billy could both get laid. He needed it too. He had only been laid once and that was when he was like 12. At least that's what he told me. I had no reason to doubt it.

Dad went to work Friday, afternoon. Before leaving he asked what I was going to do. I told him me and Billy were going to the movies in El Paso. Dad insisted that if Billy were driving me to the movies, (Billy was 17 or 18) we would buy the gas. This was working out pretty well. I had already saved myself 14.00 in bus tickets for me and Billy. I pretty well footed the bill whenever Billy and I went anywhere. If Billy ever did have a spare penny, it went to his dirt bike. He wasn't lazy he just wouldn't get a job. He would gladly work all day on anything with an engine and not get paid.

Billy and I hopped in his Mom's Monza and off we went to "Pussy Town" also known as Juarez, Mexico.

We parked in El Paso and walked across. I figured I'd find a cab driver and ask him how to get to a whorehouse. Billy wanted to eat first. He said he needed to get his energy up. I thought he was getting cold feet. We had some tacos from a street vendor that were so good, I'll never forget them. Billy puked them up within 10 minutes, and then went back for more. They were that good.

We found a cab driver and told him what we wanted. He told us to get in and it would cost us five dollars for him to take us there. On the ride, (which turned out to be about three blocks) Billy started in with, "We should save our money, we can get laid somewhere else." Billy then started naming off girls that we knew, I finally asked him if he thought his sister might be willing. Just to shut him up. Little did he know I had already made a couple of attempts at his sister who wasn't willing?Billy was starting to whine.

As we pulled into an alley, I saw a single red light above a doorway. No signs or windows anywhere. I was getting nervous, which meant Billy was about to shit himself. I could hear music coming from the other side of the door so figured it must be the place. The cab driver led the way in, I followed and as I stepped into the dimly lit bar, I quickly stepped to one side (as any good Louis L'Amour character would) while my eyes adjusted. Billy followed the cab driver. We went to the bar and bought Tecate beer for all of us. Billy said he would just have a beer, he didn't much feel like anything, "Besides they're all ugly." He said.

"Yeah, but they have pussy, I haven't had any, and they're here and so are we, your sister ain't." I replied. That shut Billy up. Billy hated his sister anyway, I didn't see the big deal about me fucking her, but he didn't like the thought of it.

The first girl that walked up was in her mid-thirties. She asked me to buy her a drink which I did. I told her I wanted to get laid and that it was my first time. She said she knew that already.

She popped her tit out and asked me "You suck on these, while you fuck me?" My eyes about popped out of my head and Billy freaked. He started laughing and told the girl that had walked up next to him that, no he didn't want to buy her a drink and he was just waiting for me.

Me???? I couldn't have been happier in my whole life that I could remember. This was *better* than a new gun! I was going to get laid! The girl led me upstairs and into a room. She told me to give her the money which I did. I was down to 10.00 dollars, after the cab ride, and the beers. She wanted more. "I don't have anymore. I bought you a drink, remember?" I said. This was bad. I had to get laid now. She told me to wait here and she would be right back. A few minutes later she came back and told me to strip. Whew! I had been really worried.

I lay down on the bed and she quickly started going down on me. I was in heaven, but this was not what I really wanted. I tried to lay back and enjoy it, but damn this was good. I didn't know how long I would be able to hold out. I reached for her leg and started my hand up her thigh, she slapped my hand away and kept sucking. After a few more attempts it was apparent that a blow job was all I was going to get, so I might as well as enjoy it. Afterwards she got up to leave. "Where are you going?" I asked. We weren't done, as far as I was concerned.

She said "You through."

"No I'm not!" I argued, I pointed at my hard on to emphasize the point.

She looked down at me and said "You want again?"

"Yeah, I want again!" Was she stupid or what? I thought, *why wouldn't I want again.* The blow job had felt great, I wanted at least one more if not two or three, especially if I wasn't going to get laid.

She giggled and said "Ok." and I laid back down and got another blowjob and my hand slapped a couple more times, because I was still reaching for places I wasn't allowed. I couldn't talk her into a third one. But I did feel better. I had just had sex with a woman for the first time in my life! It was wonderful as far as I was concerned and I really didn't care all that much that it was a whore. Weighing it out later, I thought sex now and impersonal was better than sex two or three years later with someone I "loved." Screw that. I wouldn't make it that long. Sex was great. Sex was fun. And for that matter, it still is.

On the way home, I thought about what I had accomplished and what I had set out to accomplish.

Then it hit me. *I hadn't got laid in a whore house!* This was about as embarrassing as it fucking got! If Billy ever told anyone, I would just freakin die, but in the end he kept it pretty quiet. I finally realized he was embarrassed that he hadn't done anything.

But regardless, I had learned sex was available, I started planning my next trip before I had even gotten home. Without Billy.

Exactly two weeks later, I went back. (I would have gone back the following week, except for a shortage of funds) This time I had money, and no Billy to slow me down. I was a little worried about being there by myself but figured, if I had money and I was spending it, no one would bother me. At least not until the money ran out. You can rationalize anything if you try hard enough. And if something did happen? Well, by that time I would no longer be a virgin and dying or suffering some other terrible fate wouldn't be quite as bad.

I mean, after all, with something this important, there just wasn't any sense in taking chances!

This time it went smoother. I found a cab driver, told him I wanted "po'nocho" (pussy) and hopped in. He pulled out and turned the wrong way down a one way street, and onto the sidewalk.

"This is a one way street dude."

"Es ok, mang, I'm not on the street." He replied. Which was true and really didn't seem to bother anybody except me. Cab rides in Juarez are an experience in themselves. I highly recommend it, if you ever get the opportunity.

After arriving, we went in and I bought him and me a beer. I loved Mexico. No legal drinking age, and you could get about anything you wanted, as long as you had money. This place was great, even if it was decadent, and dangerous.

This time around, I took my time however. I watched and talked to the girls. About the third one, I decided I liked. We went to a room, and she asked if it were my first time. I told her it was and asked how much it would cost me per "time." She looked at me kind of funny.

"Twenty dollars, no more time."

I didn't quite know what the hell that meant, but I was more than ready and had enough for two "times" if needed. I mean, does cumming count as a "time" or just when we went into the room and I had enough? Whose decision was this anyway? And why the hell didn't they have some "rules" posted up somewhere. They made this shit difficult. If they're going to have rules in whorehouses, fine. No problem, post them!

I paid my twenty and she left for a few minutes and came back. Being more than ready, and hornier than any one person should be, this first "time" didn't take long and I didn't want to stop so I never broke rhythm and just kept on pumping, she didn't seem to notice. I guess a "time" was up when I stopped. Fine by me, I would just keep going. The second "time," I paused and rested. She giggled and asked me if I was ok.

"Hell yeah, I'm ok." I thought. "Why wouldn't I be?" She started to get up.

I climbed back on, she looked at me and asked "You want more?"

"Yeah, I want more, you're beautiful." I told her. She had me lay on my back and climbed on top of me.

"Alright! New positions already." I thought. She seemed to get into it quite a bit, and let me have a couple of more "times." This was pretty cool, I wished I had realized that all this numerous "times" stuff, would fade as I got older. If I had known, I might have tried to squeeze in a few more.

When we were done, I went into the bar and found the cab driver. I wanted to celebrate, so I bought him another beer and me a shot of Mescal. I had never had it before and wished I hadn't afterwards. On the way out to the cab, I puked. That shit was rough.

I strolled back across the bridge, into the United States, walking a little taller, a little prouder and a lot happier. In the back of my mind I could hear Muddy Waters singing *"I'm a Man."* I believed it.

I was a little worried about my personal security on these little forays. After all, I was just a kid in age and size, even if I were a "man." I started to wonder about how to defend myself if things got bad. I fought a lot at school, but I was realistic about it too. I couldn't expect to fight off a couple of grown men, if it came down to it. I would have to start thinking about an "equalizer."

Since I still dressed western style, sans cowboy hat, I started wearing the belt buckle with a knife built into it. It looked stylish, never got noticed at school, and I could get it out lightning quick. It was small but made me feel a little better. I could always slash like all get out and run like hell if it came to it.

The knife would be okay to carry all the time but I needed a pistol too. Dad was a little protective of his .38, and felt handguns were for killing only. Carrying a gun into Mexico wouldn't be a real bright idea either. Personal protection just had to be addressed though. After saving up quite a bit of money, I finally talked Dad into buying me a pistol. It was a Browning BDA 380 automatic. It held 13 rounds in the magazine, one in the chamber, and was fairly small. I felt that if I couldn't fight my way out of a situation with 14 shots, maybe I needed the kind of gun that came on wheels. I started to carry it and practice with it. A lot.

Shortly after this, I was witness to an incident that drove the personal security issue home. More on that in a little bit.

Around this time, (maybe a year or so earlier) I got into something else that I probably shouldn't of. I started smoking a little weed. I could have gotten rip roaring drunk, (and had several times with Colter) more fights, and all kind of other things and not got into too much trouble over it, but if my family ever figured out that I had tried Marijuana, they would have flat out freaked! Drugs were something for hippies and commies. Not for us. We were, however, in very close proximity to the U.S./Mexican border. Drugs and drug trafficking were a fact of life, and could be a very lucrative life at that.

Over the next couple of years, I spent quite a lot of time by myself in Juarez. One night, I was at yet another whore house while I was supposed to be spending the night at Billy's but had come over here instead. It was very late, probably about 3:00 a.m. (I had a capacity for staying up forever back then.) I was sitting at the bar drinking Tecate, I was stoned out of my mind and wondering where the hell Luckenbach Texas was and if I should go there, as Willie and Waylon suggested or just head home. There were only one or two girls in the place and they were mainly cleaning up. The bartender was pretty much ignoring me, which was fine. He looked like a bartender out of a bad western movie. A big fat Mexican guy wearing jeans and a mostly white, wife beater t-shirt. His hair was beyond greasy, oily or whatever the hell it was, combed straight back, almost to his shoulders. He had a thick, greasy, mustache that screamed "Machismo." A white guy came into the bar. I had my head laying on the bar wondering what to do next, when the newcomer, placed both hands on the bar, at the opposite end from where I was, and said something to the bartender. It sounded derogatory.

The bartender walked over to him. "Que?" he said, meaning "What?"

The white guy, leaned over into the bartenders face, supporting himself on the bar with his hands now, and repeated, "I said, get me a fucking drink, Spic."

I saw the bartender reach down toward his hip and his hand flashed up, then down. The switchblade knife had opened on the way up, and as the bartender brought it down, he squatted, putting his weight into it and speared the white guy through the back of his hand and pinned it to the bar!

"Fuck you, Put'o." the bartender said.

The white guy looked down and started screaming. He tried to pull away from the knife which brought on a whole lot more blood and screaming. It was time to leave. I headed for the door. I had not gone half a block, when

I saw the first Federales heading for the place. I glanced at them with a questioning look, like I wondered what was going on. As soon as I rounded the first corner, I was in a full sprint. It was time to go home! I definitely wasn't taking any chances where this was concerned.

Another life lesson here. Don't go to other peoples turf and tell'em how things are going to be. It pisses them off. Go by their rules, or at least act like it.

I have to admit, I didn't go back for awhile. But, as we all know, pussy makes men (and boys) do stupid things.

Juarez had become a regular part of my party life. On weekends, I would go over, drink, smoke dope and hit the houses of ill repute. It never ceased to amaze me, that when I got back to school, somebody would be talking about how they were making out with so and so and got to rub her tits, and everybody thought they were so with it. I would just laugh to myself and think *"I got more pussy this weekend than this idiot has had in his life."* I mean it wasn't like any of us were looking to get married and find our mates for life at that age. We just wanted sex. Our mates could be chosen later, as far as I was concerned. Like *after* we had matured a little bit, and had educations, and/or jobs. Maybe when we knew a little more about what we wanted out of life. And don't even think about giving me any shit like "Yeah, but I never had to pay for it." BULLSHIT!!! Those guys spent more money on flowers, dinners, clothes, gas, movies, stereos, and music, *trying* to get laid than I ever did in a whore house! And usually they came up empty handed, going home, with a hard on, beating off, and making up bullshit stories to their friends. The problem was, the boys were ready, but the girls *were not*. When I realized this, I realized something else along with it. *Older women* were ready, and willing. This was a revelation and quite a good one I thought. Definitely worth checking out.......

Shortly after this, I turned fifteen and having graduated Driver's Education, I got my regular driver's license. Now I was really mobile. Not just by motorcycle anymore.

Several small towns around Southern New Mexico would have dances every so often. Animas might have their dance on the 1st Saturday of the month. Lake Valley might have theirs on the 2nd Saturday of the month. My point is this, if you were willing to drive, you could hit a dance every Saturday night, at least during the summer.

I thought this *might* be a good place to start finding the older women, maybe a hot divorcee that had been out on the farm too long. At least that's what I had in mind.

It was one such Saturday morning that Dad was getting ready for work, when he asked me, "What are you going to do tonight?"

I was honest, as I usually was with Dad.

"There's a dance in Hatchita, I was thinking about going to."

"There kinda clannish, nobody'll know ya down there." Dad informed me.

"I thought Granddad settled it? Don't we have relatives down there?"

"Not anyone that would know ya., I wouldn't go, if I were you."

Dad went to work and I got ready for the dance. After all he didn't tell me *not* to go he just said *he* wouldn't go. After showering and trimming up my beard, (I told you puberty hit me hard) throwing on cologne, I jumped in the pickup, lit a bowl and headed off to Hatchita.

I had decided to skip the interstate and take a long route to do some rabbit hunting on the way. Passing through Columbus New Mexico, I knew that my Aunt Ulla, (actually my Dad's Aunt) had hidden behind a bush in 1916 and watched Pancho Villa raid this small town when she was about twelve years old. This same Aunt had lived in Mexico on our family farm and ranch, when Pancho Villa had ordered them off of it.

I Looked Columbus over as I passed through it I tried to picture in my mind how the attack would have taken place. I couldn't figure out how it would have gone down, but I did come to the conclusion that Pancho Villa had been a major asshole and that I didn't like him. Not that I particularly wished our family was still living in Mexico, but making my family leave, well, it just pissed me off. Even if it was fifty years ago.

I continued on the back roads and shooting rabbits on the way, I was having a hell of a good time and was quite stoned, when I got to the dance.

I paid my money, got my hand stamped and walked in and looked around. I didn't recognize anyone, not even the band. Hmmm. After dancing a few dances, I was standing on the edge of the dance floor, next to a cowboy.

As I looked him over, I realized he was probably only two inches taller than me, and a year or two older and had at least sixty pounds on me. He had short stubby fingers, and was square jawed, looked like a bull rider to me, and not someone to cross. Hell, I didn't want to cross him anyway.

"You from around here?" I asked.

"Yep." He replied.

"You ride bulls?" I pressed.

"Nope." He answered.

This wasn't going real well. Maybe if I tried humor. About then this little chubby girl came dancing by in a pea green pant suit, but I didn't care, I was after *older* women.

"Man, that chick has a case of the galloping uglies." I said.

He started laughing. *"All right, he's ok."* I thought.

"Which one?" He asked.

"The one in the pea green pant suit."

His smile faded.

"That's my sister, fucker!"

I saw the right cross coming and ducked it. I countered with a left to his jaw that I thought was pretty good and hard. It didn't seem to do anything to him except piss him off a little more. I didn't see the left jab coming that knocked the wind out of me. Fuck this. I couldn't stand toe to toe with this stumpy bastard and win. All those hours of wrestling with Colter and Dad kicked in, and I took him down, quick and hard. He had no sooner hit the floor and I was dragged off of him. He got up. I took him down again, before he could hit me. This time when I was grabbed from behind and lifted up, I was ready. I elbowed my rear attacker in the stomach, and tried a head butt. I got the elbow in, but missed the head butt. Dropping down I brought him over the top of me into Stumpy. As I dove into both, with fists flying I was stomped from behind in the kidneys, back, and kicked in the ribs. I think the chubby chick even got in a kick or two.

I don't really know how many of them there were, and I don't know how long it took me to get to my pickup, but I do know that when I finally did get to it, my ass had been whipped. And it had been whipped good. I had fought all the way to the truck and had gone down several times on the way, I don't think I really ever hurt anybody, but damn I was glad to get in that Chevy and shut the door.

"Wow! What an ass kicking I had taken!" I thought.

I headed home. I probably beat Dad home by two hours.

Early next morning, Dad came in and woke me up.

"Breakfast is ready."

Pulling my jeans on, I walked into the living room and sat down next to Dad, who had set out two plates of steak and fried taters.

As I started to eat, Dad asked me, "Clannish ain't they?"

"Yeah, sure as hell are." I wonder who had told him. Maybe a relative recognized me and called him, but he hadn't been home.

"Didn't know anybody did ya?"

"No, not really." I quietly answered. We continued eating.

"You were hungry, you want some more?" Dad asked as I finished my steak.

"Naw, I'm fine, thanks Dad. I'm going to go take a bath and clean up."

"Ok."

I walked into the bathroom and as I passed the mirror, I glanced over. I had a huge shiner under my right eye, my bottom lip was swollen, and a scrape from the gravel parking lot on the right side of my face topped it off to positively make me look like shit.

I was glad I hadn't tried to lie to Dad.

On Monday, Dad had gone to work and I drove out to the truck stop on the edge of town to eat dinner. This was a fairly usual occurrence for me. (There were two truck stops actually.) One was owned by lifelong friends of ours that had worked with Dad, and the other one was also owned by friends of ours. I was known at both of them. The waitresses made sure I stayed fed and always talked to me.

Nikki (one of the waitresses) as well as with her husband John, who was a cop in town had become friends. Nikki knew I was always on the lookout for girls.

After our "Hello's" I had to explain what happened to my face. Nikki was getting quite a kick out of it.

"You know for a little feller, you sure get in lots of fights." She pointed out to me.

"You think I ask for it, Nikki? Maybe I'm an asshole."

"No Joe, I don't. I think you're a nice guy, a nice guy that doesn't think before he talks. You don't back down when you're wrong either. Maybe you should."

I could always depend on Nikki to talk straight up.

"That oughta learn ya though." Nikki said in her best bumpkin accent. I cracked up laughing and opened a scab on me doing so.

"Damn, Nikki, don't make me laugh. It hurts." I told her.

"Got a new girl started today." Changing the subject as she put my Pepsi in front of me. Just then, I saw a blond in a knee length white dress step into the kitchen. She had legs to die for.

"The knock out little fox with the hot legs?" I asked a little too loudly.

Blond hair poked out from the kitchen and looked me over and smiled at me.

Nikki had her back to the kitchen, and didn't see it. She laughed. "That would be the one. You want your usual?"

"Please." I answered.

When the order came up, the new girl snagged it quickly and told Nikki she would get it, as she brought it over to me, I got an even better look at her. With strawberry blonde hair, nice trim figure, she stood about 5'4", I guessed her to be about 35 years old. She introduced herself as Nellie. I told her my name, and commented that not too many women had legs that looked so good they didn't wear hose. Nellie thanked me and asked how old I was. I told her I was fifteen, which was the truth. She told me she had just turned forty. Nellie looked at me.

"That's a lot of difference, don't you think?"

"Sure it is, but the good thing about it is, that we are both in our sexual prime." Nellie and Nikki both started laughing.

"Is that so?" Nellie asked.

"And how would you know that Joe?" Nikki asked.

"I read it. Don't you have something to do Nikki? You're embarrassing me."

"*I'm* embarrassing you? I think you might be doing that to yourself, Joe."

Nellie came to my rescue.

"Aw, I think he's cute."

"Yeah Nikki, she thinks I'm cute. Can we *please* talk?" I gave Nikki my best "sad" look. She grinned and walked off.

I was terrified but scared I would run out of time and nerve, I had to hurry.

"What time do you get off?" I asked.

"Three, are you doing anything?" She asked.

"Would you like to get some coffee or dinner?" I pressed on.

"Sure, do you know where 5th street is?"

After giving me directions, I told her I would see her about 3:30. Nellie winked at me.

"I'll look forward to it." She replied.

I thought I would die from excitement right then and there. I thought maybe I should shut up while I was still ahead.

On the way out as I paid at the register, Nikki smiled and said, "John was supposed to pick up his new gun today, come on by tonight, *if* you get time." She teased.

By 2:30, I was shaved, bathed, swimming in cologne, and *way* excited. Not to mention a little nervous.

I showed up at 3:30, sharp. Nellie answered the door, still in her waitress uniform.

"I'm glad you could come. I didn't know if you would or not."

"I wouldn't have missed it for the world. I would never stand anyone up."

"Do you have a girlfriend Joe?"

"No. Not right now." I answered.

"Good. Let me go change into something more comfortable. Have a seat, make yourself at home." She said as she walked down the hall towards the bedrooms.

Looking around the house it was clean and modest, with a lot of purple. Nellie seemed to like purple.

I was nervous as hell. How was I going to pull this off? I wanted her bad. What should I say? Or not say?

Nellie walked back into the room. She was wearing a bath robe.

"How's this look?" She asked as she dropped the robe and stepped towards me.

"You're beautiful." I gasped as she wrapped her arms around my neck and kissed me.

The next few hours I just lost myself with Nellie. She was every young man's dream. An older woman who was a patient teacher and tremendously erotic lover.

I didn't make it to Nikki and John's that night.

I continued to see Nellie for a few more weeks. I couldn't figure it out at the time, but all of a sudden women seemed to be noticing me, or trying to get me to notice them. "What the hell?" I wondered. If I don't have a girlfriend, it seems I can't land a date, if I do have one, they seem to want me. I know it wasn't a jealousy thing because no one knew I was seeing Nellie. We had decided early on we should keep a low profile, because of the age difference. It seemed to be something that other women could *sense*. That kind of frightened me, and still does. When people talk about "women's intuitions" that ain't no bullshit. I'm here to tell you, God gave women something that can make them downright spooky.

During this time, I met another girl. While ordering a burrito, a cute blonde about my age was standing in line.

"I've never seen you before, are you from around here?" She asked me.

"Uh, yeah. How about you?" I replied, trying to be polite. I went back to the menu. I had all I could handle right now, I didn't need anyone else.

As it turned out, we went to different schools. Our paths had just never crossed.

"Well if I give you my number, will you call me sometime?" She asked me.

I couldn't believe this, more of that "woman's sense" thing.

"Sure." I answered, not really interested. She wrote down her name and phone number and handed it to me. I shoved it in my pocket without looking at it, with every intention of throwing it away when I got home that night.

How different my life would have been if I had thrown that piece of paper away.

Not because of her, but so many things got linked to that meeting that led to more meetings that led to a different life, as you will see. Fate can truly be a fickle thing. This was not in any way a decision put before me, or a morality issue, or an "if I would have done this and not that" thing either. It was a simple phone number. Nothing else. But what it would lead too, well that's a story in itself.

Well, what can I say? Let's get on with it.

A few days later, after an all-day love making session, Nellie dumped me. "It's time for me to move on Joe." She told me. True to her word, the next day she left town. I was stunned. This having been absolutely the best piece of ass I had ever had to date.

Having gone to John and Nikki's house, Nikki counseled me.

"You let her get under your skin."

John chuckled.

"She was a *hot* fuck, wasn't she, Joe?" John asked.

I could talk about damn near anything to John and Nikki, and often did. I grinned broadly at John.

"Man, I can't even begin to tell you, she would do *any-thing*. In fact, it was usually her idea."

"Hard to go wrong there, buddy." John answered, grinning.

"You let her get to you, Joe. You knew it couldn't be long term, too much age difference. We've talked about that before, remember?" Nikki asked.

"Yeah, but damn, she was *good*." I said.

John jumped on the band wagon with Nikki, sort of.

"If your dog dies, get a new dog."

"Keep talking like that and you won't be getting "dog-gie" or any other."Nikki said as she shot John a dirty look.

"Uh oh, just trying to help Joe out baby, you know what I mean, you're irreplaceable, Honey." John quickly answered. "Joe just needs to get laid." He continued.

Nikki turned her attention back towards me. "Any other recent girlfriends, you could call up Joe?"

"Nah, Dana's nuts, and bitchy, Penny moved to El Paso, she was a pain in the ass too." Just then I remembered the girl that had given me the phone number in the restaurant, and told the two of them about it. I also explained my "women's sense" theory to John and Nikki.

Nikki said," It's the confidence you carry, they can see it."

John had his own theory.

"Its bullshit, they're teasing you, cause they know there's not a fucking thing you can do about it. But hell, I'd call her."

"You should, Joe." Nikki added.

"Yeah, I just might. Get my mind off of Nellie."

John and I went out shooting shortly after that. He had picked up a new Ruger Blackhawk in .357 magnum. I brought along my .380. John and I took turns at the dump, shooting cans. We would line up a few and if I made the shot, I got to take the next shot and so on, until I missed. Then it would be John's turn. We called this little game. "Makers Takers."

I let John go first. He drilled a Campbell's soup can with the 1st shot, recocked the gun and put the 2nd one into a soda can, making it jump into the air. The next shot he jerked and we both watched the shot go low.

"Seems to shoot pretty straight, don't it? Your turn." John said.

There were 8 cans left. I took a sight picture on the 1st can and squeezed it off. As the gun bucked I could see the can flying and slid the front sight over to the next can and squeezed again. I did this until I ran out of cans.

John looked at me.

"Damn Man, eight for eight, you just keep getting better every time we go out."

"I've been practicing a lot." I answered. Which was true, I loved shooting. I couldn't think of anything more fun to do than shoot.

After blowing through a couple of boxes of shells each we switched guns for a few rounds then we headed back to town. Dropping John off, I headed out, thinking about Nellie all the way home.

I walked into my bedroom. As I looked down on my nightstand, I saw the piece of paper with the phone number on it, where I dumped the day's change, and assorted stuff I tended to bring home. Separating the paper from the rattles off a diamondback I had killed the day before, I unfolded it and looked at it. Written in nice writing was the name "Jennifer" followed by a local number.

"What the hell." I thought. I walked into the living room, picked up the phone and dialed the number.

A girl answered, "Hello."

"Hi, Jennifer?" I asked.

"Yeah, is this Joe?"

"Yeah, how are you?" I was surprised she knew it was me.

"I didn't think you would call, I'm glad you did."

"Oh, I've just been busy." I said, as I thought about Nellie sitting on top of me fucking my brains out.

"Do you have a girlfriend?" She asked

Uh oh. More of this *"sixth sense"* shit, I thought.

"No, we broke up."

"Oh, sorry to hear that. Well not really, but you know what I mean."

"Yeah, I do. Maybe we could go out Friday to a movie and dinner, if you're free?" I asked.

"Sure, I would love too, but, um, you, well, you would have to meet my parents first, they're kind of strict." She stammered.

"Not a problem." I told her. "That is, if you really do want to go out."

"Oh, I do, it's just that not many guys want to meet parents." She explained.

I told her it didn't matter to me. After talking awhile more, I gave her my number and said I would see her Friday, and hung up.

Dad came home from work and after awhile decided we would have chili verde burritos for dinner. I went into town and picked up five. Two for me, three for Dad. As we ate dinner and watched M*A*S*H*, we talked.

"Some girl called for you, while you were gone. Jennifer, I think she said her name was." Dad informed me.

"You still seeing that Nellie?" Dad asked.

"No, she broke up with me."

"Good, she was too damned old for you, anyway." Dad said. *How the hell did Dad know how old she was?* I thought.

"Well I didn't think so, she was hot looking." I argued.

"I don't give a damn how she looked. She was still too old for you." Dad said.

This wasn't going anywhere and was a moot point as far as I was concerned. The woman was gone.

Switching subjects, Dad told me. "We might be going on strike when our contract is up next month."

This happened every four years of so anyway and was really nothing new.

"Thing is, the Company says if we do, they'll just shut the doors." Dad continued.

This was new.

"Does that mean you would be out of a job? What about your retirement?" I asked.

Dad explained. "I've got over thirty years in, I just need to wait to be old enough before I can draw it. I won't lose it. I just have to find something else until then."

"Like what?" I asked.

"Well the Teamsters Union would put me to work at another trucking company, but the run may not be as good. Or I might go to work at the smelter with your oldest sister."

The smelter was 150 miles away.

"So we would move?" I asked.

"Well, maybe not, you're going to be a sophomore, next year. I don't really want to pull you out of school here. We'll see what happens." I'm not too worried about it."

Well if Dad wasn't worried about it, I didn't see any reason I should be.

After dinner, I called Jennifer back, thinking she would break the date for Friday. She just wanted to talk, and boy could she talk. I also figured out she went by "Jenn."

The next day, which was Friday, Dana's brother-in-law called me. Ben and his wife lived about a mile down the road from me, although Dana lived near El Paso. I had known them for years.

"Hey Joe, I'm going to a rifle match, today, just outside of town, do you want to go?" Ben asked.

"Yeah, sure. Hang on, let me run it by my Dad."

I asked Dad if I could take the 30-30 or his "Ought Six" out to a shooting match with Ben. Leaving the house with my pistol or my .22 was one thing, leaving the house with high powered rifles, well that was another. I didn't want to push my luck after the cotton trailer incident.

Dad made sure Ben would be around and gave me an ok. He was going to work anyway. I told Dad I had a date that night and would probably get home about the same time as him.

Ben picked me up and after loading the rifles into the truck, we took off. Ben explained the rules to me on the way, and also explained that it was not a "formal" match. I thanked him for bringing me. I had never been to a shooting match, of any kind.

When we got there, we had to sign in. One of the officials asked what gun I was shooting. I answered "Winchester 94, 30-30". Silence.

"Uh, these targets are a long way off son, and kind of small, is it scoped?"

"Nope." I didn't care. I was going to get to shoot.

"Well do you have anything else?" The official asked.

"Got my Dad's 30-06." I answered politely.

"Can you handle that? That would be better, what is it? Do you know?"

"It kicks a little. It's a 1917 Enfield." I replied. I had seen that on the barrel every time I had ever picked it up.

"Does it have a scope?"

"Nope, Dad don't believe in letting me use them."

The official smiled. "Well, tell you what, I'll put you in the iron sight division, there's not a lot of people in it. And good luck to you. That'll be ten dollars."

As I handed the official the money, Ben spoke up.

"Put him in the scoped division too, he can shoot mine. I'll pay for him. You can pay me later, Joe."

I was kind of surprised. "Oh, ok, so I get to shoot twice?"

"Yep, you do." Said the official.

"What kind of gun do you have, Ben?" I asked.

Ben answered the official and me at the same time. "We'll be shooting a .300 H&H in the scoped division."

The official chuckled. "Ok. He's your responsibility, Ben. Don't let him get hurt."

Whoa! What was this all about? Hurt? A *three hundred what*? This brought a flood of questions from me.

"Uh, Ben, what is it you shoot?" I stammered.

Ben smiled. "A .300 H&H, or 300 Holland and Holland."

"I've never heard of it, does it kick?" I asked.

"You can't get too close to the scope, or it will hit you above the eye and cut you open." Ben explained.

What the hell? "But does it kick, Ben? How hard?" I pressed.

"Just a little more than the 30-06 will." He answered.

"Ben, I've already got my *right* eye blackened this month, I don't need another one."

"Yeah but that was probably due to your smart mouth, I'm sure. You'll be okay." Ben teased. Ben knew me well.

The iron sights were called to the shooting line first. Watching the other shooters get ready, I noticed most of them had slings on their rifles and were wrapping their arms in them while standing up. I had never seen this done before and didn't have a sling anyway.

Ben told me I had to fire 3 shots, standing up. I asked him how far the targets were.

"100 yards for these three. Do you know where the gun is sighted for?"

"Dad tells me to take a fine bead at 200, so it'll hit high, right?" I asked.

"Yeah, aim about 2 inches low for the first shot." Ben said.

I shouldered the rifle and lined up the sights. Moving around as little as possible, I let my breath out and as the sights drifted just below the bullseye, I started squeezing the trigger. When it drifted back to the bullseye, I squeezed a little more. The rifle fired, and I let the gun down.

Ben called the shot. "Pretty close. You know where it's hitting. Do it again."

Raising the rifle again, I repeated and felt like I pulled the shot to the left a little. My arms were getting tired. Ben confirmed my thoughts. "That was a little left."

Other rifles were going off up and down the line.

Chambering the third round, my arms tired out before I could get the shot off. I lowered the rifle.

Ben asked. "What's the matter?"

"My arms got tired. Need to rest a second."

Re shouldering the rifle I tried again to align the sights. Taking a deep breath and letting it out, I pulled the rifle

JOSEPH JOHNSON

in tight to my shoulder and started the trigger squeeze. As the rifle bucked, Ben called the shot. "Perfect!"

After the line was clear, (I had taken the last shot) the officials walked out and brought the targets back.

I heard three of them talking on the way back. "Well kids are steadier, you know." One said. Another offered his opinion. "They don't have all that caffeine giving them the jitters, either." The last one said, "Either way, the kid can shoot."This was a good sign.

Moving out to the 200 hundred yard line, we got to sit down to shoot. I thought this was good because I had always been taught to get my gun as steady as possible before taking a shot at game.

Again I watched some of the shooters loop their arms through their rifle slings. I would have to ask Dad about this later on. I had asked Dad about a sling one time while hunting. His reply had been, "You can't shoot a deer with the gun hanging on your shoulder. Why? You want one?" That had ended that conversation.

Ben asked, "You know where to aim?"

"Yep, just take a fine bead." I was already starting to concentrate.

Resting the back of my elbows on the front of my knees, I squirmed around until the rifle was supported square above my knees. This was easy compared to the standing at 100, I thought.

I took a fine as sight picture as I could and squeezed the trigger. As the gun recoiled and I chambered the next round, I heard Ben let out a low whistle.

110

"Wow, dead center, Joe."

I put the next two shots in the bullseye also. I was one of the first ones finished. The shooter next to me spoke too Ben.

"He kind of hurried that. Bet he ain't as lucky with that string."

Ben glanced at him. "Apparently he didn't need it. It looks like all three are in the bulls to me."

The man's mouth dropped a little. "You're full of shit, Ben."

"Want to put some money on it?" Ben asked him. The man turned away muttering.

"What's his problem?" I asked Ben.

"He's an asshole. That's his problem." Ben replied. He had seemed like a pretty nice guy before. But if Ben said he was an asshole, then I guess the guy was an asshole.

"Oh well." I thought. No sense worrying about him, I was having too much fun. I wondered who would win. Maybe I was beating this guy, and that's why he was cranky.

Moving out to the 300 yard line, Ben asked me, "Do you know where to aim for this Joe? It's 300 hundred yards."

"Dad says at 300, I should aim at the top of a deer's back, but not over it."

"Then aim at the top of the bullseye." Ben instructed.

"Like in the top of the target, or the top of the circle?" I asked.

"Top of the circle." I was told.

This time some of the shooters were lying down, and some were sitting. I got back into my sitting position and took a fine bead at the top of the circle.

Squeezing the round off, I heard Ben say, "A little low." I thought I might have jerked the trigger a little, so I held in the same place. I was starting to get a little sore from the 30-06. I held in the same place and concentrated on the trigger. The shot broke clean and Ben told me it was low in the bullseye.

The next shot I held just a little higher and after taking a couple of deep breaths, let the trigger break.

"Damn, Joe. That was a *good* shot." I heard Ben say.

Immediately after we finished, the announcement for "Scope shooters, flight one, to the line." was given. There were enough shooters that they had to be divided up into two different groups. Ben was in flight one, I was in flight two.

I watched Ben set his rifle case on a bench and pull out a rather average looking rifle. It was a Winchester Model 70, also known as "The Rifleman's Rifle." It wore a Leupold scope on it. Next Ben took out a plastic case of ammo that he had reloaded. As he slid the top of the case off, he pulled out one cartridge and handed it to me. My stomach turned. In my hands I was holding the largest cartridge I had ever seen at that time. This thing was HUGE. Especially compared to my 30-30 cartridges. It was bigger than Dad's 30-06!

"Fuck You, Ben! I'm not shootin that big sumbitch. You're outta your freaking mind!

"Aw quit you're whining, you can handle it. Don't be a baby." Ben scolded.

My stomach started to churn some more. The butter-flies were really taking flight now.

"I'm kinda sore from Dad's ought six. Maybe I outta sit this one out." I pleaded, as I handed the cartridge back to Ben.

"You're already paid for, don't worry about it. Just watch."

The rules for the scoped match were slightly different. They would not shoot at 100 yards standing. Instead they would shoot 2 strings from 200 yards. One string sitting, and one string from a bench. 300 hundred yards would also be from the bench.

As I watched Ben slide the first cartridge into the chamber it reminded me of a torpedo being rammed into a launch tube. My stomach lurched some more.

Ben took aim. I was holding his binoculars, or as he called them, his "far lookers." Ben touched off the first shot with a roar. I about jumped out of my skin.

"*Holy shit!* That thing was *loud!*" I thought. My stomach churned again. I found the hole in the target and told Ben it was 10.

"Where in the 10?" he asked.

I looked again. "A little low and right." I answered.

"Four o'clock? Five o'clock? Where?" Ben asked.

I was confused. It was closer to eleven in the morning.

Ben seeing my confusion, explained, "Think of the bulls as the center of the clock. Where is the shot at, *if* it were a clock? You said it was low and right, so is it like where four o'clock would be, or five o'clock? Six o'clock would be lined up perfect, but low."

"Oh, ok, I get it now." I looked again. "Five o'clock." I confirmed.

Ben fired again. "Ten, dead center." I called out. Shooting his last shot it also went into the 10 ring, although high and left.

"It's on the line between the 10 ring and 9 ring, Ben, at eleven o'clock. Does that make it a 10 or a 9?" I asked.

"If it breaks the line, you get the higher point. So it's a ten." Ben informed me. That was good. I wanted Ben to do well.

Ben laid the rifle on the bench and took a seat behind it. With me spotting his shots, Ben fired three more 10's, with two of them perfectly centered.

After pulling the targets and putting up targets at 300 yards, Ben took a seat behind the bench again. Spotting for him, I called his first shot low and right in the 9 ring. "Five o'clock." I said.

"Yeah, I jerked it." Ben said. The next one went into the 10 ring. Chambering his last round, Ben fired again. It looked low at 6:00 o'clock, I couldn't tell if it were a 9 or a 10. It turned out to be a nine, giving Ben a final score of 88 out of a possible 90.

Elsewhere up and down the firing line, I could hear various mutterings and curses. Apparently the 300 yard line was tougher than it looked. From what I could tell Ben was surely ahead of everyone else, but there was still one more flight to go.

Changing targets again, the 2nd flight (including me) took our places at the line.

"I'm not sure about this Ben." The butterflies in my stomach felt like a flock of vultures by now.

"Just try one shot. If it kicks too much, you don't have to shoot anymore." Ben answered me.

I immediately felt better. I had a way out! I could handle one shot. After that I would be done.

As I sat down for the two hundred yard string, Ben handed me one of the small versions of the Intercontinental Ballistic Missile he called a "cartridge."

"Pull it in tight to your shoulder." Ben said.

"No shit!" I thought, as I took the cartridge and placed it into the magazine and closed the bolt. Finding the bullseye in the scope, I pulled the rifle into my shoulder as tightly as I could as I lined up the crosshairs and pulled the trigger, eager to get this over with.

As the gun roared, I felt a long hard shove rearward, as Ben called out, "Low in the 9. You jerked the shit out of it, didn't you?"

I quickly took stock of myself. My shoulder had not been dislocated, I had not been knocked on my ass, and my head was still attached. The rifle did not seem to snap me as much as Dad's ought six. It had been harder, but *different*. More like a "hard shove" than a "kick."

"I could handle this." I remember thinking. I had ignored Ben's comment but was reaching up for another cartridge as he continued to instruct me.

"*Squeeze the trigger,* this time."

Where had I heard that before? Forget it one damned time, and the whole world acts like you didn't know any better, and that I had never done it before. I had numerous memories flood through me as I recalled Mom, Dad, Colter, Zeb, and everyone else that ever watched me pick up a gun say, "Don't forget to *squeeze* the trigger." My sisters even told me that shit, and I can't remember ever seeing either one of them shoot. I think they just liked telling me what to do or liked to sound like they knew what they were doing.

As I closed the bolt on the 2nd round, I lined up the crosshairs again. Settling them on the bullseye, I *squeezed*. As the shot broke, I worked the bolt and reached for another round. I knew it was good.

Ben called out, "10, dead center." Putting the next round in, I lined up the crosshairs again and squeezed. As the rifle boomed, I jacked the empty case out. Ben was quiet. "I think you miss....no, right on top of the last one Joe, almost one hole!" Ben said excitedly.

"This scope makes it easy, Ben. It's like cheating." I told him.

He chuckled as he answered, "Well let's see if you can keep it up."

Moving to the bench, I settled the gun in and loaded it. Not having to brace on my knees now, the gun was rock steady. I lined up the crosshairs and squeezed the next three rounds off fairly quickly. There didn't seem to be much to do. The gun was supported, just line up the crosshairs and squeeze'em off. Ben was looking at me strangely as he said, "That's a pretty good group, Joe."

"What do you mean by group?" I asked.

"Group" means how close together your shots are. Most of yours are touching." he explained.

"This gun shoots really well, Ben. I like it."

"I bet you do. Except for the 1st shot you jerked, the rest are all right in the bulls. That was damned fine shooting." Ben said.

I thought he was just trying to encourage me, but I said "Thanks" anyway.

While the targets were changed, Ben and I talked about the 300 yard string coming up.

"On my gun, to hit the bulls at 300, you need to aim high in the 10 ring. If you aim at the bulls, you'll hit a low 10 or a 9. If you aim at the top of the 10 ring, it will be a little bit high off the bullseye, so cut the distance in half." Ben told me.

"Not quite as high as the ought six, then?" I asked.

"Nope, it shoots a little flatter, just high in the ten."

"Ok." I answered. It sounded easy enough.

As everyone else settled in, I also got behind the gun. I noticed my shoulder was getting sore, from all the shooting. As I chambered the 1st round, Ben told me.

"Don't forget to squeeze."

"Ok." I answered as I lined up the scope with the target and raised the crosshairs, just a little, and squeezed off the round. Firing the round off, I knew the shot broke well.

Ben called out. "Good shot. 10. Do it again, if you can."
The next shot, the trigger went off just a little lower than
the 1st one had.

"Bulls eye." Ben called.

"Was the 1st one a little higher, than that one?" I asked.

"Yes it was, but it's still a 10." He confirmed. Now I
knew where to aim. On the last round, I aimed the same
place the second shot had broke at. As I squeezed off the
shot, I worked the bolt and ejected the last round. I was
done and kind of glad. My shoulder was feeling kind of
loose and tender.

Ben stood behind the binoculars. "Touching the same
hole as the last one." he sighed. "Damn. That's good. You
just out shot me, with my own gun." Ben shook his head
as he said it.

I smiled. "Right. I really like this gun." I thought it was
nice of Ben to say I had out shot him, but I knew better.

"You'll see." Ben said. I was a little confused. I really
didn't know what he meant.

As we cased the rifles and put them in the truck, the
scorekeepers collected the targets and tallied the scores.

For the most part, all the shooters seemed pretty happy, except for a few grumpy ones that were making excuses
about one thing or another. Scopes, rifles and hand loads
were being talked about and generally it seemed like cel-
ebration was in the air. This was a good time.

I had come to realize that I actually had a chance to
win this, if it were allowed. I didn't put much stock in that
happening though. Colter and Dad both were better shots

than I, but it seemed that I had shot well compared to everyone else, and Colter and Dad weren't here.

One of the scorekeepers spoke up.

"Ok, listen up everyone. First, we'll call the iron sighted. In 3rd place, is Dan Spaulding." Dan stepped forward and as the scorekeeper handed him the money, he said "Good shooting, Dan." Continuing the scorekeeper said, "In 2nd place, Greg Dewitt." Mr. Grumpy stepped up, and took his money. He still didn't look happy.

"And in 1st place, we have a new winner, Joseph Johnson. Congratulations, damn fine shooting, son." As the scorekeeper handed me the money, he pumped my hand and grinned at Mr. Grumpy.

"Moving on to the scoped division, we have some good scores to announce. In 3rd place, Dan Spaulding." I watched Spaulding step up and receive some more money. He had been at the opposite end of my line. I wished I could have watched him shoot. He had taken two, 3rd places. The guy obviously knew what he was doing.

"Not a bad day, if you ask me. Got a little shooting in and a little change in my pocket." His grin was irrepressible. This man had come to have a good time, and did. I understood how he felt.

The scorekeeper continued, "In 2nd place with an 88 out of a possible 90, Ben Coles." As Ben stepped up and took his money he thanked the scorekeeper.

"In 1st place, we have a new winner, with an 89 out of a possible 90, Joseph Johnson, again." Everyone started clapping, this was great, as the scorekeeper handed me the 1st

place money he asked me, "What happened to that one point, Son?"

Looking up at him, I ashamedly said, "I forgot to squeeze." This brought a roar of laughter, as well as some back slapping and teasing to Ben as well.

"Been a long time since Ben got beat, he'll be more careful who he brings next time." Dan Spaulding said with a grin.

"This oughta be limited to adults only." Mr. Grumpy said. Dan Spaulding fired back at him. "What difference would it make, Dewitt? Ben would still out shoot you."

There's always one in every crowd. This was a lesson well learned. I haven't been to too many matches, that there wasn't "one in every crowd."

"Well, everybody, that wraps up the rifle competitions. Let's head over to the shotgun range for the skeet shooting." The match director announced.

Shotguns? Skeet? Ben hadn't mentioned this. This is another story entirely, and it's not going to be told here. (Yeah, I got my ass kicked.) But I had money left over even after paying Ben back.

When I got home, Dad had left me a note, saying he had gone to work at four o'clock. He would be home between midnight and two in the morning. I had no sooner set down, and the phone started ringing. It was Jenn.

"Hi, Joe?"

"Hey Jenn, what's up?" I braced myself for her to break the date, although I really didn't care.

"Not much. I was wondering if we were still going out tonight? I've been trying to call you all day."

"Yeah. I just got home, I was getting ready to clean up and give you a call. Dinner at Grigg's and a movie sound good?"

"Sounds great, I'm excited. What have you been doing all day?" She asked.

"I went to a shooting match with Ben, a friend of mine. I used to date his sister-in-law." *Now why in the hell did I say that?* I thought to myself.

"Oh? Who's his sister-in-law?" She curiously asked.

"Her name's Dana, doesn't live here, near El Paso." I said, as casually as I could. I needed to get away from this subject.

"The girl that you just broke up with?" She tried to casually ask. I could tell she was on high alert.

"No, that was another one, Dana was an old girlfriend, I haven't dated her in quite awhile." I replied honestly. I was digging my hole deeper. This sucked.

"Is she pretty?" she wanted to know. Damn right, she was pretty I thought, but what am I going to say, that I only date ugly girls?

"Well, yeah." I tried to sound unsure. "But she's crazy, a big pain in the ass. I haven't dated her in over a year." I quickly added.

"Wow, you have a lot of girlfriends huh?" She wasn't making this any easier.

"No. Right now I don't have any. It's just that Ben and his wife are friends with us. We go camping, fishing, and stuff. He just invited me to the shooting match this morning, was all." I really needed to get off this subject.

"How did you do?" She finally was going to let it go.

"I won!" I said, happily.

"Was there a lot of kids, in it?" She wanted to know.

"Uh, no, there wasn't. I was the only one." I was feeling better about this and a little proud too.

After talking a little more and narrowly avoiding the subject of Nellie too, (I pretended I didn't hear and answered one of her other thousand questions.) we agreed I would be there at 5:30, meet her parents, dinner at 6:00, movie at 8:00. What can I say? I'm a planner.

I pulled out the Hoppes #9 and cleaned Dad's Ought Six, and put it back into its place in the closet next to my 30-30. I reeked of gun oil, and started a bath.

Cleaning up and trimming my beard a little bit, I put on a new pair of jeans, and a nice western shirt. I slapped on some after shave that Crazy Dana had given me and made a mental note *not* to mention that.

I found Jenn's house and after passing by once, drove around killing time. I then decided to stop and buy some condoms, (just in case.) At 5:30, I knocked on the door. Jenn met me at the door wearing jeans and a low cut top. I hadn't noticed before but she had nice tits. For the second time today, I wasn't thinking about Nellie. Jenn assessed me up and down.

"You look nice, smell good too." She said approvingly.

"Thanks. You look real nice too." I answered, although somewhat bashfully.

Jenn introduced everyone. "This is my Mom and Dad, Dave and Karen. This is Joe."

Dave was dark haired, almost six foot tall, with broad shoulders. His nose had been broken at some point in his life. Looking at him, he could have been anything from a day laborer, to an accountant. I looked Dave in the eye as I shook hands with him. The look was returned, with some coldness, I noted.

Karen jumped into my rescue. "Dave, don't be mean." What grade are you in Joe? How old are you? I politely answered this and every other question that was thrown at me. Dave wanted to know what my Dad did. I told him, and asked what he did for a living.

"I'm a pilot." He answered. I was impressed.

"That's a pretty good job isn't it?

"Not bad." He admitted.

"Do you fly jets? Like for American Airlines or who?" I was very curious.

"No, I fly rotor wing, and fixed wing. I'm a charter pilot." He explained.

I wasn't even sure what the hell he had just said.

"Where did you learn to fly? I always wanted to be a pilot but my eyes suck." I explained.

"I flew slicks in Southeast Asia, and then multi engines for a contractor."

I had never heard of "slicks" or Air America as I found out later the "contractor" was called. Asking the obvious, "So you were in Vietnam?"

"Yep, I was in Vietnam, two tours on the slicks, and then some time on the C-130s." Dave answered.

"I have a lot of respect for Vietnam veterans. Actually all veterans." I told him. I was trying to make points, but it was, and is the truth.

"Is that a fact?" He asked, somewhat curiously I could tell.

"Yes Sir, I do."

"And why is that?" Dave pressed.

"It's obvious that the only reason we have the freedoms that we have today and the country that we live in is because people have fought for it. We owe everything to our vets." I replied.

Dave stared at me for a long time without saying anything.

"Really? He finally asked.

"What the hell was this all about?" I thought. He was kind of spooking me.

"Yeah. Really." I answered politely.

"Was your Dad or Brother in the service?" Dave asked as he continued to stare at me.

"No, they weren't. It's just the way I feel about it, is all." I quietly answered.

This seemed to satisfy him. He nodded agreement with me as he stood up and left the room. I apparently had touched a nerve or something. *That was just plain weird,* I thought.

Jenn invited me to sit down on the couch as she poured us sodas. Karen sat down opposite me and asked what our plans were.

"I thought we would go to Griggs for dinner, then a movie." I answered.

"What movie?" Karen wanted to know.

"Whatever Jenn wants to see, I guess." I replied. I hadn't really thought about it but I had picked up on where Jenn had gotten her tits. Her moms were huge.

Dave walked into the room carrying a rifle, and cleaning kit.

"Dave!" Karen said harshly.

"What?" Dave innocently asked.

"There is no need to scare the boy." She told him.

"I'm not trying to scare him, I just need to clean it." Dave said.

I stood up and moved over for a closer look.

"No Karen, it's ok, guns don't scare me. I just cleaned mine, well my Dad's. Is that a 30-06? It's not a Winchester, or Remington, but it's not *quite* like my Dad's either. His is an Enfield." I explained.

Dave looked up from his chair and handed me the rifle as he explained.

"It's a Mauser, the Enfield is based on it. Different company. You have a good eye for guns. Do you know much about them?"

"Yeah, well, a little I guess. I have a 30-30, a 20 gauge, and a .22 and a .380. I love to shoot." I explained.

"Are you any good, Joe?" Dave asked. I told him about the match today and how I had won it. I left out the part about the shotguns.

"He's just trying to scare you Joe." Karen reiterated. I was slow catching on.

"I like guns." I replied. I didn't realize that I was supposed to be scared of Dave.

"Well Jenn, he may know guns, but he isn't all that sharp." Dave laughed.

"Dad! Don't be rude." Jenn said angrily.

"I don't get it, did I miss something?" I asked Karen. Now she was laughing.

"Yeah, you did. But that's ok. It's not often Dave's plans backfire on him." She replied.

Changing the subject, Karen looked at me.

"Joe, may I ask you something?"

"Sure, go ahead."

"What happened to your hands?

"I got burned." Jenn looked shocked as she seemed to notice my scars for the first time.

"How?" Jenn asked as everyone got quiet and riveted their attention on me.

I very solemnly looked at Jenn and her family and replied.

"Fire."

She blinked, like she couldn't believe what I had just said.

"Great. He's a smart ass, too." Dave said as everyone laughed.

Now that it was out in the open, I pointed out my ear that was partially melted off, and showed off some of the rest of my scars. This brought out the rest of the story about me and Mom being burned along with my Mom dying later of Cancer. This was a pretty routine conversation in my life. It seemed to make everyone else uncomfortable initially. I explained it and that was that.

Jenn asked if I was ready to go. I said "Yes" and looked at Dave.

"What time do you want her back by, Sir?"

Dave stood up and reached to shake my hand, replying as he did so.

"10:30" Dave pointed at my belt buckle with his left hand. "Keep your mind above, that."

"Dave!" Karen said somewhat loudly.

"Oh all right. Eleven o'clock then." Dave said.

"Yes Sir!" I replied and grinned.

Walking out to the truck, I opened the door for Jenn. She climbed in and I walked around the truck, got in, started it up and left. As soon as we were around the corner, Jenn looked over her shoulder, as if her Dad might be following her and scooted across the seat next to me. Putting her hand on my knee, she said, "I'm glad we're going out."

"Me too." I said.

"That's nice cologne, what is it?"

I told her the brand.

"That's expensive stuff. Where did you get it?" Jenn asked.

More of that *intuition* thing, again. This was starting to freak me out.

"Uh, from my Aunt." I lied.

"Well, it's nice. I like it."

"Thanks." I said. This night might not turn out too bad after all, I thought.

Jenn wasn't really very hungry so we caught an earlier movie. I don't remember what, but it was probably a scary one, knowing me. My theory was all first dates were taken to scary movies. That way, they had a good reason to get close to you.

After the movie, driving home, Jenn asked where we could go park. Finding a place wasn't really a problem. As I turned the truck off, Jenn came close and kissed me. She was a good kisser. I was warming up fast. Knowing she was still young, (compared to who I had been seeing) I didn't expect this to go much further. But hell, I was a red blooded American teenager, I *had* to try. Sliding my hand under her breast, she stopped me.

"Wait." She said. Then leaning back, she untucked her blouse and unbuttoned it. Pulling it open with her breasts swelling out of a pink bra, she looked at me and spoke.

"There, that's better." I hadn't expected that, I thought, as she slipped her tongue into my mouth and made me forget all about Nellie.

Jenn wasn't a virgin, but she didn't have a lot of experience. She knew what she liked though, and I did my damndest to make sure she liked it all. Getting back to her house about 10:45, we stood outside her front door and made out until 11:00. I went home happy, with ZZ Top, playing "Tush" on the cassette deck.

The next morning Dad poked his head into my room.

"Breakfast is ready." I saw his nostrils flare.

"Was that Nellie gal here, last night?"

"No, I told you she broke up with me." I answered as I reached for my pants. Pulling my boots on, I realized I reeked of sex. Which was fine by me, but may have put Dad off a little. While cutting up my steak, the phone rang. Dad answered it. I listened.

"He's eating right now, have him call you back? Who's this? Ok, bye."

"Call Jenn when you finish breakfast. Was she over last night?" Dad wanted to know.

"No, I went to meet her parents, and we went to a movie." I told him. I left the part out about eating and fucking her and making her cum five times, but I was dying to tell *somebody*.

"What's her folks do?" Dad asked.

"Dave's a pilot, Karen's a housewife. They seem nice."

"How old is she?"

"My age. Fifteen, I guess." Damn, I hadn't thought to ask.

Dad nodded, I guess he approved.

"Don't forget to call her back."

"I won't." I answered, as I wondered why the hell everybody wants to know what everybody else does.

Dad hadn't asked me if she were pretty. Her folks hadn't asked what I wanted to do with my life or what I liked to do, or even very much about me. Her parents and my Dad had both asked about how the others made a living. This needed some thought. Later, though. I finally did get back around to this, but it was several years. I shouldn't have put it off, more life lessons and all that crap.

Calling Jenn back resulted in me being invited over to dinner at her house that night. I accepted. The next night, I was over there again.

On weekends, Jenn and I would go out to a movie and/or dinner and depending on her mood, out to the river to watch the "submarine races." Sometimes I couldn't talk her into it, other times, there was no stopping her. Go figure.

Evenings with Jenn and her folks became pretty regular, when Dad wasn't home. I was over there enough that in a rare moment of humor for Dave, he asked me for my social security number. When I asked him "Why?" His reply to me was, "You spend enough time here, I can claim you as a deduction on my income taxes."

I was usually there when Dave was, as well as when he wasn't. Dave's schedule would put him out of town for four or five days at a time and then back home for a few more.

About a month had gone by, when Dad's company went on strike. I asked him if we were going to walk the picket line, like we had in the past. His reply said it all.

"Nope, time for me to find a new job. Just for a few months, until my birthday."

Dad started his new job, one week after leaving the old one. He told me, "It's a good outfit to work for." And he seemed just as pleased as ever.

As summer rolled past, and into the windy days of fall, Dad started planning his retirement. He had decided to go to work at the smelter and stay with my oldest sister and her family. We talked about it over venison and fried taters one night.

"Do you have a problem with me going to your sister's? He asked.

"No. Not really. Should I?"

"Well, my schedule would be seven days on, one off, seven on, two off, and then seven days on, four off, which works out to five, because I start on days the last week, and come back on graveyard of the fourth day, so it's like having five days off."

I could barely contain my excitement. I was going to have the house to myself, *if* I didn't blow it.

I considered my answer carefully.

"Hmmm, well it is only a 2 and half hour drive."

"Three." Dad corrected me. "You need to slow down."

"I can pay the bills when I come home on my four day weekend, and on my two days off, I can do the laundry and dishes and stuff."

"I can do my own laundry Dad, dishes too, ain't a big deal to me."

"You really don't mind me being gone that long?" Dad asked.

"No. You gotta work. I just wonder why you don't make me move with you though?"

"Well because I am not ready to give this place up. I don't know that I want to stay there or here either, for that matter. Besides it'll be easier on you, than switching schools this late in the game. Especially with your mouth." He added.

"Thanks, I appreciate that. I guess."

Dad looked at me and after considering for a bit continued.

"I promised your Mom, that I would take care of you and see you got raised. I just want to make sure you're going to be ok. Will you be okay? Here? By yourself?"

I could hardly contain my excitement as I considered my answer, again.

"I don't see why not, if I run into a problem, I can always give ya a call." I told Dad as I thought about any women or girls that I knew that would be willing to move in.

"Good. You know I'm proud of you, don't you pard'ner?"

"Thanks Dad. I'll be ok, don't see why I wouldn't."

"Well me neither, but I still worry about you." Dad said.

Dad retired, and moved in with my oldest sister, and started a job at the smelter. He came home pretty regularly in the beginning, and I was responsible while he was away. I was almost always in bed by 10:00pm and didn't bother to skip school. Weekends were a different story. Generally it involved, going out with Jenn or a whole lotta dope smoking with Billy, Rob, and Brad.

Billy was still pretty much worthless, although he had been graduated for over two years.

Brad, I had known since I was about 12. I used to say, that "Brad has been stoned since the 5th grade." He was the "peace, love & joy" pothead of our little group, and still is to this day, as far as I know.

Rob, I had met the year before through Brad at a party out in the desert. He was a good guy. Originally from back east, his family had moved to El Paso, when he was young. Rob and I became lifelong friends and still stay in touch. Over the years, Rob has stood by me as a friend more times than I can count. Rob also took great pleasure in helping me terrify Brad over the years. Brad smoked so much dope he was constantly paranoid. It took little from me and Rob to freak him out. Spinning a pickup or car out, was usually enough to start him down the road of paranoia and smoking more weed to calm down.

When bars and drinking were concerned, it was always just me and Billy. Brad and Rob were both too young to drink. The drinking age was eighteen then, and although I wasn't even close, I had a full beard, and never got carded.

As spring came around, Jenn and I were dating more, and we both thought we were in love. One thing for sure, I was over Nellie. Well, pretty much. It was hard to replace a woman that kept coming up with ways to surprise you.

One night coming home from a date with Jenn, I heard a tire start making noise, just before it blew out. I eased off the gas and pulled into a convenience store parking lot. Looking down at my watch, I realized, we would have been back to Jenn's house five minutes before she was supposed to be. Now we would be late. I was never late, especially with Jenn.

I reached into my pocket and pulled some change out and indicated the pay phone on the outside wall of the convenience store, while handing it to Jenn.

"Go call your Mom, let her know we broke down."

"No, that's ok."

"No, it's not ok Jenn. Call them and tell them what happened and where we're at. Tell'em we'll be 15 minutes late. I don't want your Mom pissed at me."

As Jenn walked off to the phone I was already pulling out the spare tire, jack and lug wrench. I was hurrying.

When Jenn came back we talked as I changed the tire.

"Was your Mom mad?" I asked.

"My Dad answered." Jenn replied.

This wasn't a good sign. Dave should have been asleep.

"Did you tell him what happened? Is he mad?" I didn't want to face a mad dad, when we got there. But we did have a flat and I had the blown tire to prove it.

"No, it's ok. We just need to get home." Jenn didn't sound so sure.

"When we get there, just drop me off, I'll handle it." Jenn continued.

"No, we didn't do anything wrong. If your Dad is mad, he can tell me. I have a blown tire. It's not like we're lying to them." I sounded cool, but I sure didn't feel that way.

I pulled up 10 minutes after the hour. As I walked Jenn to her door, she was still trying to talk me into going home. As we stepped up onto the front porch, the door opened and Dave stepped out. He was fully dressed.

"Dave, we blew a tire, man. I fixed it as fast as I could." I quickly explained.

"Ok. Jenn time for you to get to bed. I'm going to work." Dave answered.

Inside, I breathed a sigh of relief. I hadn't even thought about him getting called to work. As Jenn shut the door, Dave looked at me.

7

SMUGGLER

Dave, after deciding I would be "solid" as he put it, suckered me into a "little something."

"You want to go?" Dave asked quietly.

I considered his question, but didn't really understand. Did he mean leave the house or go with him?

"Go where?" I finally asked.

"With me. To work, dumbass." He answered.

"We're gonna fly somewhere?" I asked excitedly.

"Well we're not walking. We'll be gone for three days. Do you want to go or not?"

I had to make a decision, quick. I wasn't about to call Dad in the middle of the night and ask him, if I could take a three day flight. He had left the day before. I wouldn't hear from him for a couple of days at least. I could skip school on Monday, I hadn't missed a day all year. I could leave him a note just in case he did come home unexpectedly.

"Yeah, I'll go. I need to run by the house, first. What all do I need to bring?" I asked.

Dave told me a couple of essentials to bring, and said he would pick me up at the house. Ten minutes later, I was turning into my house, followed by Dave. I ran in, grabbed a few things and wrote Dad a note that I hoped he would never see.

> *Dad, I went with Dave.*
> *He just needed some help.*
> *I'll be back Monday.*
> *Josey*

As we climbed into Dave's pickup, and drove to the airport, I asked where we were going.

"We're heading down Mexico way." Dave answered as he stared straight ahead.

"Uh, do I need a passport or anything?" I was a little unsure of myself now.

"Nah. Not unless we get stopped. Then you might have a problem." Dave chuckled.

"Oh shit!" I thought. "Dave. We really did have a blowout. It's in the back of my truck if you want to look at it."

Dave laughed for the second time in one day. This was rare.

"I know you did. I looked at it when you went into your house. I'm surprised you didn't wreck." Dave said, glancing at me.

"My Dad taught me to drive young. I can handle a blowout. Just don't hit the brakes, is all." Did he think I was stupid?

"You seem pretty resourceful, for your age." Dave added.

"Thanks. I just do what needs to be done." I was glad Dave thought that much of me. I didn't really think he had noticed much.

Dave explained to me a few things I didn't know. He would fly fishermen, hunters, businessmen etc. down to Mexico, Honduras, El Salvador, or any of the Central American countries. Since charter flights were longer, fuel and money was not spent to come back only to turn back around and go get them. Dave would wait for a day or so, before bringing them back.

Arriving at the airport, we went into a hangar. Inside was a twin engine airplane. It seemed pretty big to me. I was checking it out, mesmerized. I don't think I had been this close to a plane like this. I had flown a couple of times in airliners, but that was it.

On this first trip, I helped Dave load the plane. The first items loaded were crates and boxes. I assumed they belonged to the clients, or were supplies, airplane parts, etc. I really had no idea, and didn't ask. I also helped load all the clients gear. Looking back, I should have asked about the "supplies."

After arriving in southern Mexico while unloading, Dave told me as I was reaching for some boxes and crates, "Those stay." I slid them back into their respective places.

After confirming arrangements to pick up the clients, Dave indicated we were getting back into the plane. After taxiing out and turning west, we started flying over mountains.

"I thought you always fueled when you land?" I asked Dave, curious about where we going.

"Usually we do, but we don't need the extra weight for where we're going and we have plenty of fuel. And it looks like we're going to be a little early too." Dave answered as he looked at his watch.

As we started to descend I could see a dirt strip in the distance. There were no signs of habitation that I could see from here.

"What are we going to do here?" I wondered out loud.

Setting the plane down on what I originally thought was a dirt road, I realized this was a rough strip and it seemed pretty remote to me. I was starting to worry. Just what in the hell was this all about? In the back of my mind, I could hear the theme to the "Twilight Zone."

Dave didn't answer me as he was busy with the plane or just chose to ignore me.

Slowing to a stop at the end of the runway, I saw movement in the tree line. Before I could grasp what was happening, Dave dropped the engines to an idle and pulled a .45 automatic pistol from somewhere on his side of the cabin.

Cycling the slide and chambering a round, he thumbed the safety up and handed the gun towards me.

Panic started to set in. Butterflies took flight in my stomach. Was this one of Dave's jokes to scare me? But the gun wasn't pointed at me. I involuntarily reached for it, thinking better in my hand than someone else's. I looked at Dave questioningly. I'm sure my mouth was at least half open.

"Wha...wha...what's..going on?" I hesitantly tried to ask.

Dave looked at me and gave me my instructions. Short concise and to the point.

"You do *not* shoot, unless somebody else shoots first. Then you're on your own."

I freaked! As Dave's words sunk into me, my eyes darted to the men approaching the plane and back to Dave. They had guns. *Machine guns!*

Holy Shit! I thought.

"WHAT THE HELL, DAVE? WHAT'S GOING ON? DAVE, WAIT YOU FUCKER!" I yelled as Dave climbed down out of the plane.

Full blown panic set in as I saw what seemed like twenty armed men, walk up to the plane. (There were probably more like seven or eight.) But with that many machine guns looking back at me it seemed like a lot more!

As the rear door on the left side of the plane opened, I spun in my seat and looked over my left shoulder. A dark face stuck its head in and looked back at me. I couldn't shoot at him if I wanted to. I moved the .45 to my right hand. Could I hit him from here, if I needed to? What the hell was I thinking? I couldn't shoot it out sitting in a plane, with a pistol against these people. Whoever the hell they were.

The dark faced reached for the first crate and drug it towards him, as he pulled it out, someone took it and he reached in for the next one. In less than a minute, he was done and shut the door.

Dave closed the door behind him, slamming it as he climbed in, carrying a canvas bag. I jumped in my seat, finger on the trigger of the .45. It was a damn good thing Dave had put the safety on. Otherwise he would have just got shot by his own gun, or there would be a hole in the plane or worse, the people outside took it as a hostile act and opened up on us.

Dave spun the plane, shoved the throttles to maximum and set the flaps as we started accelerating toward the trees. Pulling up at what I thought was too late, and starting to climb, I took stock of myself. I was still alive. And scared, *real scared.*

As we continued to climb, Dave reached over and took the pistol from my hand. He placed the pistol into the canvas bag and pulled out a stack of money. He peeled off five, one hundred dollar bills. Handing them to me he spoke. "Here's your cut. You're in."

I was speechless, which was pretty damned rare for me.

I took the money. If I was in half as much trouble as I thought I was, I may need it. No sense taking any chances.

My stomach churned. I needed to use the bathroom.

My first thought was to get to a major airport, use the money Dave had given me and buy a commercial flight back to El Paso. Fast. On second thought, it might eat all the money up and I had no passport. Would that be a problem? I wasn't sure. Going back and forth from Juarez it wasn't a problem, but that was a border town. I could call Dad. I imagined the conversation in my mind. Calling Dad up, while he was at work, "Dad, I'm in Central

America. Can you come get me?" I didn't want to take this thought any farther. Dad would have been so ashamed of me I don't think I could ever face him again. To say nothing of the retribution that would follow.

It was time to take stock of the situation. I needed to lay my emotions aside, which were running wild and try and think logically. Stick with the facts.

To begin with I was a teenager in a foreign country. It was all I could do to keep from crying when I thought about this. I had no one to rely on. I couldn't trust the person I was with or could I? I wasn't dead, I was 500.00 richer, but I sure as hell hadn't seen this coming. Could I depend on Dave or not? I couldn't reach an easy answer to this and at any rate, it didn't stick with what I was trying to determine. I needed to determine what I *knew* as fact. Should I call Colter instead of Dad? Another damned question, again no facts. I took a deep breath, and started over in my mind.

Fact: I was in a foreign country. I was a teenager, this could work for me or against me.

Fact: I knew no one, except the person I was with.

Fact: I had money in my pocket so therefore I had *some* resources. I may or may not be in danger, and I had no weapons, to speak of. I felt for my knife.

Fact: I was due back sooner than it would take Dad or Colter to locate, reach me and return. This didn't mean I would make it back though.

Fact: I couldn't trust the person I was with. He had gotten me into this thing, but I had not been harmed. Yet.

Harming me would serve little purpose that I could see. If my personal wellbeing were part of the equation, the bad part was *probably* behind me. Not fact but still, I considered it. I went over this again in my mind and boiled it down a little more.

Fact: I didn't trust Dave, but I had no indication that I was not returning with him and no attempt had been made to harm me. This did make me feel a little better.

I took another deep breath, I was fucked. Royally, one hundred and ten percent fucked, with no way out, except playing it out to the end. See where the cards fell and hope for the best. This sucked.

I looked over at Dave. He was smiling. The arrogant, psycho bastard was actually smiling. I had to know what had just happened and decided to just flat out ask him.

It came out as a screaming accusation. "WHAT IN THE HELL, DAVE? WHAT IN THE HELL WAS THAT ALL ABOUT? ARE YOU TRYING TO GET US KILLED?"

Dave started laughing, from the belly up, long and loud. His head rocked back and forth as he tried to cover his mouth. Tears welled up in his eyes. He tried to speak but every time he glanced at me, even for a moment, he would start laughing again. I sat there like the dumb ass that I felt I was, waiting for an answer. After a while, Dave's laughter started to become contagious, and I was laughing as well. I was still scared, and didn't understand why I thought anything was funny, but I couldn't help myself. I couldn't stop laughing either.

142

"You should have seen the look on your face." Dave said as snot blew out his nose from him laughing. "Have you ever fired a .45?" He asked, as he tried to calm down. Turning his head away, he pulled out a handkerchief and wiped snot from his face.

"Once. They have some kick to them." I answered.

"Good. Learn to keep your finger off the trigger, unless you're going to shoot. If that safety hadn't been on, we'd both be in trouble right now."

"No shit. More trouble than I am right now with my girlfriends Dad in a foreign country and no one knows where I am?" I said sarcastically, making Dave and I both start laughing again. I couldn't figure out why I was laughing. I was scared half to death. The handkerchief came back out. Dave was enjoying himself tremendously.

Dave, with some seriousness, explained somewhat of what had just occurred. "Those people have a very oppressive government. It is so oppressive, that they would rather fight and die, than continue living the way they are living now. Have you ever had it that bad in your life, or seen people live in those conditions?" I was somewhat ashamed, to answer "No" although I had no reason to be ashamed. I had seen living conditions in Juarez and it was pretty bad, and told Dave so.

"These people would love to have it that good Joe. That's how bad it is. Every day is a fight for survival. Finding food, avoiding harm, and trying not to get sick. Any and all those things can, and do kill them, everyday..." Dave let his words sink in, before continuing. "If me providing them guns helps them out, then so be it, not to mention the money to be made."

Well that explained what was in the crates, and made me feel somewhat better about what had just happened. I had a question though. As I considered it, Dave watched me, somewhat suspiciously.

"Well, what do you think?" he pressed.

"My question is, if they have money to afford guns, why aren't they using that money for something else. Like food, clothing or medicine?" I asked.

Dave smiled, "They would and do, but they *need* the guns for survival, and they don't generally have the money. They get the money from drug sales to buy guns. Most just turn to drug sales, it's a lot more lucrative, we could make ten times the money we just did, if we traded the guns for drugs instead of cash. It's easier for them too."

"Then why don't you?" I asked.

"Because I'm not in the drug business. It's the scourge of our country. I won't have any part of it." Dave said somewhat defensively.

I wasn't even sure what the hell he said, but I did understand his meaning.

"Also, getting drugs back into the United States is risky business, *any* cargo going north is suspect, and nothing going south gets checked, well hardly ever. Dope has to be smuggled in, split up, sold and all the associated risks that go with it. There's a lot of money to be made, but you're just a common criminal. You're a doper, nothing else. What we're doing may be illegal, but it's not *wrong*."

Dave had said "We're" as in plural, or "us."

"What's this *we* bullshit? You gotta mouse in your pocket or something." I asked, trying to be funny. "It's not exactly like I knew what we were doing." I continued.

"True, but you still committed a crime, and you still helped those people out, and you did come away five hundred dollars richer. Next time, you'll make probably more like four thousand. You need to think about it."

Four thousand! That stuck in my head a lot more than the *next time* did. Looking back, I'm sure it was meant to be put to me that way.

"You do this a lot, Dave?"

"Whenever I can. Not as much as I would like to. They really do need the help, more than we can give them. But still, every little bit helps."

"Enough to make a difference? What if we get caught?" I asked.

Dave quickly answered, "We've never been caught, and yes it's enough to make a hell of a difference. These people are fighting for their lives, their independence, their kid's lives, and their future. We just help them out. Like British smugglers helped arm the colonists during the revolutionary war. We couldn't have done it without them."

I didn't know that. Made sense though, where would the colonists have gotten guns if the British didn't want them to have any? I don't remember hearing about *that* in history.

I was quiet for a while. Dave broke the silence. "Here's how it works. I will show you how to purchase the guns, and which ones. I'll even help you out the 1st time and get you started. You can pay me back later. Basically you can bring down about five guns per trip. I bring five and some medical supplies. Each gun will cost you about two hundred and fifty dollars. I'll show you what needs to be done to them. When we get down here, you'll get anywhere from five hundred on the low side to fifteen hundred on the high side."

I did some quick math in my head. 5 times 250.00 equaled 1250.00. I saw what seemed like a scam to me. "If I give 1250.00 and only get 500.00, that doesn't sound like much of a deal to me."

"No, you'll pay 1250.00 *total*, and get back 2500.00 to 7500.00, that's a 1250.00 to 6250.00 profit."

"Oh." I replied. That was the way I heard it, but I wanted to be sure, and that it wasn't a play on words. I knew what Dave had said, I just didn't think it would be that easy. As it turned out, it pretty much was.

I noticed we weren't flying east, the direction we had come from. Instead, we were now heading southeast. I asked Dave where we were going.

"We're going to spend a day or two of down time. Give you some time to think this over. Maybe introduce you to some people, and have a good time. Sound fun?"

"Yeah, sure. I don't know who we're meeting Dave, but I don't really want to be in anymore situations like that. At least not right now, anyway." I added as Dave shot me a concerned look. "And I don't really want to be threatened by anyone either. I've had enough threat for one day."

Dave said, "You won't be threatened. If I introduce you to these people, you will come to trust them like no one else you know. You'll see."

We landed on the out skirts of a small city. The thought crossed my mind "I *don't even know where I am*" After taxiing, and fueling, we tied the plane down. I watched and helped as I could, keeping my distance and feeling extremely vulnerable.

Walking out of the airport, Dave yelled and waved for a cab. A yellow car, spewing black smoke and sounding like it was barely running chugged up next to us. As we climbed in, Dave spoke in what sounded somewhat like Spanish, as the driver hit the meter and pulled out into traffic without looking.

Ten minutes later, we were pulling up to a raggedy two story motel. It was a wooden building, with a saggy awning out front and windows so dirty you could hardly see through them. Dave paid the driver and we walked inside. After paying cash for a room and trying to understand what the clerk had been saying in the most heavily accented English that I had ever heard, we headed upstairs. Turning up the stairs, I noticed in the back of the lobby, a wide arch that seemed to lead into a rather nice restaurant. Music seemed to be coming from the back and the smell of steak wafted across the lobby. It suddenly hit me that I was ravenous. I hadn't eaten since yesterday and had a huge adrenalin dump since then. And I had five hundred dollars in my pocket, along with an enormous erection, although I had no idea why.

"Dave, I'm gonna grab a bite to eat."

"Let's hit the room first, put our stuff up." Dave answered. I followed obediently.

Entering the room, I saw two twin beds, with a lamp on the table between them. The bathroom was on the left side of the room. I put my bag at the foot of the bed on the right. Dave set his bag down on the left side bed and opened it. Grabbing a clean shirt he headed into the restroom and washed his face and shaved, while I stared at the wall wondering what the hell had I gotten myself into and thinking about food. Returning from the restroom, Dave was carrying the dirty shirt in one hand, and his shaving kit in the other. The .45 automatic was riding in a leather holster on his right side, inside his pants. Buttoning up his shirt, he announced that he was ready.

Bouncing up off the bed, I headed for the door. Seeing the .45 had brought back to mind what an eventful day I had so far. I was ready for it to be over, but I was hungry. Following me down the stairs, I decided I needed a little break from Dave. The opportunity came a few seconds later as I walked through the archway of the lobby into the restaurant. Immediately on my right was a bar, one patron was sitting towards the far end of it. The bartender standing on my end, was wiping down glasses. He nodded at me and asked if I wanted a drink. Knowing Dave didn't drink, I answered, "Tequila. Please." Dave continued behind me to a table and sat down. I walked past him and sat down two stools away from the guy on the other end of the bar. Behind me, I heard Dave order a beer. I glanced over my shoulder. *So much for him not drinking* I thought.

I looked to my left, the man that had been sitting alone two stools away was sipping a beer looking at me.

With what I thought was a thick British accent he spoke. "Hey mate, what you up to now?" I answered. "Rough day. Ready for a drink and a steak." I politely answered.

As I looked him over I saw that he had sandy blond hair, short enough to stay out of his grey eyes. I decided he was about 6 foot tall and probably over to 200 pounds. With defined arms and barrel chested in a long sleeve shirt that looked like something a professional hunter would wear. He had tan pants and was wearing hiking style boots. The back of his right hand was badly scarred. I also noticed he had some small scars on his face, from small lacerations and whatever a life time of whatever his profession had dished out to him.

"Rough, eh?" I wasn't about to tell a complete stranger about being in a Central American country with my girl-friend's dad committing felonies.

"My name is Joe." I offered my right hand, and as he took it, I could feel Dave watching us cautiously.

Shaking my hand, I could feel raw strength. This guy was strong. "How'd you get that burn on the back of your hand?" I asked. Never looking away, he answered, "Working, Mate. How did you get yours?"

I told him about the fire that had burned my Mom and me. He listened politely, and then said. "Well life can be tough, it's what you make of it mate." Well at least we shared the same philosophy on that.

"Where are you from?" The accent sounded cool to my young ears.

"Australia." He answered.

"I didn't catch your name."

His eyes seemed to twinkle.

"That's because I didn't give it."

The silence seemed a little uncomfortable. Was he teasing me, or what? I watched him as he stared back at me smiling and took another drink of beer. He didn't give me his name. *"What an asshole."* I thought. I spun off the stool and went and sat across from Dave who seemed to be watching me with some suspicion.

Picking up Dave's menu, I saw that a 16 ounce T-bone was only about three dollars. They had a 32 ounce also, and it was only five dollars. As I sat the menu down, the waiter came over and took our orders. Dave ordered a chicken fried steak and another beer. I ordered the 32 ounce T-bone and another shot. Dave and the waiter looked at me.

"That's a big steak." Dave said.

"I'm hungry." I had no doubt about finishing it.

Dave didn't seem in a talkative mood, and I wasn't sure I was either. Behind Dave, through the arch that served as the doorway into the restaurant, I watched a man duck his head as he came through it. I couldn't see his facial features well at first, but as he drew closer, I saw that he was black, and he was big. *Really* big. Standing about 6'9" with muscles everywhere, was a soft face, shaven head, wearing blue jeans, and a loose t-shirt. He was wearing lace up boots. He glanced at Dave and me, smiled and nodded. I was glad. That had to be the biggest son-of a bitch that I had ever laid eyes on. We nodded back. Walking past us, he turned and sat down next to the Australian, ordering a beer he greeted the Australian. Good. I thought. Maybe he'll get smart with him and get his ass kicked. I was still a little put out by the re buff about his name.

When the food came I tore into the steak. After I finished it off, I ate some of the baked potato too, and ordered a Coke as the waiter took our plates.

The two at the bar seemed to know each other and were talking quietly. I couldn't hear their conversation, but they looked our way more than once. I had the impression they were discussing me, or me and Dave. I didn't like it and started wondering what they were up too. Dave didn't seem to notice, or if he did, he didn't care. *Were they going to try and rob us?* I thought. The Australian had his back to me, but as I looked up at the bar our eyes met in the mirror. They continued to talk quietly as he watched me with cold grey eyes. This guy was scary. Mentally, he might not be all there. I couldn't tell if he was threatening or mocking me. Finally I broke eye contact with him. Something was up. I could feel it, I was certain of it. It was time to get out of here. I had already had way too much excitement for one day and still hadn't processed all of that yet. Now the two at the bar didn't seem like simple working men to me anymore. They seemed dangerous. One by his demeanor and one by his sheer size. I couldn't handle these two and didn't think Dave could either. But of course Dave had a .45, so maybe he could handle them, if he would or got the chance. That was the question. He seemed oblivious to them.

"Dave…" I began.

He cut me off in midsentence and said, "We're done. Let's go, I got the check."

Heading out the restaurant door and turning up the stairs, I looked hard right, trying to see what the two at the bar were doing. They seemed to still be drinking, but they were watching us.

Walking into the room, Dave took the .45 out of his holster and lightly tossed it onto his bed.

"I need to piss." He said as he walked into the bathroom.

As I sat down on the edge of the bed, I could hear Dave pissing and mumbling something about beer going right through him.

There was a knock at the door. My stomach turned and fear set in fast and hard. My eyes, going from the door, towards the restroom saw Dave's .45 lying on the bed. I dove for it. As I grabbed the gun, my finger reached for the trigger, as I felt it, I took my finger back off of it and flipped the safety down. Scurrying could be heard just outside the door. Dave walked out into the room zipping his pants, glaring at me.

"Put that thing away before you hurt somebody." Dave said loudly as he walked over and opened the door.

"Come on in, guys."

Outside the door, a baritone voice asked, "Is he going to shoot us if we do?"

"If the little foker has a gun, I'm shooting back Dave." The Australian!

"He's putting it away. Right, Joe?" I blinked and looked at Dave. As I lowered the gun, I flipped the safety up. *"Weird, I don't remember raising the gun."* I remember thinking. Dave reached over, taking his gun back from me for the second time in the same day.

"It's all clear." He stated.

A huge black face peered through the door. His eyes were locked on my hands. As he stepped through, his right hand was going behind his back. Obviously he was armed too. Following close behind was the Australian. As he stepped through the door, I could see his right hand leaving the butt of a semi-automatic pistol in the front of his waistband. He dropped his shirt back over it.

"What in the hell have I gotten myself into?" I thought.

Dave introduced them. "This is Bro and Aussie. You don't need to know anything more than that."

"Who's who?" I asked sarcastically. Bro, let out a roar of a laugh that startled the hell out of all of us.

Aussie said to no one in particular, "Pommy lil bastard, he is." Whatever the hell that meant. I found out later, that he thought I was a little full of myself, and possibly an asshole to boot.

"Were you going to fockin shoot us? After all, I thought we were going to be Mates." Aussie's eyes twinkled as he asked me.

"Dave didn't exactly tell me who you were. In fact, he didn't tell me a damn thing. I thought you were going to rob us."

All three looked at me, apparently dumbstruck. Before the question could come, I continued.

"Look, it's been a really eventful day. There's been a few things Dave didn't tell me about. All I knew for sure is that between the two of you, you were damned dangerous to me."

Looking at Aussie, I said, "You're damned strong." I nodded toward Bro, "And that dudes big enough to block out the sun. What the hell was I supposed to think?

Aussie smiled, just a little bit, as Bro laughed.

"You have good instincts, Mate. That's a good thing."

Bro, in a deep slow southern voice, that sounded like it should be in a Mississippi church choir, addressed me next.

"Dave spoke highly of you. Said you had some potential. I personally don't see how, as young as you are, but you did ok today. At the meet and here too."

My puzzled look, gave Bro cause to continue.

"We were there today. Dave wouldn't have it any other way. We don't do nothing on our own. Too easy to get killed." Bro drawled.

Eventually I found more out about Bro and Aussie, but not as much as you would expect. I never learned Aussie's real name, or his last name for that matter.

Bro, was obviously from the South, although he could drop the accent on demand and sound almost plain and monotone, with no accent. Like he was from California or some place that talked flat and proper. Dave said Bro had been a "Snake Eater" which meant he had been in Special

Forces. He had served at least two tours of duty in Vietnam. He told me once that the last few months had been the worst. I was also pretty sure he had attained the rank of Staff Sergeant. He was trained as a medic, knew mechanical stuff much better than most and damn he could handle an M60 machine gun, as I would later find out.

Aussie was a little older, perhaps. He had fought in the Rhodesian war, and I suspect hired out in a few conflicts across the globe. Where his initial training and fighting had been, I don't really know. But I do know his training was good. It was good as he was. Aussie was so cool he pissed ice cubes, and it wasn't an act either. I don't believe I ever saw Aussie get mad, lose his temper, look scared, (although he claimed to have been scared more than he cared to remember) or show any emotion such as regret, hesitancy, meanness or sadness to any appreciable degree. Aussie just *did*.

Bro and Aussie were an unlikely pair, as Aussie had met Bro in Africa, and I had heard them mention the war in Angola. They were tight and they were a team. Aussie told me more than once in our conversations that regardless of skin color, everybody bleeds red. I carry that with me to this day.

After a little more talking, it was time to call it a night. I knew I wouldn't be able to sleep and dreaded a night of tossing and turning. It turned out, that I was wrong. I was asleep within seconds of my head hitting the pillow.

The next morning bright and early, Dave and I were up and out on the street. Parked in front of the motel was an old Jeep. I knew it had not been there the night before. Dave indicated for me to climb in the passenger side. After fishing around under the seat, he came up with a key. Putting it in the ignition, he cranked the jeep and pulled away. Heading west out of town, Dave explained that we were going to meet Bro and Aussie and have a little fun.

Twenty minutes later after driving down a dusty dirt road, we turned up a wash. We followed it for about two hundred yards where I saw Bro and Aussie were standing next to a beat up pickup truck. We pulled into an open area, next to them, surrounded by what looked very much like pine trees to me.

As we got out of the jeep, Bro opened up what appeared to be a large lockable toolbox in the back of the pickup. Peering down into it I could see guns. Lots of guns.

"See anything you like?" Bro asked me.

Reaching inside, I pulled out the rifle on top of the pile. It looked like an M-16 to me. I looked at Dave.

"Armalite AR-18, 5.56X45 millimeter NATO, 18 inch barrel, 6.7lbs, 37 inches long, 800 rounds per minute. 20, 30 and 40 round magazines. Give it a try." Dave said.

I looked the gun over, it had a magazine in it. Finding the cocking handle, I pulled it back and saw the magazine had rounds in it. Releasing the charging handle chambered a round. The safety selector had 3 positions. I flicked it through the 3 positions, finally leaving it on safe.

Aussie pointed out a bottle that had been placed on the hillside about 100 yards away as well as others further out. Lifting the gun to my shoulder, I lined up the first bottle and squeezed off one round. With much less recoil than I expected, I saw that I had hit the bottle. I moved up to the next one and saw the shot strike low. Hmmm, 200 yards and the bullet was already dropping. I aimed a little higher and connected. Moving out to 300 I aimed a little higher still. I couldn't hold still enough so I sat down, placed my elbows on my knees and easily hit one of the far bottles.

Bro let out a low whistle, which boosted my confidence.

In reply I heard Dave say, "He's damned sure steady."

Aussie suggested I try it on full auto. Turning the selector switch, I aimed at one of the closer bottles and squeezed the trigger. Hitting the bottle with the 1st shot, I watched the next two rounds hit high before I could let go of the trigger.

"Man it's hard to hit with on full auto. I can't control it very well after the first shot."

"Let that be a lesson then to you, Mate. It's a waste of ammo, except at close range."

Standing up, I walked back over to the box. Dave reached in and pulled out another gun. Handing it to me, he described it. "

FN FAL 7.62X51 millimeter NATO, 21 inch barrel, 9.8 lbs. 43 inches in length, cyclic rate is 650 rounds per minute, 20 round magazine."

Cocking it, I took aim again at one of the closer bottles. Squeezing the trigger was much different than on any of my guns. These were long and sluggish. Going off with a much louder boom than I expected, I vaporized another bottle. This was *not* the same caliber as I had just shot.

I asked to no one in particular, "What's all this 7.62 by whatever NATO shit? What's all this crap mean, anyway?"

Dave explained. "Military uses metric designations, but for your purposes, a 5.56 is a .223. A 7.62X51 is a .308. NATO stands for the North Atlantic Treaty Organization, which basically is a big list of countries that are on the side of the United States."

"This doesn't kick as much as my brother-in-laws .308. How come?"

"Well Mate, it's not a hunting rifle, it's a battle rifle. They're heavier, have gas or spring recoil systems that help with the recoil. Otherwise you couldn't control it, a'tall. Try that one on full auto."

Moving the selector lever, I quickly found a bottle and pulled the trigger. A burst of about five rounds went down range before I let off the trigger. Not hitting anything except dirt, I staggered back. I had not been prepared for that, but it didn't hurt. Aussie reiterated his point.

"Single shots are much more accurate."

Next up was a Heckler & Koch G3 or as Dave said;

"H&K, G3, 7.62X51 millimeter NATO, 18 inch barrel, 9lbs, 11ounces, 41 inches in length. 20 round magazines, cyclic rate of 550 rounds per minute."

The sights were different than the others, a drum on the rear sight. It had 3 peep holes in it and a buck horn style sight, unlike the others that had one peep hole or an "L" shape flip affair that had 2 peep holes. The different holes were marked 200, 300 and 400, and the open notch was marked 100. This just had to be a better system.

Bro showed me a bottle that I had not seen yet.

"That's about 450 yards, can you hit it?" He asked.

"Well yeah, now that I see it I can. Why wouldn't I?"

"Well we're waiting, smartass." Dave said.

"Ok." I shrugged. Sitting down, I turned the drum on the rear site to 400. Aiming over the top of the bottle, I took up the trigger with what felt like 3 inches of slack. As the shot broke, I knew I had hit it. This gun was nice, accurate too.

Bro was grinning ear to ear. "Damn, the boy can shoot, cain't he Dave?"

"Yeah, he can. Let's see how he does with pistols. You know anything about pistols, Joe?"

I told them that I had done some shooting with a pistol and that I owned a Browning 380 that held 13 rounds. Dave pursed his lips and glancing at Aussie nodded his head as if in approval while still considering. Considering what, I don't know.

Aussie, reaching under his shirt and pulling out a large automatic, said "This should be familiar to you then."

It did *look* a lot like my Browning, only a lot bigger, like my Browning on steroids.

"This is a 9 millimeter. 15 round magazine. That's 16 shots total. It's a double action/single action." Aussie explained.

I didn't think I knew what double action/single action meant. Turns out I did. It was the same as my Browning.

"It's not as powerful as a .45, but it's fine if you load it with hollow points, but as your Confederates used to say, You can load it on Sunday and shoot all week." I thought that was quite funny.

Handing it to me, Aussie showed me the safety and told me there was already a round in the chamber.

Dave tossed a soda can that he had just emptied. Not going very far, he walked over and picked it up and continued to about 15 yards and set it down. Walking back, he looked at me, challenging me with his eyes he asked, "How many times do you think you can hit that?"

As he walked past me, I raised the gun and sighted. Firing the first shot, I realized that it kicked less than my .380 due to the weight and size of the gun. And it shot true. As the front sight came back down, the can was still rolling. I lined it up and squeezed the trigger again. By the 7th or 8th shot, the can was about 50 yards away and torn to hell.

"I like this! This is a hellva lot better than my 380. I exclaimed.

Aussie was chuckled softly, Bro grinned ear to ear as they both looked at Dave. He didn't look very happy.

"He'll do. If he doesn't get killed. Let's go." Dave told them as he went to the jeep and got in. Now Bro busted out laughing in earnest.

"My o my, but the worm do turn, don't it Aussie?

"Appears that way, Mate. Be careful going back Joe. Dave's not used to that."

Sternly Dave looked at me and told me to get in, as it was time to leave as he glared at Aussie and Bro. I handed the 9mm back to Aussie and thanked him and climbed in the Jeep, not sure what had just taken place. Apparently I was still slow on the uptake about whatever joke I had missed.

On the way back, Dave explained how we operated as well as giving me some ground rules.

Open bolt weapons were to be bought back home and converted to full auto. He would show me how later. I was to have several different sets of identification, which he would help me obtain and would be used to buy the guns. (Which he did.) Five sets, different names, and a passport for one Mr. Joseph Johnson, with my picture in it. This involved meeting a rather scary individual that I hoped to never meet again, and haven't yet. Thankfully. No more than one purchase at a time from any one store. All meets were set up by Dave, (no exceptions) we should always be early at meets, and no drugs were to be exchanged for anything we had. Period. This was nonnegotiable and not to be even considered. Ever. If medical supplies were obtained by Dave, they would be given away, not sold. This occurred several times. I usually tried to include gauze bandages or anything else I thought of that could be of use. The words "Contras" and "Sandinistas" were used a lot. I was warned about using either one of these terms, as sometimes even the Contras themselves didn't like it, and preferred "Commandos." While we were against the

Sandinistas, we weren't necessarily for the Contras. It depended on the group. As it was put to me by Bro, "If's they shootin at ya, they's ain't friendlies." That made sense to me.

Getting back to the motel, Dave had a message waiting for him. After a lengthy phone call, Dave told me that we would be flying out today. The clients had decided to stay longer and we were not going to sit around and wait for them.

Bro and Aussie showed up and we all met in mine and Dave's room. Dave told them that we would be going back this afternoon and said he had some things to do first. He also asked if Aussie could get me to the airport at 1700 hours, while he ran his errands, and pointed out that it would give me time to get to know Bro and Aussie, as well as having them show me a couple of things.

As Dave left, Aussie and Bro led me back to their room. I hadn't even known they were staying at the same place. Reaching between the mattress and box spring, Aussie produced a machine gun. It looked much like the FN FAL that I had shot earlier in the day, except shorter. How the hell had he gotten that in here without any one seeing it, I wondered.

"You shoot right fine, Joe, spot on, I would say. But I noticed a few things. Like do you know how to reload? In a hurry?"

"Push the button and stick in the new mag?" I answered.

"Listen to him, Joe." Bro drawled. "He's fixing to teach you something."

I nodded my head in agreement and studiously watched and listened to Aussie.

"First of all, have your ammo, where you can reach it fast. The farther the reach, the slower the reload. Second, be ready to reload. I load a tracer as my 2nd round, into my magazines. That way when I see it, I know I have one shot left. *(I started putting a tracer in 3rd from the bottom, so I would know when I had two shots left. It's a habit that continues with me to this day.)* You being left handed, things will be a little different for you. You really do need to spend some time, working it out and practice it, until you get it down."

Aussie then held the magazine in his left hand, rifle straight out at the shoulder, with his finger off the trigger, reached up and pushed the magazine release button with his left hand and as the magazine fell out, rotated his hand and rocked from front to rear the new magazine into the gun. It was fast. As if reading my mind he then told me.

"Don't go for speed, Joe. Go for smooth. Smooth is fast."

"Aaamen Brother." Bro emphasized.

After showing me a couple of other small details that if overlooked could "git ya kilt" as Bro put it, we started talking about pistols.

Aussie offered his opinion right off the bat.

"Pistols suck. If you need it, then fine. But they're piss poor fight stoppers, and should only be used, if you're out of ammo or can't carry a rifle. Also, don't hesitate to shoot a lot with a pistol, but you'll definitely do better if you make your shots count. Carry hollow points when you can. They work much better."

"Where the hell am I supposed to get all of this?" I asked.

Bro chuckled. "I wouldn't worry about that, Dave will set you up. Worry more about staying alive."

"Well I am worried about staying alive. I'm not even sure how I got myself into this, or if I want to do it. I wasn't told about any of this shit." I was really ready to start crying and had not realized for a few hours how scared I really was.

Aussie didn't even blink. Bro looked at me, with the slightest bit of sadness he spoke.

"If you want out, you need to tell Dave. Quick. Nobody would think any less of you. I don't think you will though. You know why?"

I shook my head no. This was kind of deep for me, but I was riveted. I really didn't know why, and wanted to know why I was going along with any of this. I wasn't much of a follower.

"Cause you have a good sense of what's right and wrong, and you're eager fo the fight. You love being scared, don't ya Joe? Look me in the face and tell me I'm lying. You want to help, and you want to know what it's like don't ya?" Bro said.

I nodded my head yes. Aussie spoke next, fixing me with those cold grey eyes.

"Now's the time to get out. Not later, not when we're in the shit and you decide it's too tough. You will do what you're told, and when to do it, or you will die. There are no prisoners in this business. Understand?"

Before I could answer, Aussie thankfully changed the subject.

"Another thing you need to know. Seems like somebody is always trying to kill Davey. If you're going to be around him, get used to it."

"Man, ain't no lie there. That's the truth!

"Ok, no problem."

"That's where you're wrong, it is a problem. First off, they'll try and kill you too. Second, Davey's not going to be tolerant of you standing around doing nothing while someone is trying to kill him. Don't ever forget, you're the most expendable."

"Got it. I'll handle it."

"Really? Then you damn well better keep a gun on hand at all times, would be my advice to you, my little Mate."

For some reason, I felt much better. Like I was capable. These two men, opposite of each other in so many ways, had taken me in. Taken me under their wing. They seemed to know what was in my soul. They knew my fears, but didn't hold that against me. They gave me credit where I had earned it, no matter how little, as I was yet unproven. They had told me the truth, in a way that I didn't want to hear, but was still in fact the truth. And after all, I was *expendable*. Whatever that meant. I made a note to look it up in a dictionary when I got home. It sure as hell sounded cool though.

Expendable. Neat. Yeah! I could do this. Let the ride begin. I thought.

We continued to talk. Bro and Aussie both showing me all they could about anything they thought I might need to know. Formations, flanking moves, gun handling, medical emergencies and anything else I could think of to ask about until it was time to take me to the airport. They also suggested that I start weight lifting and running.

Bro stayed behind and Aussie and I climbed into the beat up old pickup for the ride to the airport. On the way, Aussie talked.

Reaching under the seat, he pulled out a book and handed it to me. Looking at it, it appeared thick. The covers were gone, but inside the pages were filled with guns, lots of guns, and their descriptions. Included next to the picture, was the manufacturer, weight, length, caliber, magazine capacity, barrel twist rate, and country of origin.

"You need to spend some time reading this. Memorize it."

"The whole damned thing?" I asked incredulously.

"Well, as much as you can, Mate. Particularly the NATO arms, Soviet bloc too, if you're inclined. Good info in there. You seem to like it and take to it."

Aussie also told me to start exercising. Particularly running. Little did I know this was starting a friendship that would shape my entire life. Outside of Dad there were few men that had as much influence on me as Aussie did. His lessons have allowed me to survive deadly situations, time and again.

Arriving at the airport, we met Dave. He had the plane ready to go and told me to go get in, he needed to talk to Aussie.

I had a feeling I was the subject of the discussion so I gave them their room. I think I had passed muster so far.

Shortly after takeoff, Dave said he would get us to cruising altitude and set the auto pilot and we would talk, since we would be alone. And talk he did. The rest of the years I knew Dave, I never heard him talk as much as he did on the way back to El Paso, after that eventful trip.

Admitting nothing, Dave informed me on several significant points. To begin with, after the wars in Korea and especially Southeast Asia, the American public didn't want our government or our soldiers fighting in "some foreign place" that didn't affect or appear to affect the U.S.A. That didn't mean atrocities weren't happening elsewhere and it didn't mean that we didn't have an interest in it. If nothing else, the Cuban Missile crisis had taught us that. It just didn't seem prudent, reasonable, or strategically wise to let a communist regime set up shop next door. Poor dictatorships, ok. Corrupt democracies, we could handle. Communist support from a world superpower during the height of the cold war? Not a freaking chance. With that being said, anything that was done to help these countries "privately" well, that was ok by the government. If those people got caught? Well, they were just "smugglers, criminals, or entrepreneurs." No link to any government agencies, I was told. I work for myself. No one would know me if

I got caught, no one would come to help, and bottom line was that we were on our own.

"Another thing, Joe. If you learn nothing else from this, you better learn what I am about to tell you. You listening?"

"I'm listening." I replied.

"Good. Look at me and listen good. No one, and I mean no one, is to know about this. Not Jenn, not Karen, not your Dad and certainly not *any* of your friends. If anybody at all knows or hears about this, Joe, The whole thing is fucked! Do you understand me? If you tell one person, ever in your life Joe, it's not a secret. Just one, and now someone knows, and they will eventually tell someone else. People want to talk, if you want to talk, talk to me, or one of the guys, but *never, ever,* talk to anyone else. Do we agree on this? If you do, I will trust you and take you in."

Dave was looking hard into my eyes. Not intimidating, just serious. I don't know that anyone had ever been that serious towards me before. Deep down inside, I knew he was right though. I sure as hell couldn't tell Dad or Colter. They would flip out. Billy would just tell everybody. Jenn, I didn't even want to think about. *Who* was there to tell? No one, was my conclusion.

"That makes sense to me, Dave." I agreed. "I won't say a word, to anybody."

Arriving in El Paso, *hours* later, we headed home. We were both ready for sleep. Jenn had other ideas though. She wanted to hear about the entire trip. Did I have fun?

Was Dave mean to me? What did we do? Did I meet any girls?

Dave immediately jumped into this conversation and said that I really seemed to like the fat ones, and that one named "Juanita" was all over me.

Karen wanted to know where I met Juanita, and what were we doing where there were "Juanitas" or any females.

Dave said she was our flight attendant and laughed. That seemed to ease Jenn and Karen's minds. Later, after more prodding by Jenn, I told her that it had been a long flight. We went to a motel, crashed out, ate, and came back. That seemed to satisfy her, and that was that.

The next day, Karen asked me if Dave had been mean to me on the trip. I told her no. She then informed me that she thought he had a girlfriend or even another family elsewhere. This stunned me!

"He's awful secretive, doesn't talk about his work at all, did you meet his girlfriend, Joe?" Karen asked me, while folding clothes. She appeared to be so casual about it, but I knew she was watching my response, closely.

"*Not Jenn, not Karen, not your Dad and certainly not any of your friends.*" I could remember Dave saying.

"I didn't meet any girls. Karen, I think Dave thinks his job is boring. He doesn't like to talk about it. He just flies." I offered.

"I wish he would take me, sometime." Karen responded.

"I am sure he would, if you asked Karen. But it sucks, I mean I find it interesting. I would love to be a pilot someday, but do you really care about alto cumulus clouds and stuff like that, and not having a regular toilet?"

"No, I suppose not. Thank you, Joe." Karen said, without looking up.

"For what?" I asked.

"For telling me the truth, I guess."

"No problem." I said, and got up and walked into the kitchen. I felt like shit. But the point had just been driven home with me. I was a liar, and would continue to lie. This sucked, and I was going to have to get used to it. Quick.

The next day, Dave had me go into El Paso and meet a guy, for my false identifications. He was an ugly old Mexican guy. He obviously drank too much, didn't bathe near enough, and he was carrying a Rapala filet knife that I sort of figured he might be pretty handy with. All he did was take pictures and threaten me.

"Don't tell your friends about me. Forget you ever meet me." and "Tell Davey, he owes me, beeg time."

After a couple of days of down time, Dave and I went into El Paso. Stopping at a storage area, we swapped out vehicles to an older Chevy truck. Dave said it was "clean" and not traceable to him directly. Whatever that meant. Next up, was picking up my identifications. All had me at 21 years old. Since I wasn't even 18 yet, Dave thought going any older was inviting trouble. There was no question that I looked well over 18, but maybe a little young for 22 or 23. I agreed and off we went to the gun shops. This also consisted of sporting goods stores, hardware stores or any place that did sell firearms, which was quite a few.

With Dave providing the cash, (which he seemed to have a lot of) I purchased five guns, and Dave bought two. The ones I had bought were, largely Ingram Mac-10's, made by RPB Industries. Rumor had it, that RPB stood for *Rape, Plunder & Burn*. While this wasn't exactly true, it seemed to stick with the "Cocaine Cowboys" though, and they just flat loved these guns. As explained to me, "The profit margin is huge." Another advantage to us about these guns, believe it or not, was their high cyclic rates of fire. Meaning the guns were capable of firing about 1200 rounds in one minute. How was that an advantage to us, if we didn't carry them for our own personal use? While true that the very guns we sold could and sometimes were used against us, we sure didn't want to equip anyone better than ourselves. At 1200 rounds per minute, that meant a 30 round magazine only had about 1 and one half seconds of sustained fire power. That's not very much. And while the guns shot so fast they sounded like a little buzz saw, if you weren't hit in the very first burst, chances are, you weren't going to be hit. They were a bitch to control, and if the person firing the weapon was even a little scared or inexperienced, they tended to lock down the trigger, and empty the gun, in 1.5 seconds, while the gun climbed hard and to the right. The range on them was short too. Sometime later, I would see this point driven home first hand. But they were small, relatively light weight, and intimidating as hell. The cool factor was very high for the people that wanted confidence that didn't relate to skill level. KG-9's were also used, or any open bolt weapon for that matter, that were easily converted. Later in the early 1980's, manufacture of open bolt weapons were banned in the United States because of the easy conversion factor to full auto.

All this was taken back to the storage room, where Dave had power drills, grinders and other tools. I was shown how to do the conversions, which was surprisingly easy. We then packed everything, and left it there until ready to fly out.

Dave also asked me which personal guns, that I would prefer to carry and did I like anything that I had shot with Bro, Aussie and himself. The H&K G3 immediately came to mind. I told him so.

"Then you'll have it. What about handguns?"

"I liked Aussie's 9mm. Can we get one of those?" I asked hopefully.

"We can get anything we want, and you'll have one of those too."

In the background, Glenn Frey was telling *me* about the Smugglers Blues.

Then Dave dropped a bombshell on me.

"Do you remember meeting Denny, my brother in law?" He asked.

Taking a second, I remembered, I had in fact met him, briefly, at a family dinner.

"Yeah, I guess so. The one you don't care for, much. Right?" I asked.

"Right. Well you'll see him on some of these trips. He used to be okay. But being married to Karen's sister, and not being able to hold a job, or save any money, he's a pain in the ass. He is good under fire though. And that's pretty damned important."

I didn't know what to say. I sat in silence a minute. Finally I spoke.

"How the hell did you get him into this? I thought you didn't like him."

"I've known Denny for a long time. Since Vietnam in fact, we served together. I was the one that introduced him to Karen's sister."

"Bet Karen's not happy about that, from what I've heard." I said sarcastically.

"Yes, Joe, I am reminded of that from time to time by Karen. I don't need you reminding me too. I will handle Denny." He answered defensively.

"Ok." This was just getting better and better. But what the hell, after all I was *expendable,* and I bet Dave's brother in law wasn't, so I still had that going for me. I still hadn't gotten a chance to look that up in a dictionary. I kept meaning too, but I just kept forgetting.

"Oh well, I'll get around to it." I thought.

Since it was summer, I wouldn't have to worry about school, and when Dave let me know when the next trip was, I was ready. Or as ready as I was going to be. We flew out on a Monday night.

Dave had some weapons and crates that I had not seen him purchase, and I didn't ask. I was sure you couldn't buy that stuff at a gun shop. At least not any gun shop or sporting goods store that I had ever been to. Everything had gone without a hitch, and I had seen once again, how it was done.

All the reservations and fears I had seemed to magically disappear when we got back and I got my cut.

After Dave taking out what I owed him, I cleared six thousand dollars.

8

BITCH

Trip three *sucked*. I was ready to make some more money. I hadn't even spent half of what I had made yet. Dave had cautioned me about buying expensive items that drew attention.

Morning. Hot already. The humidity felt like it was 110% and rising. I hadn't slept well, and I still felt tired. Swamp coolers and fans were as good as it got. I had decided that I just had to live feeling "sticky." This sucked.

Dave had insisted on rising early. As we walked a few blocks from the house, I took in the still unfamiliar sights, sounds and smells. Street vendors had not really set up their wares yet. But the one that was setting up seemed to have strips of what looked like snake in his basket. It certainly smelled reptilian, even from across the street. I wasn't going to try it.

Dave indicated a restaurant, or what passed for one, that we were headed too. He said he had something to do, and would meet me there. I told him I would see him there, but I was going to try and find some aspirin first and have a smoke. I turned into a small mom and pop store. A Spanish version of "It's a heartache" was screeching from a transistor radio. I bought the last bottle of Bayer that they had. They had coffee too. I gave the old man a dollar for the coffee that was only twenty five cents. Pouring myself a cup, I took three of the aspirin, stepped outside and lit a Marlboro. Damn it was hot. I was glad to be standing in the shade. I hadn't seen where Dave went, and was a little concerned. I could find my way back to the house, but other than that, I wasn't sure. We had just gotten in a few hours prior, and it was dark when we arrived. This was a rather large town. Finishing my coffee I walked back inside and poured another cup. The old man had made a fresh pot, and made it clear that I could help myself to all I wanted, if only I could spare a Marlboro? Handing him the smoke and lighting it for him, I refreshed my cup and went back outside.

Finishing my smoke, I ground it out on the ground and took another drink of coffee. I leaned against the wall and relaxed a little bit. I was starting to feel better. Considering having another cigarette, I saw Dave step out of a door, probably forty yards to my left. He looked right, then left, then right again, towards me. Leaning against the wall in the shade, he might have had trouble seeing me, as bright as it was outside, so I raised a hand so he would see me.

The sun just seemed to sear, and screamed light out. He nodded towards the restaurant directly across from him, about 20 or 25 yards away. I dreaded leaving the shade but pushed myself off the wall and stepped towards the restaurant.

Leaving the very door we were headed to, was a woman. Carrying a paper grocery bag in her left hand with her right hand inside, she seemed to be fumbling for something in the bag. As she let go of the paper sack with her left hand and it fell away, everything went into slow motion as I saw the machine pistol in her right hand. The muzzle was down but coming up.

In awe, I saw her turn slightly away from me as her left hand pulled the bolt back and then let it go forward as she chambered the first round. She pulled the trigger as soon as the bolt closed, firing from her hip. As the gun fired a burst of about eight rounds in less than a half second I saw brass fly out of the ejection port on top of the weapon, spraying bullets everywhere and brass straight up! She was shooting one handed. *Skorpion!* They had top ejection. Releasing the trigger and moving her left hand down to help control the gun, she mashed the trigger again. Firing from the hip, empty cases flew out of the gun at a rate of nine hundred rounds per minute. Having already fired one burst, she had less than one second of sustained fire power left. Turning her head slightly to avoid the stream of cases striking her face, a conical mist of gray and red appeared from the back of her head. Ever expanding as it widened into a brief shower of blood and brain matter, speckling the wood building behind her. Her gun empty, her knees buckled, and the gun dropped muzzle down, barely in her right hand now. As she fell, I could see a single bullet hole in her cheek. Face first into the dust, her gun now half underneath her waist, arms down along her side. One and one thirds seconds worth of sustained firepower from a 20 round magazine, delivered in two bursts, and now she was obviously deader than hell. I looked further to my left, towards Dave. His right knee was in the dirt with his left elbow propped on his left knee for support. I could see the .45 automatic was extended in front of him. Like he was at a shooting match or something. Which I guess, in a sense, he was. And a damned important one at that. I had never heard him shoot. No sound came from anywhere. The place was quiet. Then somewhere a chicken clucked. Dave was on his feet and running towards me. His lips were pulled back in a snarl, and his eyes were wild. He looked positively crazy. He ran up to me and grabbing me by my t shirt with both hands, he screamed into my face.

"DID YOU FUCKING SEE THAT SHIT?"

I was stunned. Of course I had seen it. Did he think I was blind? Maybe he just wanted a rundown of what I had seen, although now didn't seem the time to talk about it.

I looked down at his hands. He was hurting me. I looked into his face and replied.

"Skorpion, 32 a.c.p. 2 pounds, 13 ounces. 4 and half inch barrel, 10.5 inches long. Cyclic rate of 900 rounds per minute."

Dave's mouth dropped open and his face relaxed. I saw him mouth the word "What?" Then just as quickly his lips curled again. Grabbing me by the shoulder he spun me around and yelled "*Run!*"

Bolting through a doorway of a shop, I followed Dave in a blind panic. Drawing my pistol as we went out the back door, and across another street scattering small animals and people. Dave yanked open a screen door and sprinted through what may have been a cloth or tailor store, Dave tripped over a stool and went down hard. Spinning around I pointed my pistol from the way we had come. I was ready now! No one seemed to be following though. As Dave got his feet under him, and exited out the back door he barked at me.

"Head to the house and put that damn thing away." Slowing to shove my gun back into my pants, I realized how stupid we must have looked. As I secured my gun, I sprinted to catch up to Dave as we went through a bar and out yet another back door, into a back yard and by a house. I could feel my gun working loose.

Holding my gun underneath my shirt, while we ran, I came around the corner at full speed and ran smack into the back of Dave. Staggering, he caught himself from falling and looking over his shoulder, Dave gave me a strained smile. From a distance he would've looked happy.

"Walk." he said quietly.

I fell in next to him.

"Smile, and try to look cool and casual. We'll make our way to the guys. We don't want anyone to remember us looking scared or running away. But you be ready, it may not be over. Watch everybody, but don't make eye contact."

I looked up at Dave and smiled stupidly. It was all I could do. My heart was pounding and about to beat out of my chest. I was sweating, and Dave had sweat just rolling off him.

It was a hot day though, and as we walked past a street vendor, I noticed he was sweating too. Not looking him in the face, he went back to straightening his fruits and seemed to ignore us. It was working. Other than the fact that we were white, we didn't stand out. Well Dave was obviously a gringo, but I could easily pass for a Mexican.

"Should we separate, so there's not two of us?" I whispered at Dave as I walked and smiled.

"I was thinking about that. I don't think anyone saw you with me, until after. What do you think? Think they're looking for one or two?"

Trying to reason it out as we walked, I continued to speak quietly while smiling like an idiot.

"Not sure, if they saw you, then they saw us leave together, so they would be looking for two. But if they did see us both, they damn sure saw you *first*, so they *know* what you look like. Sticking together, at least we're a team."

"Sounds reasonable, if you're a part of the team. Far as I could tell, you drank coffee and smoked." Dave said through clenched teeth.

"Well what the hell, Dave? I'm standing there minding my own damn business and the bitch pulls a gun, what the hell was I supposed to do?"

"Shoot her? Did you ever fucking consider that?" Dave hissed.

"It happened quick." I answered defensively.

"Lower your voice, damn it. We'll talk about it later. Smile and walk."

Arriving back at the house, Dave knocked once, paused and gave two quick raps before entering. Closing the door behind me, Aussie and Bro were both putting down weapons as we entered.

Dave having held in the adrenalin, and now feeling somewhat safer, let it all out.

"Some bitch just tried to blow my damned head off! Comes at me with a damned machine pistol in the middle of the damned street! Broad daylight!

Aussie picked his gun back up and swung it towards the front door.

"Did you get away clean, Davey?" He asked.

Bro picked up his weapon and moving over aimed it loosely towards the back door.

"I'm not sure. We're not hit though. That's a plus."

As if suddenly remembering all over again, Dave turned towards me accusingly and yelled.

"And this little bastard. Guess what he does? I shoot this bitch while he stands in the street and watches, and then when I ask him if he had seen her, he says;"

"Skorpion, 32 a.c.p. 2 pounds, 13 ounces. 4 and half inch barrel, 10.5 inches long. Cyclic rate of 900 rounds per minute." Dave mimicked.

Bro and Aussie both turned at looked at me.

"I couldn't believe it, the little shit. Never lifted a damn finger to help me. What in the hell was that all about Joe?"

"You asked me, if I had seen it. I assumed you meant the gun. Hell Dave, everybody saw her trying to kill you. I didn't think you were asking me if I had seen *that*. And as you said, she was damn sure trying to kill you. I wasn't prepared for that. What did you do to her anyway?" I tried to reason.

Bro and Aussie both started busting up laughing.

"Sounds like a hell'va show, Mates. Are you sure it was a Skorpion, Joe?"

"Yeah, I'm pretty sure. It ejected out the top. She lost control of it. The cases ejected into her face. Seemed to fuck her up." I explained.

"That's a Skorpion all right." Aussie answered.

Bro while watching toward the back door said to no one in particular.

"Skorpion is Czech. That means Russian. I wonder how that found its way down here?"

"Right good catch on Joe's part, but Bro's got a good point, Davey. How *did* that find its way here? Did it look new, Joe? Could you tell, or was it junk?"

"Didn't look dirty or worn out to me." I answered.

"Yeah, that definitely needs some serious consideration, I would say." Dave quietly answered.

"Well, at any rate, the meet's off. We can't take a chance now." Dave continued. "No reason stepping into Dodge City. This deal is one hundred percent screwed. It's off, and we need another place to stay."

I sat down, hard. I can't even remember what I sat on. Blood seemed to be rushing through my ears. Shock started to set in. I had just seen a woman get her brains blown out of her skull. That could have been me. Or anyone for that matter. What in the hell was I doing here?

Looking up, I saw that Bro was talking to Dave. I hadn't heard a word of it. Aussie was staring at me. He stepped closer. Placing his hand on my shoulder, he squeezed quick and hard. I flinched in pain and looked up at him wondering why he had done that.

"First time you've seen anything like that, Joe? Don't be going sour on us now. Head shots can be nasty. Everybody's got brains and everybody can lose them. Gunshot, auto mobile wreck, or a rock, no matter. Dead is dead. Snap out of it and think. There may be some more coming and you need to be mentally and physically with it. Dish some out, Mate. Don't take it. Do you hear me, Joe?"

I nodded my head, and got up and picked up the H&K out of the corner of the room. Checking the chamber, I confirmed that it was loaded and had a full magazine. I pulled a chair into a corner with the rifle on my lap and facing the door, sat down to wait. For what, I wasn't sure. Again, I was in way over my head. Sometime after that I wondered *why is everybody trying to kill Dave?* In the end, I decided it didn't really matter. Survival mattered.

9

PURLE HAZE

Returning to El Paso, I was in a daze. I had seen a woman killed. Hadn't lifted a hand to help Dave, and I ran like hell. In spite of that. Bro, Aussie and even somewhat Dave had stated that I did ok. I did gather important information, concerning the woman's weaponry. Aussie pointed out that I must have been studying the book he gave me very diligently. Which in fact, I had. I found it totally engrossing, and studied it everywhere I went. Even Dad had noticed me reading it. After that, I kept it out of sight.

Jenn had started acting a little weird too. After telling me she was going to spend a weekend at her Aunt's house, I made my own plans.

I called Rob, went and picked him up and started partying. Hendrix sang about Purple Haze. I could relate right now.

Rob had suspected for a while, that something was up with me. Although we both liked guns and shooting, Rob and only Rob, had detected a change in me, as far as I could tell. The stress of living a lie was starting to show, at least to him.

We were out in the desert, I had a bottle of Jose Cuervo that we were sipping from. Sitting on the tailgate, staring across the desert into Mexico. Mt Cristo Rey loomed on our left. Its zig zag trail could easily be seen. On top of the mountain at the head of the trail, was a Cross.

"Dude, what's up with all the weaponry? You've always been a little paranoid, but for Christ's sake man."

"Nothing. Just like shootin is all."

"Bullshit. You've got a 9mm, with enough ammo to take down a fucking bank. I seen the spare magazines too. You going rabbit hunting with a case of ammo? You that piss poor of a shot?"

I started laughing. Rob always had a way of exaggerating that would crack me up.

"No man. Just seems better to have it and not need it, than to need it and not have it, is all."

"Yeah, right. You expect me to believe that bullshit? You're into some serious shit, aren't you?"

I looked down towards the ground, watching my feet swing back and forth while I sat on the tailgate.

"Naw man, I'm fine." I replied.

"Look man, you're my friend. If there's anything I can do, let me know, and I'll try and help. But I ain't coming to rescue you out of no fucking whore house, just cause you didn't wanna pay." Rob grinned at me.

I started laughing again, and picked up the bottle and took a hit from it, handing it to Rob when I was done.

Taking a sip, Rob watched me.

I told him that I thought things were fixing to go bad with me and Jenn.

"So? Fuck her. There's more women dude."

I was exasperated.

"Rob, what the fuck? You tell me something is bugging me, and I tell you."

"No you didn't. You told me things were going bad between you and Jenn. You planning on shooting her, you crazy bastard?"

"No, I'm not planning on shooting her. What the hell would give you that idea?" I asked, laughing.

"I don't know, maybe the ten fucking million rounds of ammo you have."

"I am not going to shoot Jenn." I said defensively.

"I know you're not. So that doesn't really explain all the firepower, which is illegal in Texas by the way, to carry in your truck."

"Yeah, I know that."

"So what's up with Jenn, that's got you carrying a gun? Scared of her Dad? Good God man, what did you do to that poor girl?" Rob pressed.

Rob had me laughing uncontrollably now. He charged on, he was enjoying this.

"Oh, I know. You're done with her, and I know how you like older women. You want to fuck her Mom, huh? That's why you need the gun. Fuck them both, Mom and daughter. You're a sick bastard. Why don't you just include the family pet and her Dad and brother too while you're at it?"

By now I was laughing so hard, I was about ready to piss myself. Rob always had a way of taking a serious situation and turning it into comedy.

"Oh my God, Rob. Where do you come up with this stuff?"

"Well brother, you are a source of pretty good material. I have to get it in now, before I see you on the news."

Rob then broke into his "baritone newscaster" voice.

"In Juarez Mexico today, a man armed with a pistol and ten thousand rounds of ammo, decided to take on the entire Mexican army from the roof of a whore house. Apparently he was still horny after his girlfriend dumped him and he ran out of money. Why he didn't sell the ammo to pay for the whores? No one will ever know. That alone would have got him through till Christmas. Wait, wait, we have breaking news. It's not over folks. Apparently he had some more bullets on top of that whore house and he's still in the fight. Will he ever get laid again? Check in at 10:00pm for more updates."

I laughed until I had tears in my eyes. There was just no winning with Rob.

After dropping Rob off, I got home about two in the morning. Walking in the house, I saw a stack of books that I had left out. The word "dictionary" popped into my head. I found it, and was getting ready to open it up, when the phone rang.

I checked the time. It was after 2:00am. This couldn't be good. Apprehensively, I answered.

"Where the hell have you been?" It was Jenn.

I breathed a sigh of relief.

"Why the hell are you calling me at 2:00am? You scared the shit out of me. I thought someone was dead." I was relieved and pissed.

"Question is, where were you all night?" Jenn asked again.

"I was out with Rob. I thought you were spending the weekend at your Aunt's. I didn't realize I was supposed to check in."

"I'm still there. I just missed you, is all." Jenn sweetly changed the subject and softened me up.

"Did you and Rob have a good time?"

After a few more minutes, we called it a night and I went to bed. This shit was exhausting. The dictionary was forgotten and I dreamed of Central America, someone in the dream, called me the "expendable one."

Next morning, after getting up, cleaned up and dressed up, (for what, I have no idea) I had a coke for breakfast.

I opened the dictionary on a TV tray and flipped it to "E."

ex-pend-a-ble (ex spen'de bel)
Adjective

1. *Subject to use or consumption: an expendable source.*
2. *Not worth salvaging or reusing.*
3. *Not strictly necessary; dispensable: an expendable budget item; expendable personnel.*

4. *Open to sacrifice in the interests of gaining an objective, especially a military one.*

Noun

   A person or thing considered expendable.

I sat in silence. I was stunned. How fucking stupid could I be? I was the *most expendable*. I was furious. Who the hell did they think I was? I kicked the TV tray across the room, and leaving slammed the door behind me. I started the truck and headed to Dave's. He had an ass kicking coming as far as I was concerned. How had I let myself get suckered into this? As I drove over, I realized that Dave had not been the one that told me that I was *expendable*. Aussie had. I wasn't feeling angry toward him. He had been straight up with me. Actually they all had.

Life lesson here. If you don't understand something, don't pretend too. You'll make a total ass of yourself.

As I drove, I started to calm down. Well, at least lose my anger, but I was still scared. It seems I had been scared forever. I was scared of getting caught while I was at home, and I was scared of getting killed when I wasn't. I felt like my stomach had a hole in it, every waking minute.

I kept driving. Turning onto the old highway known as the Don De Ornate trail, I continued towards El Paso. It had hardly any traffic, was a slow paced two lane, mostly with tractors and pickups on it. It gave me time to think. Instead my mind went blank. I wound up down on the Rio Grande, by myself, watching the swirling, muddy water roll by.

On one hand, I felt like I was in way over my head. But on the other, I had learned a lot from the guys. I had made a lot of money, and there was more to be made. But could I do anything to make a difference down there? I wasn't really sure, but I knew I wanted to try. Although I had not seen it too rough yet, I had heard the stories.

I sat there until one in the morning. With no decision made, I headed home.

10

CHEAP THRILLS

S unday afternoon, Jenn called and asked if I wanted to come for dinner. I was getting ready to make an excuse not to.

"Didn't you miss me? I thought you would want to see me."

"Ok. I'll be there in a few hours. I have some laundry to do, and I need to clean up, first."

"That will be ok. Oh and my Dad says hurry up, you can ride with him into town. He needs help picking something up, I think."

"Well, I can be there in an hour, I suppose." I replied as flat and as uninterested as I could.

After relaying my response to Dave, Jenn started in on me.

"My Dad says that will be fine. So for me, you can be here in a few hours, but for my Dad you'll hurry it up? Are you seeing someone else Joe?"

Placing my hand across my forehead, I squeezed my temples. I could feel the headache coming on.

"Funny, I was thinking the same thing. I told you, I was with Rob. You want his number?" This was such childish bullshit, I was thinking. I don't have time for this.

"We'll talk later." Jenn icily replied.

I threw in a load of laundry, more to give me time to think, than because it needed done. Then I jumped in the shower, got dressed and left. I still couldn't figure out what was going on. With anything.

As I pulled up to Jenn's I saw her glance out the screen door. By the time I got parked and locked my truck, Dave was walking out the front door.

"Hop in." Indicating the car, I walked to the passenger door and got in. Jenn was nowhere to be seen.

As we pulled out of the driveway, Dave told me his plans.

"We have another place to stay. I want to pick up our stuff tomorrow morning, and get out of here by tomorrow afternoon. A meet is already scheduled. It's a safe group, and one we've done business with before. Do you have a problem with that?" Dave asked.

"No. Sounds ok to me. I can make it." It had to be better than sticking around here and dealing with Jenn, I thought.

Dave pulled into the local grocery store. Walking in, he picked up a loaf of bread, and we went to the checkout line. Walking out, I saw Dave turn his head and look at me. As we got back in the car, Dave paused.

"You and Jenn having problems?" He asked.

"Fuck. I don't know. I mean, I think so. Depends on when you ask her I guess." I answered truthfully.

In typical Dave style, he didn't respond in any way. His question had been answered as far as he was concerned. We went back to his house. Walking in, Jenn informed me that we were going out to dinner and a movie. I didn't know that, but what the hell. This was just getting weirder and more stressful by the minute.

Walking out the door, Dave told Jenn to be home early. She needed her rest. Knowing that it was directed at me, I gave a slight nod to Dave. We had a big day tomorrow. I needed to get all the rest I could.

Climbing into the pickup and pulling away, Jenn informed me that she wasn't hungry and didn't want to see a movie. I braced myself for the impending argument.

Leaning over and sliding her hand into my shirt, she whispered. "Take me to a motel, honey."

That wasn't exactly what I had been expecting. Women, who could figure them?

Waking up the next morning, I was still thinking about the night before. Getting up to piss, I realized, I reeked of sex. I definitely needed a bath before climbing into an airplane with Dave. And as I found out later in the day,

Denny came along too. I was really glad that I had decided to bathe before leaving the house.

By the time all the weapons were picked up, worked on, and we were airborne, it was late afternoon.

Denny talked little more than Dave. From the conversation, I had the feeling he really didn't mind *too* much, me being around. He asked me some "what if?" scenarios on the way down, as well as some advice on how to handle certain situations. After that, little was said.

Arriving just before daylight, at what by now I had figured out was Managua, we met Bro and Aussie at the airport.

I rode with them, and Dave and Denny took their own way, to the "new" house that Bro and Aussie had found us. It was a dive, but as Bro pointed out to me, if needed, it was somewhat more defendable than most. After my last dash to safety, I did appreciate this fact.

We spent the day, fixing the place up a little bit, at least on the inside, picking up old furniture and what not. There seemed to be some clashes going on around the city. Staying in seemed like a good idea. This was the most potentially violent place I had ever been in my life. One minute everything was fine, and the next, you would hear machine gun fire.

The following morning we retrieved everything we needed from the plane and drove outside of town in two pickups.

Barely out of town we met with a group of men. I noticed some of them were about my age. I also recognized some of them from the very first time that Dave had landed without telling me what we were doing and they unloaded the plane. Following Bro's prior given instructions, I stood off to one side where I had a good field of fire. The ones that recognized me thought it was kind of funny that I went from spooked the last time to trying to look like a badass this time. Dave spoke with them and cash was exchanged for the guns. Other than being somewhat cautious, the meet went off without any problems.

I made another seventy five hundred dollars.

11

LIFE'S BEEN GOOD

As summer waned on, we made more and more trips. I actually lost count. There was no rhyme or reason when we went. Middle of the week, weekend, sunshine or bad weather. We might not go for three weeks, and we might go twice in one week, but that was hard to do.

The money was starting to add up, and I didn't know where to put it. Dave would occasionally remind me not to buy a lot of stuff, which I hadn't. I had it stuffed into a gunny sack and hidden. I wasn't worried about it being found though. When I wanted some, I just took out a hundred or so and used it for a week or two. Unless I went partying or to go do something for the weekend, then I might take more, depending on what I was doing. This couldn't last. I would have to get a bank.

Dad noticed on one of his monthly trip homes, that I had plenty of money left over. He was very proud of that fact, but wondered if I was getting enough to eat. I told him I had been eating mainly at Jenn's house. After that I made it a point to spend a little more of what Dad would leave me.

When I did have a weekend to myself, I would get with Billy, Rob, and Brad. I usually footed the bill, and lately I didn't seem to mind any of it. Pulling into a supermarket, we would fill a cart with booze, and drink for the weekend. We made it a game to try every type of alcohol available. More often than not though, we came back to what we called "Jungle Juice." which was nothing more than Hawaiian Punch with Ever Clear in it.

Rob was still worried about me, he started pointing out to Billy and Brad how much hardware I was carrying with me. I tended to go nowhere without my 9mm. And I kept a couple of rifles behind the seat of my pickup. Brad told Rob, that I had obviously lost my mind, and was paranoid. Nobody liked to rabbit hunt that much and it was a matter of time before they saw me on the news.

When Rob told me this, we used it several times to scare the hell out of Brad. It was great fun, Billy loved it also. On several occasions, with Billy and Rob's help we convinced Brad that I had "suddenly" decided to rob a convenience store. They would just "barely" talk me out of it. You would think Brad would have stopped coming around after awhile, but he said he just couldn't miss it when I finally went over the edge. He wanted a front row seat and just hoped I wouldn't get him killed in the process. As this got old, we found new ways to terrify Brad. Launching a car at fifty miles an hour over a set of railroad tracks resulted in some damages one night, and made me realize again, that I didn't need to be drawing any unwanted attention to myself. I just needed an outlet for all the stress, was all.

I had come to realize that I loved adrenaline. It was the ultimate high. I couldn't get enough of it. I looked forward to every trip to Central America, and the danger it presented. I would have rather have had a good adrenaline rush, than drink, or smoke weed. Probably the only thing that came close to it was getting laid.

As things with Jenn seemed to be "on again, off again" I found other ways to relieve my stress.

After Jenn broke up with me, (again) I grabbed some cash and headed to Juarez. It was a Friday night when I got there. Starting at a discotheque, I finished up my own personal little party on Sunday afternoon, in what I had come to call "sporting houses." I felt much better. I had come to realize that whores were a hell of a diversion for most anything bothering you.

School was getting ready to start and I needed to figure out a way of continuing to go on my little forays. I actually thought about just quitting school altogether, and moving down there with Bro and Aussie. After some thought, this didn't seem all that wise. It couldn't last forever.

Colter was going through a hell of a nasty divorce. Occasionally he would show up, and we would get some drinking in. He didn't seem to notice that I had no problem getting into bars, and didn't really seem to care. I thought this was because he had started to think of me as a man. Turned out, it was simply because he was too deep in his own misery to give a damn. This came out in a conversation we had and bout scared the hell out of me.

"You're getting ready to graduate. What are you going to do? I was thinking you might go to a trade school." He said, answering his own question.

"Actually Colter, I've been giving some thought to becoming a mercenary, the moneys good."

Colter grabbed me by shirt front, and yanked me to him.

"*Are you out of your fucking mind?*" He screamed at me.

I kicked out at his groin and tried to loosen his grip. Even half drunk, he was still a lot stronger than me. I tried a swing at his jaw, and he shoved me backwards away from him.

"*You'll get your ass killed, you dumb little bastard! What are you thinking? It ain't like a fucking movie. What the hell even gave you that idea?*"

This conversation wasn't going any direction that I had wanted it to. I immediately went back into my "hide everything" mode. I certainly wasn't going to tell him shit now. Instead I just defended myself.

"*Fuck off, Colter. I'll do what the hell I want. At least I didn't go off and marry some stupid bitch.*"

"*Did you tell Dad about this?*" He yelled, a little less loudly.

"Did you tell Dad about you coming down here getting drunk and chasing women?" I countered.

"Fuck you. You little bastard! You're gonna wind up deader'n hell." Colter hollered back at me.

This subject was never brought up again. What the hell did Colter think? That I was going to be a Welder? Not that there was anything wrong with being a welder. Hell, I wish I did have a skill along those lines. I just wasn't mentally geared that way, and still not for that matter.

As school came around, I got a little bit of good news. The first thing was that I would have enough credits to graduate by December. The second windfall was I only had to go for half a day, in the morning, *if* I got a job. So with the help of a hot looking school guidance counselor, I got one.

I let Dave know what was going on, who said he could get by without me for a bit. But to let him know when I was available, and we would try and work then.

I hated the job, but stuck it out. We're not going into it here.

Weekends were pretty much spent during this time, partying in Juarez, and chasing women.

Colter found his "true love" while working his new job. He was now a miner, and while he didn't have a lot of money, he was getting his divorce paid off. I would occasionally see him and liked the new girlfriend. In the past I had liked several of Colter's girlfriends, but this one did seem a little more in it for the long haul. They were eventually married and still are to this day.

When December came around, I turned in my two weeks notice and started getting ready.

The first thing to do was see Dave. However, arriving at the house, Jenn thought I was there to see her, and she seemed quite happy about it. Dave invited me to stay for dinner.

After dinner, Dave and I stepped out into the garage. Plans were tentatively made for the following Wednesday. Come Wednesday, we were on our way. Dave seemed to have some extra cargo. On the way down I asked him about it. I was told "You'll see."

One thing that I never had figured out that I asked Dave about, exactly who were the players in this little conflict.

Basically it boiled down to this. Nicaragua had a President named Somoza who was pretty much a dictator. He was thrown out in the late 70's. The group that opposed him were the Sandinistas. They were supposed to do all kinds of good things for the country. Unfortunately, they thought their changes needed to come at the end of gun. So another group started opposing them. They were called the Contras. Meanwhile, in El Salvador, which is practically next door, *was* having a civil war. The United States actually supported the El Salvadorian government at one time but then began supporting one of the leftist groups. For a while anyway. During this time, United States Special Forces were reputed to have training camps there.

All this simply meant, for me anyway, that El Salvador had potential customers also. The Honduras was another story altogether. The United States had a military presence there for the sole purpose of supporting the Contras. This could be done without actually establishing a United States Military presence in Nicaragua, and "getting involved" in some other countries dirty little war. This would come into play occasionally. Landings, weapons, fuel points etc., could generally be done in Honduras without any problem or anyone asking many questions. This also served on a couple of occasions to transport items to Nicaragua. As the Contras actually got training eventually, they did become a much more effective fighting force. This seemed good on the surface, but when a native was a trained Contra, (excuse the hell out of me, I mean "commando") one day and then flipped to the other side...well, that could be a problem. It caused problems in more than one family and village.

One thing for sure, when we landed this time around, I could tell right away that Dave and Denny's attention levels were way up from normal. Even more so than before. On the way to the house, (which had been moved again, in my absence.) Denny kept one hand on a pistol tucked underneath his leg. I just *had* to ask the obvious question.

"Anyone try to kill you lately, Dave?"

"People have tried to kill all of us, at one time or another, lately. Double crossing each other seems to be the order of the day." Dave replied earnestly.

Before I could process this and ask what had occurred, Denny piped in.

"It's hot, man. Really hot. Everywhere, all the time."

As we pulled up to the house, I thought I saw a barely perceptible movement from one of the front curtains. It appeared dark inside. What passed for a yard had a fence around it. Large rock columns at least three feet by three feet square, sat about eight feet apart, separated by wrought iron panels. The columns were entirely too close together, making it look like a rock wall had been planned and then changed in the building process into a fence. It was however, great cover.

Going into the back door, I was greeted by Aussie and Bro. As they put down weapons, and shook my hand, I noticed they were well armed and appeared ready to go. Pieces of steel and metal were leaned up against the wall below the windows for additional protection. Heavy blackout curtains covered the windows also.

Pumping my hand furiously, Aussie grilled us.

"Any problems motoring over, mate? No sign of surveillance Davey? Right good then. How ya goin, Joe?"

"I'm good Aussie, been missing you guys." I meant it.

"You might not feel that way too much longer. Things have been touchy lately, Joe. You really need to watch yourself. If you make a mistake or somebody senses a weakness, they're gonna move on ya." Bro added, and with that, he brought my H&K out of backroom and handed it to me.

Checking it showed that it was already loaded with one in the chamber. My guess is they had it in a backroom near a door or window. Having already set his own weapon down, Aussie retrieved Dave and Denny's rifles from what I assumed to be bedrooms.

As I looked around the house at last, it was laid out with a main room that consisted of the living room and kitchen with a front and back door, almost in line with each other. On one side of the room, was a hallway. This led to bedrooms and a bathroom. Two bedrooms on the left, bathroom and another bedroom on the right. Aussie had taken the 1st bedroom on the left and Bro had the last room on the right. Dave and Denny bunked together in the last room on the left and Bro gave me a sleeping bag to lie out on Aussie's floor. Worrying about snakes, spiders and other creepy crawlies, I convinced Aussie to pull down a cot he had stored in the closet. I very much appreciated this. The bedrooms had carpet in them but everything else had wood floors, except for the bathroom. The floors creaked like an old rusty hinge. Nobody would sneak into this place. My rifle lay on the floor next to me within easy reach. Aussie's leaned on the wall, next to his bed.

Before lying down, Aussie lifted his mattress and indicated some items in a plastic bag.

"It's my bail out. Got spare identity stuff and cash there. Feel free to put yours there, if you like Joe."

I did have spare credentials, and stashing them was always a pain in the ass. I thanked Aussie for the offer and made a mental note to do it the next morning.

I laid on my cot, staring into the darkness, Aussie and I caught up a little.

"What you been up to, Joe?" He asked.

"Quit my job. On the weekends I've been pretty much living in whore houses and drinking tequila."

"Job? What kind of job did you have?"

I told him truthfully that I had been a clerk typist.

This brought a chuckle from Aussie. "Rack off, you have not!"

"I did, and I hated it." I answered.

"Did you do it for the Sheila's?" He inquired.

"Weren't many women there. I just needed it to stay out of school, till I could get back here." I explained.

"I hope you haven't been dipping your stick recently, mate."

"Why's that Aussie?"

"It's one thing to be randy all the time, especially after a mission, it's another to go into the bush with a case of clap." He explained.

"I never thought of that." I honestly answered. It had been at least a week and I had never caught anything. Besides that I always used protection. But the idea of being so far from a doctor and not having access to any medical attention of that kind….well that would not be pleasant. I filed this for future reference.

"Well, now you know. While we're on the subject, I know you need to start thinking about what you're going to do, but don't do it out here. We need you sharp and ready. This place is heating right up. Most civil wars do eventually. Can't see it lasting another year. Two at most. Could be wrong though mate. Nam sure as hell lasted a long time."

"What will you do next, Aussie?" I was curious about this.

"Probably Afghanistan. Russians invaded it. You knew that right? So far the Afghies are getting it handed to them, for now. But things will open up. There'll be work there."

Afghanistan. I wasn't even sure where the hell that was. I knew it wasn't on the North or South American continents. Other than that, I had no damned idea.

"Bro's got a ell of a brekkie planned for us in the a.m. though. Let's get some sleep and try not to disappoint the big fock." Aussie added.

"Ok. Goodnight Aussie."

"Night Joe."

That night I dreamed of the woman's head exploding as Dave shot her. Waking up, I figured that was about as bad as it could get.

Bro had indeed, made a hell of a "brekkie" as Aussie called it. Fresh eggs and biscuits from a Dutch oven. Some type of sausage patties that I had never had, and I didn't ask what it was. They were flat out delicious. The butter was locally made and the jelly was some type of fruit that I wasn't familiar with, that just rocked. When we were finished, the food was gone.

Denny kept checking out the windows while Dave gave us a rundown of the days planned events. Bro and I washed up the dishes while coffee was made again.

As I dried dishes, Aussie asked me, "Dave tell you somebody tried to kill him again?" This confirmed what I had suspected.

"Yeah, fuckers almost got me with him, this time." Denny proclaimed, as Dave rolled his eyes.

"Go ahead, tell him about it Aussie. I can tell you're dying too. Denny was worse to have around than Joe." Dave said.

Aussie grinned. "About a month ago, Davey and Denny go to a cantina. There's a foreigner standing in there. So Denny sits down on the man's right, and Davey is standing to the right of Denny. As Davey is talking to Denny they hear glass break behind them, and as this happens, the foreign guy, starts to draw a pistol. Denny seeing the glass break, realizes it's a grenade, but before he can say or do anything he sees Davey drawing a pistol towards him, not realizing the guy behind him is arming himself."

"I thought Dave was going to shoot me." Denny said ashamedly.

Aussie, barely suppressing a laugh continued. "So Denny here does about the only thing he can, he *ducks*. He ducks so fast slammed his chin into the bar and split it open. Now Aussie paused to giggle a little. "So as Davey's gun comes over the top of Denny's 'ead, he shoots the guy, in the face. Twice, right Davey?"

Dave nodded in the affirmative as he took a long drink of milk.

"So by this time, our stranger has his Browning out, but since he just got shot twice in the face, he never gets it up. But as he gets hit, his reflexes manage to trigger off a shot." Aussie paused for effect and grinned.

Denny couldn't stand it anymore. "Yeah, and the fucker shoots me in the leg with his dying breath!

Aussie's eyes were positively twinkling. He was enjoying this.

Bro quietly added, "You barely got nicked."

Denny was adamantly defending himself. "Bullshit. It was through and through. I was lucky it didn't get a bone or artery."

"You shot him *twice,* in the face with a .45?" I asked Dave.

Shaking his head, Dave paused from his glass of milk. ".38 special."

Still trying to suppress a laugh, Aussie continued. "Before Davey and Boy Wonder here can process all this and the fact that there is a grenade rolling around on the floor, from the front window, somebody starts screaming at the back door. As Dave turns back around to see what that's all about a burst from an Ingram comes through, and this little dude comes in screaming and shooting. Fortunately for Davey, in that order, so Dave empties his gun at him."

I stared wide eyed. This had to be bullshit. "With a .38?" I asked incredulously.

"I didn't hit him. Honest. He just dropped the gun and ran. It wasn't even empty."

"Man." Bro exclaimed while smiling and shaking his head from side to side as he put up the last plate.

"What about the grenade?" I asked.

"Didn't go off. It was a dud. Looked like an old Chinese stick grenade." Dave answered as he rinsed his glass.

I looked around the room. Aussie was still grinning.

"Uhm, Dave?" I started hesitantly.

"Yeah?"

"How do you know that the guy with the pistol, wasn't trying to help you? He could've been responding to the grenade and the yelling too." I pointed out.

Aussie looked ready to bust a gut. "Wait for it Joe, wait for it." He emphasized.

Dave looked at me. "I didn't. He looked more like *one of them* than *one of me.*"

Aussie containing himself no longer started laughing out loud. Bro just shook his big head from side to side. "Man you guys are brutal."

Denny defending himself says, "He did shoot me, Joe."

"By fucking accident! He was fucking dead, Denny." I exclaimed.

Now Aussie was laughing himself so hard I thought he would piss himself.

I looked at Dave questioningly, as his eyes met mine, he answered.

"There was no time to figure it out, Joe." With that he turned and walked down the hallway.

With that for me to think about, we got back to the business at hand.

Dave and Denny would take the first pickup to the airport. Bro and Aussie would ride in the second one. I would ride in the back of their pickup to provide protection from the rear. From there, we would transport the guns to the meet. Be ready. Stay guarded, and watch for ambushes. Aussie suggested that I have more ammo and magazines, which I immediately got.

Guns were taken out and loosely stashed in the pick-ups. I was given a folded tarp to keep my H&K covered. Concealed but very accessible was the order of the day, as were all days in populated areas. Climbing into the back of the truck, Bro pointed out a rope anchored to the front of the pickup bed on each side, down low.

"If we have to go high speed, push your feet out against it, so you don't get bounced out. I wouldn't have it across my waist though. Case you need to get out or move in a hurry. Up to you though." Bro casually explained.

Butterflies started in my stomach. I couldn't believe how good it felt. I jumped in, and put the rope out in front of my feet. I couldn't reach it. Bro or Aussie must have set it up for them. I wasn't tall enough to reach the damn thing sitting down. Untying it quickly on one side, I shortened it up, until I could lock my boot heels on it. Dave was getting impatient with me, but at last we were ready.

Dave pulled out, and Aussie followed, quickly dropping back about half a block. Several times we drew looks and I noticed a lot more "soldiers" or whatever the hell they called themselves, out and about. There was certainly no shortage of weapons here. How had they all gotten here? I knew we hadn't brought enough in to arm an entire country. I made a mental note to ask Dave about it.

At one point as we went around a corner, a man carrying an assault rifle in fatigues, made eye contact with me. He stepped out into the street and watched us as we drew away from him. I pulled my rifle into my lap, flicking the safety off as I did so. All I would have to do now is lift it and fire. With my right hand I gave a quick wave and smiled. He watched us go, then turned back toward the shade from which he had come. I relaxed and put the safety back to the "on" position.

We arrived at the hangar and Denny had the doors open for us. As we drove in, he closed it behind us.

"Joe, watch that door. Stay where you are and watch it. The rest of us will load."

Telling Dave about the man that had watched us, I was told to "Get used to it."

Aussie spoke to Dave while the unloading and reloading was done.

"Davey, if I drop back any further following you, it would draw less attention, but then we may not be close enough to react if hit."

"Yeah, I know. Let's stay somewhat tight. I like it the way it is. Not getting hit is good and it might avoid it, but getting hit and having the back up too far out, well that's not acceptable."

"I agree." Bro said.

Crates were stacked on either side of me, giving me some cover, as well as Dave's "new" crates. I still hadn't found out what was in them.

When we were done, Denny went to the hangar door and slid it open. Dave and Aussie pulled through. Denny then slid it shut and trotted up and climbed back in with Dave. As Dave pulled out, he made a motion for me to watch behind. I did as I was told.

Arriving just short of the meet site, Dave pulled over. Pulling up next to him, he issued instructions.

"Joe, hop out here. There's a clearing about 200 yards ahead. You go into it by foot. Look it over. Bro, you and Denny, we'll drop as we enter the clearing, break left and right. Joe will have that side. Me and Aussie will park the trucks and go to whatever available cover we can on the far edge of the clearing. Get everyone else located. We don't need a Mexican firing squad if it goes bad. Everybody got it."

We all answered up, and I started to walk. About 100 yards out, Aussie and Dave drove by, cloaking me in dust. I moved off the road a little where I had better cover.

As I saw the pickups brake, Bro and Denny got out on the move. Bro went right and Denny went left. I could see the clearing now as I drew closer. I adjusted my pace to match Denny and Bro reaching their respective sides. Parking the trucks in the center of the clearing, Dave and Aussie headed for the far side. We all settled into wait.

After about an hour, I caught movement in the far tree line. Bro was standing up, speaking to someone. As

Bro and another man came into the clearing, I could see they were followed by about a dozen more men. All were armed. They seemed fairly relaxed. None of their weapons were slung, but nobody seemed exceptionally nervous or had their fingers on the trigger. Dave and Aussie started towards the trucks and Dave motioned Denny and I to come in. I kept my rifle at the low ready as I walked in. I had already flipped my safety off. Looking around, I saw I had no cover available, except for the pickups between us. On the other hand, neither did they. We were outnumbered at least 2 to 1. The butterflies in my stomach really took hold and I started tuning into every small sound. Birds, crunches of footsteps, weapons being handled, and talking. Everything felt intense and sounded intense. The natural high started to come in, causing my brain to concentrate even harder on every minute detail.

The crates were opened, so they could be seen, and got an affirmative nod from the jefe. Dave also lifted the lid on two crates, and pointed out the two tubes in each. They were olive drab green and about two and a half feet long. They had what appeared to be a canvas sling attached to each end. The rebels were very excited to see them. The jefe actually gave Dave a hug. The tubes were marked; Rocket HE 66mm Antitank M72/A2. Where in the hell did Dave get these, I wondered? And since when did tanks come into the picture? I hadn't seen any armor. Not that they didn't have it, just not much of it. I didn't realize at the time, the LAW rocket, or Light Antitank Weapon had never been very good at stopping tanks, especially modern ones. They did however make instant waste out of cars, pickups, were hell on buildings and absolutely destroyed stationary aircraft.

All four tubes were removed and passed off to men who slung them on their backs. All I could think of was what if these were used against us as we were leaving? Then again, they wouldn't get their money back. It would be blown to hell.

Turned out there wasn't even money exchanged this time. In Dave's usual precautious manner, he had seen to it ahead of time. *This* time.

Later that night, while putting my spare credentials under Aussie's mattress with some money we heard a distant explosion in the city. I swear I heard Dave chuckle softly in the dark, down the hall.

Dave paid me when we got back. I made another seven thousand dollars.

12

NO MORE MISTER NICE GUY

The next two trips we made were uneventful. Dave had brought more LAW rockets each time. They seemed to be a popular item, but were having the effect of driving the price down on my guns. Not enough money to go around apparently, I wasn't complaining though. I still cleared five thousand each trip.

Dave, keeping with his pattern of not having a pattern had switched up the meets each and every time. His philosophy was that it kept them guessing, kept us loose, made it hard to put a pattern to us, and left them more room to screw something up. Which left us more room to see it coming. I didn't agree, but since no one asked me, and wouldn't have listened to me anyway, I kept my mouth shut. Dave was right.

On a warm breezy day, Dave said we would meet up with a group in a small town, barely outside of the city. It would be in public to discuss prices and the terms. The exchange would be some time afterwards. Probably within the next 24 hours. Dave decided we would take one vehicle since there were only four of us. Denny had not come the last two trips and was having some kind of trouble at home. Or as Dave put it, "He's a flake."

Over breakfast, Dave described the people as a small rebel group and probably connected with the narcos. They had been told however that we do not trade guns for dope. Word was always put out, that we didn't carry guns with us to the sale or cash. (Even if we did.) This lessened the chance of ambush, but did not get rid of it entirely. I believe they thought if they could get us, they might make one of us talk, thereby getting the weapons for free. This did not sound appealing to any of us. Also, there was a chance we were dealing with the "other" side, trying to interdict us. Usually the highest chance of ambush was delivery to a group the *first* time we did business with them.

I was told I would ride in the back. Aussie offered to ride with me, but I told him to go ahead and ride up front. I didn't mind. It really was a beautiful day. Since it was a tight fit, Bro would leave his M60 behind and use my H&K instead. I was to wait outside with the truck to watch the rifles, in case something did go wrong. All of us had our pistols though.

I jumped in the bed of the old Ford, and we headed out of town. Most of the girls around town were dressed for the warmth. Cut offs and t shirts seemed to be the order of the day. Even Aussie was wearing shorts. Watching

the day go by was refreshing. I had eaten a hearty breakfast, was with good friends and was going to make a lot of
money. Dave picked up speed as we left town and thirty
minutes later down a dusty road we were pulling into a
small village.

Once into town, Dave turned left and then right. After
another quarter of a mile, he turned right again and a
block later another right turn, bringing us right back onto
the road we had come in on. Only now we were facing the
way we had come from. The town was quiet, but it was early and was a warm lazy day. Still seemed a little too quiet
though. I started to get antsy.

I heard Dave indicate the building on the left where
we would be going. As I looked it over, it appeared to be
somewhat like a warehouse. It had one door that I could
see, and a window a few feet from it. As Dave drove past
it and pulled to the right, I noticed an old beat up green
Chevy pickup, sitting underneath a shade tree. It was
parked across from the building Dave had pointed out.

Sitting up in the driver's seat as we passed, and resting his arm out the window was a Nicaraguan male. He
looked to be in his early twenties. Our eyes met, and as
Dave brought the pickup to a stop, about thirty-five yards
past him, he nodded at me and smiled.

It was an evil smile.

Blood started rushing in my ears, and my stomach
turned. Nothing was happening though, but I kept staring. I stood up in the truck bed and placed one hand on
the tailgate and stepped over, onto the bumper and down

to the ground. I heard Bro and Dave open the pickup doors. As my boot hit dirt, I let my eyes drift right, just for a second. Still watching in my peripheral vision, I saw the Nicaraguan open his mouth as if speaking, and his passenger door started to open. Someone had been hiding in his truck. Before I could process all of this, I saw a gun barrel flash in front of his steering wheel as he brought his right hand off his seat and prepared to exit the pickup.

I had to warn the guys, but didn't know what to say. Should I yell "ambush" or "gun?" I was running out of time. As I started reaching for my pistol, I yelled. *"It's not right!"* Time seemed to stand still as he exited the Chevy. As he cleared the door he planted his feet, and braced himself. In his hand was an Ingram machine pistol. *Oh God, this is going to be bad.* My hand still wasn't on my gun. My arm seemed to be made of lead. I was running out of time. *"Dad, Colter, I need you,"* I thought. Looking down to see why my hand wasn't moving seemed to result in a sudden burst of speed from my arm and I *finally* had the 9mm in my hand. As I started to bring it up, I looked back towards the Chevy and saw the Nicaraguan was pulling the bolt back to cock the machine pistol, although he still wasn't facing us. He seemed so damned calm and collected. Then my arm seemed to slow down again. Using what seemed like every muscle in my upper body, the gun came into view and I got both hands on it and into a firing position. As he turned towards us, I saw the front sight come onto his chest, I started to pull the trigger. I had decided the gun wasn't going to fire, with all the strength it seemed to be taking, when it suddenly did go off, sending a 115 grain Federal hollow point his way. The front sight bounced up and then reappeared. I pressed the trigger again. This time, I saw the front sight blade lift and bounce back down and I squeezed again. A hole appeared in his shirt, not quite in the center, about halfway to his left shirt pocket.

Something seemed to be wrong with the Nicaraguan as he slid down from my view. I didn't notice any blood though. It seemed the least he could do was bleed properly for me. Let me know that I had hit him solid. For the first time since I had stepped off the truck, I noticed that the air was filled with gunfire and bullets cracking. I dropped into a crouch while waving my right hand crazily in the air, as if trying to ward off the bullets like angry bees.

I heard the rear window glass shatter behind me and I could hear rounds passing behind me, from my left and my right. Bullets were also cracking in front of me right to left. The tunnel vision started to fade. I became aware that on the passenger side of the Chevy, a man with a gun of some type was trying not to drop it as bullets impacted him. Glancing over my left shoulder, I rose up slightly to see Aussie, leaning into his rifle, shooting rapidly one shot at a time, towards the Chevy. Bro was on Aussie's right, barely out of the pickup door, firing steadily on semi auto across our pickup bed, while using it for cover. Across the dirt street towards the building, the incoming fire was diminishing. As Dave emptied his M16 on full auto, I heard him scream. "*GO!*"

That seemed to be the best advice I had heard in a long time. After all, no sense taking chances.

Spinning into the pickup, Dave stomped the gas. Bro dove into the open door on the passenger side, and Aussie with one hand vaulted himself into the bed. I reached for the tailgate, as the truck caught and surged forward yanking me off balance. I had a vision of Colter and Zeb leaving me out in the middle of nowhere to find my way home. I had to get my foot underneath me before I was drug away, I pulled myself up and over into the bed and fell face first into Aussie's boot. I felt my lips split open and pain screamed through my face. Landing with my finger still on the trigger, the 9mm went off, reverberating through the bed as I shot a hole in the wheel well narrowly missing a tire. That would *not* have made anyone's day that I gave a damn about. Aussie, shuffling around desperately for a magazine, scissor kicked his legs to reach it. I saw the boot coming again. Too late. It caught me square in the mouth for the second time, hard enough that I saw lights go off in my head, and things seemed to slow down and go quiet for a little bit. I was beginning to wonder whose side he was on. Completing his reload, Aussie fired short bursts over my head. Through the now broken rear window, Bro was firing also. In the back of my mind, a voice told me, *"Do Not Try To Sit Up!"* I was very content to stay where I was at. Providing I didn't get kicked in the face again.

The important thing though, is that we were away and moving. Even more importantly, *I was alive!* We didn't quit moving until we got back to the house.

I couldn't quit shaking.

Dave slowed down about a block away and pulled in behind the house slow and casual. All of us were staring at it hard. Once we scrambled out of the truck, we looked at each other and started talking excitedly.

"The truck's shot up. We need to ditch it. After dark." Dave said. Looking at the truck for the first time, I noticed several bullet holes in the side of the bed, plus the back window shot out. Five or six of them were entrance holes. One was an exit hole. I suddenly remembered triggering off the round in the bed, while face down, and decided not to bring it to anyone's attention.

"What happened to Joe's mouth?" Bro asked Aussie.

"Not sure, mate. What did happen to your mouth Joe?"

"You kicked me in it. Twice! You big bastard." I answered, spluttering blood.

"Why did you kick him in the face, Aussie?" Dave looked perplexed.

"Seemed like the thing to do." Aussie grinned, while examining my mouth closer. "I don't think it'll take any stitches though. I knew I booted you once mate, while I was trying to reach my bloody magazine. When was the other one?"

"When I landed in the bed."

"Well now Joe, that really shouldn't be my blame. If a Sheila jumps on you, who's focking who then?"

I had to laugh. "Man that was some scary shit." As if on cue I started trembling again and noticed Dave was also.

Bro stepped over to me and lifted my face up with his hands checked my mouth. "Ya done good. That was pretty close. I think you and Dave were in the worst positions. You were definitely in a crossfire dude."

"I...I didn't know what to do." I replied ashamedly.

"You did bloody good Joe, spot on. You dropped that bloke right well, I'd say."

"Did I kill him?" I asked looking down at the ground.

The silence made me look up, everyone was looking at me.

"By the time I looked at the bloody fock, he was on his knees, with his gun on the ground. Three holes in his chest, with two of them next to each other. It's a safe bet. Had it coming, he did." Aussie emphasized.

"You saw it coming before the rest of us. You followed your instincts, and it paid off. We can make more money, later." Dave said.

Bro then looked at Dave and in an authoritative voice asked, "Why in the hell were you standing out there without any cover? You know better. You're lucky you didn't get your ass shot off."

"I didn't have any damned cover. If I left the truck, who would've got us out of there?" Dave answered. Bro couldn't argue that. Or anyone else either, for that matter.

We all headed inside the house but I kept my H&K handy, and still being full of adrenaline, had to clear the house first. I felt silly when I was done, but as Dave put it. "No one is here, but it won't hurt."

I noticed Dave seemed to be the most pumped up (not including myself). Aussie seemed somewhat livelier than normal. Bro on the other hand, set about making lunch like it had been a routine day at the office.

We stood in the kitchen going over the whole incident, again (for the third time at least). I asked why all the different reactions. Me and Dave were obviously still worked up. Bro was not, and Aussie was somewhere in between.

Bro told me, basically because it was my first time participating in something like that. I asked then why Dave was all worked up too. He had lots of experience.

"Cause he's a chicken shit." Bro grinned.

"Oh, fuck you." Dave hollered.

That got all of us laughing. Anyone listening to the laughter from outside would never have guessed what we had just been through.

As Dave walked to the refrigerator for a beer, he casually dropped a hand on my shoulder and spoke as he went by.

"Thanks, Joe. I'm glad you're ok."

I don't know why, but that brought out a huge flood of emotions from me. I started to choke up. I wanted to scream at him, *"We almost got killed today"*. Oh man, this was way too deep for me. I'm in so far over my head, I don't know what the hell to do. Scream, cry or laugh. I felt like I was capable of all three.

Looking down at the floor and rubbing my temples, I could feel eyes on me. Looking up, Dave stepped past me, beer in hand. Bro and Aussie were staring at me. Glancing at each other, they seemed to come to some silent agreement. Aussie nodded his head and Bro looked again at me and turned back to his cooking. Aussie spoke.

"Joe, How about after we eat, me and you go get us a drink? We need to ditch the truck anyway."

"Ok Aussie. Whatever." I answered. I needed something to do. I started field stripping my H&K for cleaning. I then took my 9mm out and placed it next to the H&K parts, my eyes kept getting drawn back to the pistol. I relived the whole thing again and again. Becoming frustrated quickly, I picked the 9mm up and shoved it back in my waist band. Out of sight, out of mind. I tried hard to concentrate on cleaning. My hands wouldn't quit shaking. Knowing when I finished, I should clean the pistol too, seemed depressing. I started slowing down on the rifle cleaning, prolonging it, as long as I could.

When I was done, I reloaded the H&K and leaned it on the wall nearby. I stripped the 9mm and wiped off the powder residue, oiled and reassembled it. A quick function check showed it to be working fine. I reloaded and put it back into my waistband.

After lunch, as I got up to do dishes, Aussie suggested we go for a beer. I declined since there was work to be done. Dave told me to go ahead, he and Bro would finish up, and ditch the truck later. I had a feeling something was up. Adrenaline started to flow for the second time that day.

Aussie sensing my apprehension spoke. "It's been a rough, scary day for you Joe. Let's just me and you go out get pissed and talk."

"I'm not pissed at you Aussie." I answered. Why would I be pissed at someone else? Surviving this morning seemed enough. I didn't see a reason to go start more trouble with someone else. I was puzzled.

This brought a chuckle and an explanation. "Getting pissed" meant having a few drinks. It was not the first or last time, Aussie's slang had to be explained to me.

"Bro, you and Dave feel free to join us later, I'm sure you can find us." Aussie offered.

This sounded ok and I felt that maybe all the fears and anxieties were left over from this morning.

Aussie as it turned out, liked the ladies too. Walking into the bar KC and the Sunshine Band were screaming on the juke box to "Play that funky music white boy, play that funky music right." Aussie positively disco danced his way to the far corner of the bar, embarrassing the shit out of me in the process. We sat down with our backs to the wall in a dark corner of the bar. Almost as quickly two women approached us. I was still trying to size them up and decide if they were looking for company or money. They weren't dressed like sporting girls but not like women out on the town either. Looking around though, I decided that any woman wanting a night out, wouldn't come here. Aussie offered to buy them a drink if they would get our drinks for us, and give us a little time to talk business. He explained that I was from the north and had come looking for work. After fetching theirs and our drinks they smiled and walked back to the bar, chatting in Spanish.

"Did you hear what they were talking about mate?" Aussie asked me.

"No, I didn't understand it." I admitted.

"They were talking about some Americans getting shot, near here, by narcotics traffickers. A gunfight in broad daylight, they said."

"You know that's not quite the way it happened though." I said.

"No. But no matter. They can spin it any way they like." Aussie grinned.

"Speaking of today Joe, there are a few things I wanted to talk to you about. If that's ok? If not, I'm going to any-way mate."

I took a long swallow of beer, and could feel it start into my throat, and drop all the way down to my stomach. Damn it tasted good. That had to be the best beer I have ever had in my life. But I didn't really want to talk right now.

"I'll get right to it then, Joe. You killed a man today. It's got your emotions running wild, doesn't it? Feels good too, doesn't it? Look me in the face and tell me I'm wrong."

In the dimness of the bar, I could see Aussie's grey eyes watching me. Lying to him was no use. He was right, I did feel good. In fact I had never felt better. What in the hell is wrong with me? I thought.

For the second time that day, I said the words; *"It's not right."*

"Oh, but it is right my little pommie mate. What you're feeling is natural. The good feelings. The feelings of invincibility, the wanting to cry. What's the matter? Scared since it feels good, there must be something wrong with you? Is that it? Don't even bother to answer Joe. We've all been there. It's normal. It comes with the adrenaline high. Head doctors could write volumes on it, they could."

Aussie was right. For the first time that day, I started to feel just a little bit normal. Damn this beer was good. Draining it, I looked at the girls and ordered more. As the older of the two brought them over, I thought to myself that she had some of the biggest, nicest tits, I had ever seen. It wouldn't be too hard for her to undo those top three buttons on that blouse either.

Aussie let his eyes drift between me and the door, and managed to work in a smile to the younger girl sitting at the bar. Clinking our beer bottles in salute, he continued. "You did well today. Not because you killed a man, which is irrelevant by the way. But for the simple fact, you saw it coming first and hollered out. You didn't freeze up."

"I felt like it." I said ashamedly. Aussie just patiently waited, so I explained. "I felt like I couldn't move. My arm wasn't working, I was so fucking scared."

"Joe, I saw you shoot the man, there was nothing slow happening anywhere. That was your senses, lying to you. Things seem to go into slow motion, *sometimes*. Especially if you're about to get creamed. That was really touch and go today. No doubt about it, we did get lucky." Raising the back of his hand he lightly tapped my arm, and I looked up at him. "Did you see how Dave was rattled? Almost as bad as you. You know why? Not because he's chicken shit.

Because he was right on the edge. He was exposed and behind the timeline. Davey could have very easily bought the farm today, as you Yanks put it. Bro and I, on the other hand, were in good positions. We had cover and we saw what was going down. Bro passed up the passenger in the truck, because he saw the guy was screwing with his rifle. Bro just kept his circle going until he had credible threats and targets and let them have it. I took the first target I came too. The passenger in the pickup, he was just raising his rifle, but I was ready. If you're not ready, you die."

"What about the guy I shot? He was getting ready to fire." I asked

"He wasn't ready though. He would've got to us eventually, another second or so, but he was scared too. Something fucked him up." I remembered watching him try to cock the bolt back, he should've had it ready. "Believe it or not, you actually get used to it, eventually. Well as much as a man can get used to it. Just makes you breathe a little hard is all. Kind of like a good Sheila can make you do." Aussie grinned as he looked at the two girls at the bar.

He fixed me with those cold grey eyes again, Aussie became serious once more.

"You have to maintain though, Joe. Keep yourself together. Don't ever go thinking you can't be beat, or you're the best. Killing to live is ok, living to kill or murder is not, and I won't tolerate it. Not from you or anybody." He meant it.

As he bought another round, Aussie invited the girls over to the table. The youngest one decided she liked

Aussie's "English accent." I saw Aussie wince the tiniest bit, but he didn't correct her. Speaking to the older one, he told her that although I was quite young, he thought I *might* be strong enough to hire, but wanted her opinion. As she smiled at me, and dropped her hand to my knee, she glanced at Aussie and said, "We see."

Aussie laughed as I stared at her tits.

Hours later we stumbled in as the sky started to lighten in the east, we found Bro awake. Drinking his first cup of coffee of the day. I smiled stupidly at him. I was maintaining, but no doubt, I was drunk.

Bro was grinning ear to ear. "You two smell like beer and pussy. Davey's gonna be *mad*. He said, drawing out the last word.

"Well, the fock should've joined us then, eh Joe? Would've helped release some of that pent up energy now. Joe released a barrel full of energy, three or four times, I would guess." Aussie giggled.

Knowing he was referring to the women, I teased back. "Mine didn't scream as much as yours though. What was all that shit I heard about a *Tiger Snake?*"

Bro started laughing loud and deep. "Did he tell you Joe, he calls it that because it causes *paralysis?*" Bro was beside himself laughing.

"It does, and you know it you big bloke. Just ask your wife. She'll tell you straightaway."

Bro started laughing even harder, if that was possible. "Man, my old lady, would wear your little ass down, in about five minutes. You'd be begging for me to stop her.

Combat ain't shit compared to a night in the sack with my woman."

I didn't even know Bro was married. He had never mentioned it. Before I could ask any further, Dave padded in barefooted, surprising all of us. Wiping sleep from his eyes, he said, "Well, I see the whore mongers have returned to the roost. Might want to set them up with a shot of penicillin, Bro."

Aussie trying to suppress a giggle, spit his first sip of coffee out. "Ell Dave, you might want to take a shot too. Seems Joe likes the older gals. I don't think your daughter needs to worry, but you might think about getting your old lady, tested."

I could have died. I couldn't believe they were talking like this, and not getting angry with each other.

"Fuck you Aussie." Dave answered with a little grin. As he poured a cup of coffee he said, "Besides, they're not seeing each other anymore." Referring to Jenn and I.

"No we're not." Trying to get in a good one, I continued. "Good thing too, cause that one last night, that looked like your wife, about ruined me."

Now it was Dave's turn to choke on *his* coffee. "Fuck you too, you little bastard. Fuck all of you drunken whore mongers." Bro and Aussie thought it was quite funny. This was fun!

"*I'm* not a drunken whore monger, Dave. I stayed right here all night *and* helped you ditch the truck." Bro pointed out.

"If you bury your nose any further up Dave's backside, we won't be able to tell the two of you, apart." Aussie said.

Ignoring Aussie and I, Dave said, "I know. At least there's one of you I can count on."

As Aussie and I razzed Dave, he walked out of the kitchen to go get cleaned up.

I fell asleep on the couch and was woken by Bro shaking me a couple of hours later. "Time for you and Dave to head out." He said.

Getting up, I went into the restroom and pissed. I took a look at myself in the mirror and realized I looked rough. My mouth was a mountain of scabs. I grabbed my comb and started to wet my hair. As I bent over the sink to splash water on me, my stomach turned suddenly. I stepped to the side, dropped to my knees and puked my guts out into the toilet. I thought of yesterday. The fear. The smell of the gun smoke. The beer, the women and perfume, brought everything up. I must have thrown up about four times. I pushed myself to my feet. I felt much better, certainly lighter, even if just in the head. Stepping back to the mirror I rinsed my face, and started combing my hair, and while looking past my busted lips, it was still me. But something was bugging me. Something wasn't right. I stared into my own eyes, not sure what I was seeing, and not sure if I liked it either.

I went down the hallway and out the back door. There was a Ford station wagon, faded red with fake wood paneling down the side of it. Bro was going over it. I was slightly stunned.

"Where in the hell…." I began.

"We picked it up last night to replace the truck. Good idea actually, lots of storage. You guys are going to leave all your stuff you brought down, here. Give you more next trip. Now me and Aussie got a good way to transport it."

I made a mental note to ask Dave about this seemingly endless supply of old piece of junk vehicles. Every time I turned around it was different vehicle. From a tactical standpoint it certainly had its merits.

I had a mental image of me trying to dive through the back window of a station wagon while under fire. Just as quickly that image was replaced by one of Dave, Aussie, Bro, Denny and myself, climbing out of a station wagon, armed to the teeth, with guerillas laughing at us, as Bro and Dave tried to un ass themselves from it. I wondered if Bro could even *fit* in it.

"That's not a cool car, Bro. It's too slow to get in and out of." I opinioned.

"Yep, not good for that, but it is inconspicuous." He answered. Bro seemed to genuinely like cars of any kind. "Huh." I answered.

Before leaving, Aussie called me into the bedroom. In his hands was a holster. It was soft leather, with a clip slid into a reinforced tab with a slot on one side and a matching reinforced tab on the other. It could be worn in or out of the pants, just by reversing the clip. Tossing it to me Aussie said; "Try your 9 millimeter in it. You need it. Thing like yesterday, you don't want your gun hanging up. I keep telling you, it's the little things that get you killed."

The gun fit perfectly. After moving the clip over to the left side of the holster, I clipped it in my pants and holstered my pistol. "Wow man, this is much better. Thanks Aussie."

"No problem mate." He smiled back at me.

The flight back seemed to last forever. I was pent up with nervous energy, and Dave seemed flat out bored. After awhile he let me take the stick. Placing my feet on the rudder pedals, I watched the gauges Dave told me too, and made corrections as he instructed when a gauge drifted off. This occupied my mind for a few hours anyway. We landed in El Paso, while still daylight out, I had plans to go to Juarez. I was so wound up, I couldn't stand it.

I called Rob when I got home and asked him if he wanted to go to Juarez. He did not. He never did. I really don't know why I ever asked. He told me to come by and pick him up and we would do something. As much as I wanted to get laid, this sounded good too. Peeling my jeans off that I had worn for four days straight, I realized, I stunk. After cleaning up, I redressed and drove to Rob's house.

"Well Johnny Cash, lives and breathes." Rob greeted me.

"What the hell are you talking about?" I asked him.

"The Man in Black." He answered. I realized, I was wearing black jeans, a black western shirt, and my cowboy hat.

"I look *good*." I emphasized.

"Really? What happened to your mouth? Get your ass kicked again?"

"Got drunk and fell down."

Rob's older sister Liza walked out the front door. "What's up with all the black Joe? Going to a funeral? What in the hell happened to your mouth?" She asked as she walked closer.

"Got drunk and fell on my face." I replied, answering her last question first. Seeing a chance to play on her sympathy I continued. "I just wanted to look good for you, Baby."

Liza rolled her eyes. We can party together, Joe. That's it. Rob, keep your friends on a leash." Liza was older than us by about three years. I thought she was pretty hot looking and she already had a kid. Liza had not been receptive to any of my advances, but still hung out with us from time to time, and tolerated me.

With that I felt compelled to howl and let loose with the best impersonation of a howling dog that I could. I could feel the scabs pulling on my lips, and made a mental note not to do that again.

Liza turned red, and Rob laughed. "I'll give you this Joe, you never give up, do you? It makes me feel good, but it's never going to happen." Liza added.

"So where the hell you been, man? I've tried getting a hold of you for three, four days now." Rob asked.

"Aw, just trying to make some money, dude. You know how it is." As the last trip started replaying in my mind again, I drifted off into my own little trance.

"What in the hell are you looking at?" Rob asked, while slowly waving his hand in front of my face. "You look out of it."

Returning to earth, I focused on Rob. "Let's go out to eat." I suggested. "On me. Get a nice steak dinner, some good booze, drink up, come back here, and I'll marry Liza if she's nice to me."

We all agreed about the dinner, and climbed into my pickup. Liza made it clear, dinner or not, marriage wasn't in the cards. On the way, Liza started in on me. "Rob says you have a new affinity for weapons Joe. What's up with that?"

"Ask the crazy little lunatic if he has one on him." Rob suggested.

Liza looked at me. "You don't. Do you?"

"If I do, would you go out with me?" I answered back.

"Bullshit, and no I wouldn't, and you don't have one anyway." Liza was too smart for me. I couldn't let her win though, she had just called me. I reached over to my left side and pulled out my 9mm so she could see it and stuck it underneath the seat.

Liza's eyes got big. "Jesus, Joe, That's freaking illegal! What in the hell are you thinking?"

"He's probably got a machine gun or two behind the seat." Rob added, fueling the fire.

"You don't, do you?" Liza asked even more concerned. "No, a couple of rifles is all. Just in case." I answered as nonchalantly as I could.

"In case of *what*, Joe?" She asked.

Laughing Rob couldn't let it go. "In case he decides to take down a bank or convenience store to pay for dinner."

"Joe, you seriously need some help. You're getting more paranoid by the day. For God's sake don't get us busted tonight." Liza added.

"Don't worry, he won't get us busted. He'll just shoot his way out of it." Rob grinned.

"Great. Just great. Twenty years old and I'm out with my little brother and his psycho friend, and I'm going to get shot to death by the cops before I turn twenty one." Liza was starting to act like she wished she hadn't come.

At the steak house, Liza and I left Rob to get us a table and we went to the bar for margaritas.

Liza made conversation at the bar. "Rob's been worried about you. Says you're into something deep. You don't seem your normal self, everything ok?"

"I'm fine. Just thinking about what to do with my life is all." I answered.

"I hope you're not seriously considering bank robberies and stuff. Are you?"

I started to say it wasn't a bad living, but that sounded ridiculous, so I just said; No, I wasn't.

After we sat down, with the buzz from the margarita coming on, I ordered the biggest sirloin they had. Man I loved steak. I was really looking forward to it. Ever since day before yesterday, my senses seemed five times better. The smell of food made me salivate, and the smell of perfume left me with a constant hard-on.

Liza talked about her new job at Red Lobster and Rob said the supermarket where he worked, still sucked.

I couldn't imagine working at either one, and as I started to think more about it, I drifted off again. Replaying the last few days in my mind, the world seemed to be mine. The crowd of the steak house faded out. I knew they were there, but it seemed all the conversations were subdued, quiet. In my mind's eye. I watched my front sight coming up. Then Aussie leaning into his rifle that blurred into the woman at the bar taking her shirt off later that night, placing her hand around my head, pulling me to her gently.

"Sir...Sir. Would you like another margarita?" I looked up to find the waitress staring at me. "Coke would be fine." I answered.

As she walked away Liza and Rob stared at me. Liza spoke first. "I don't know what you're smoking, but I want some of it. You seemed to just zone out."

Rob added his opinion. "He's crazy. I told you he was." Looking at me Rob continued. "Ground control to Major Tom. Hello! Anybody there?" Rob said giggling. "He does that now, just here one minute, gone the next. I'm telling you Liza, he's going to be on the five o'clock news some-day." We all were still laughing, as the waitress brought my soda, and the bill.

After dinner, I dropped off Rob and Liza, with a stern warning from Liza. "Be careful, Joe. And whatever you're doing, don't drag Rob into it. He's a good kid."

"Don't worry I won't, and I'm fine." I replied, as I blew her a kiss causing her to roll her eyes again as I drove away.

When I got home, I suddenly felt very tired and decided to go to bed. The next morning, lying in bed, I stretched and decided it was time to get up, I rose to go piss when I heard the front door open. I freaked! My pistol was in my truck. Dad's pistol was in the hall closet. Going to it, would expose me to the front door. Before I could make a decision, I heard Dad's voice, in his cheerful way. "What's going on here?" Although I knew he might come home today, I hadn't expected him this early, and frankly being half asleep, I had pretty much forgotten that he would be showing up. I breathed a sigh of relief.

Walking into the short hallway, I said, "Hi, Dad."

"How ya doin, Pard'ner? He asked.

"Good, how are you? You startled the hell out of me."

"Watch your mouth, and speaking of that what happened to it?" Dad said, while pointing at my busted lips.

"Got in a fight." I replied sticking as close to the truth as possible.

"Well you can tell me about it later. I'm off for the weekend. Would you like to get some fishing in? We could go up to the dam, fish below it. Maybe get us some catfish."

It sounded good to me and we both set about packing for a couple of nights away. It also gave me time to concoct a story about my "fight."

That weekend was a good one. Dad and I both caught plenty of fish. Standing waist high in the Rio Grande, with fast current and the smell of water around me, had a calming effect. It gave me time to sort out my thoughts.

I was living a double life and could not fathom stopping it. I didn't want to either. I couldn't even begin to think about what would happen if/when I got caught.

The adrenaline highs I felt were intoxicating, and I felt like I was with friends, *real* friends. The kind that I could talk to about anything and would risk their lives for me. We were brothers in arms, and I loved them as much as I loved Colter or Dad. The difference being, we were on the same wave length. Thought about the same things, wanted the same things. Enjoyed the same things. I knew I couldn't speak to Colter about battles and tactics, and trying to tell Dad how much I liked older women with big tits seemed like a pretty awkward conversation, and not even pleasant to boot. I was ready for this stuff. I loved it.

The down side was not without effect either. I wasn't even old enough to vote yet, I lied constantly, chased women, (well that might not have been a bad thing) had killed a man, and seemed to acquire a thousand yard stare. In retrospect, the killing was bothering me. At the time though, I told myself the lying and everything else was just as bad. The lying and womanizing was causing me plenty of trouble and stress. Deep down inside though, I kind of felt like I had the Mark of Cain.

This was like an out of control roller coaster. Problem was, I was *digging* it. Way too much. I was learning and learning hard and fast, I thought. The more I learned, the better off I would be, right? After all, knowledge was power and power allowed us to survive, I wanted to survive, and learning all I could would help. There was just no sense taking chances.

"Keep learning." I told myself.

13

STUCK IN THE MIDDLE

Although things were going fine, in spite of the obvious tensions everyone felt, we stayed on edge. I knew it was a matter of time, until something really bad happened. I just didn't realize there would be so much of it. If anyone had told me you could get used to this, I would've said they're crazy. At some point, I would end up asking myself this same question. *"Am I crazy?"*

We had a made a deal that's not even important now. In fact it wasn't even important by the end of the day. As the five of us walked into a small village high in the hills, we strolled into a battlefield. The village, (whose name I couldn't pronounce) had been hit earlier in the day. Sandinistas, Contras, it really didn't matter at this point. The point that hit home with us was the fact that there were dead and dying, and carnage. We had to help. You just can't look at that and not do anything. It's against human nature.

Lying dead in the dirt was a man with a machete. He had tried to stand against machine guns with a machete. It seemed so stupid and yet so *brave* at the same time. Maybe brave was not the right word, perhaps *desperate* would've been more appropriate. Did he really think he had a chance? The blood was still fresh, and the wounds had not been tended. This must've happened just before we were close enough to hear it.

At the front door of a house was a woman sitting in the dirt, crying. In her arms was a young girl of about twelve. She had an exit wound out of her back from a rifle round. Covered in blood and breathing with a horrid rasping sound, she was barely clinging to life. My world went quiet except for the rushing of blood in my ears. How the hell could people do this to each other?

Kneeling down, I placed my rifle on the ground and reached for my t shirt, ripping it off from underneath my shirt. As I listened to the woman wail and curse, I tried to pack the wound on the child's back with my shirt to stop the bleeding. Her mother clung to her as tightly as she could, hoping that holding her would keep the precious life from slipping away.

Realizing that this was beyond my skill level and knowledge, I looked around for Bro. Not seeing him, or any of the guys, I started to turn and rise and thought about my rifle as I did so. I turned back and picked it up before rising again. I almost made a fatal mistake and hadn't even realized it, yet. Everyone had spread out and were doing what they could to help. We had come in from the southeast, and barely gotten into the village when I found the wounded girl. I hadn't even seen where anyone else had gone. I trotted north about a hundred yards to the center and the northern edge of the village looking around as I did so for Bro.

Denny was the first I saw. He was standing on the edge of the village at a trail head that dropped off the mountain, away from the village. What the hell was he doing? He appeared to be just standing there, oblivious to everything.

"Denny! Where's Bro?"

Denny just looked at me, like we got separated in a bar or something.

"I don't know. Why?" Was he fucking serious? I then started to realize that Denny was in his own little world of shock too. He wasn't doing a damn thing.

As I started to turn, gun fire erupted from the southeast and it was close. It sounded heavy, like an M60. I swung around raising my gun toward the direction I had come from. I could barely see the mother and her child through a gap in between the houses, as I took a sight picture. I wouldn't have a shot in that direction without risk of hitting them. Suddenly Aussie ran into my field of fire at top speed. He was moving fast and low.

Rounding the corner, he stopped and turned, using the corner of a shack for concealment and let loose about five shots from the direction he had come. As he fired, Bro came around the corner of the same shack, past Aussie.

Aussie's fire had to have been passing very close to Bro as he bolted past him.

"There's too many." Bro yelled. "Beat feet! Now!"

"Where's Dave?" I yelled as Bro went by. Aussie was right behind him, the only thing I could see behind Aussie was the mother and child. To the south, gun fire was everywhere. Bullets cracked overhead.

"Go, Joe!" Aussie said as he went by. As he passed I turned and saw Bro had turned down the trail and Denny was reloading as he turned to run. I started down the trail, following it to the left. In the lead was Dave. How the hell had he gotten by me, without me seeing him? Later, we figured out that while I had covered Bro and Aussie's retreat, Denny had covered Dave's approach from the southwest. Dave had passed within yards of me, and I had never seen him.

As I dove down the trail after them, running hard, I saw Dave turn right, the trail doubling back on itself, just lower down the mountain. Rounding the same curve, I had seen Dave and the guys go around, I saw Dave turning *left* now. The trail was zigzagging down the mountain. Running as hard as I could down the steep trail without falling forward I glanced back as I rounded the curve. I saw a rifle being raised and fired as I rounded the corner. Running even harder, trying to catch the guys, what I saw next, scared the hell out of me. Where the last couple of zigzags had been about sixty yards in length, this one I was facing was closer to ninety yards. This meant the guys *behind* me would round the corner behind me before I reached the next one. I was going to be shot in the back. Running as hard I dared too, I considered diving off into the forest. It looked too thick to bust through, I had a vision of me being laughed at as I was riddled with machine gun bullets while I was stuck in the brush. The hill was so steep, and I was running fast enough that I was having trouble keeping my balance. I was going too fast to stop or make the next turn. I sat down hard on my ass, and started sliding like a runner coming into home plate. As I slid, I rolled over onto my stomach and brought my rifle to bear. Rounding the last corner, I saw the same man that had already shot at me. He had his rifle up, trying to slow down and gain his balance from the steep run.

Sighting on his chest, I squeezed the trigger on the H&K as quickly as I dared, but knew I had pulled it low. Not feeling or hearing the recoil I saw the shot puff dust on his midsection, right at his solar plexus. For the briefest moment, forming a flash picture in my mind's eye, he looked surprised as he exhaled suddenly, the bullet knocking the wind out of him. And the life. His entire body relaxed and went limp. The forward momentum kept him coming towards me as he nosed dived face first into the dirt trail, pinning his rifle underneath him, his legs flopping briefly towards his head, his arms at his side. He never even twitched. Switching to full auto, I fired a burst where he had been standing as more of them came around the corner, only to find their dead companero and bullets whipping past them.

I rolled to my left, downhill, about three times, bringing me to the next leg of the zigzag. It was shorter. No one was in sight and I was up and running. Above me I could hear screaming and wild bursts of fire. I was the last one, what the hell were they shooting at? I wondered.

As I continued running down the mountain, I could still hear bursts of fire and yelling above me. After about four more zigzags, I finally caught sight of Dave. Coming to the bottom of the mountain, next to a stream was Bro, Denny and Aussie. They were knelt down behind a rock pile in a semicircle with weapons pointed towards me. Dave was doubled over gasping for breath, "I think…. they…dropped back." He wheezed. "Had to be at least fifty of them."

"Yeah. I shot one of the fuckers!" I exclaimed excitedly as I gasped for air.

"Are you hit, Joe? Your arms are bloody." Bro said as he continued to sweep the hill and trail with his M60.

I looked down and saw both of my forearms were covered in blood. They were skinned up, really good, but that was it. I then remembered sliding in the dirt and rolling over onto my arms and stomach as I did so.

"No, I'm good." I replied

"We have to move. No chance to make a stand. We could go right. Downhill." Dave suggested. "But not across the stream and up and out. We'd be done."

Denny agreed. As we started to move towards the brush along the stream, I started talking, I had to make a case for my argument, *fast*. We had no idea how much time we had. It could be seconds.

"Let's get in the stream." I said. "It won't slow us down that much and they might not know which way we went. They would have to split up. If they did catch us, it would be a smaller group."

"Hell yes!" Bro said as he stepped into the water, his actions supporting my tactic.

"They'll expect us to go right Dave, its downhill. It's easier." I reasoned. "Let's go left, instead."

Dave nodded and pointed left. As we stepped into the ankle deep water, Dave explained his decision. "Although this stream goes downhill to the east it falls farther away from the way we came in. Going upstream, it loops back towards the village, climbing pretty hard, and getting into a narrow gully. Good cover, I've seen it on the map. But the closer we get, the more careful we'll have to be. Great place to hide, fucked place to be caught in."

As we moved away, we could hear them coming down the mountain. They were moving slowly and not too quietly. I don't think they really wanted to meet us again. We kept quiet and kept moving. The water gurgling around our ankles seemed loud enough wake the dead. The thought that they might hear it, terrified me.

Dave brought up the rear.

The next half hour or so, we climbed. Slowly and quietly. I was paying attention to everything around me. My senses seemed to be on hyper alert. Every sound and smell was flooding me with information.

Coming up to a small waterfall about twelve feet high, that looked like it might stop us, Dave signaled for us to gather up.

"They're not following, yet anyway. Let's take a little breather collect ourselves. Joe, how bad did you hit that guy?"

I related the story to them as quietly as I could, describing how and where I hit him. Dave then looked at Bro. "How about you? I heard your sixty open the show."

"I got one. When I first saw them, they were trying to sneak in closer on us. They were going to cover then some jefe got them moving and firing."

"I got two, one wasn't hit that hard. His mates were heping him, before I bugged out." Aussie added.

"How about you, Denny?" Dave asked.

"Naw, I was just covering your retreat. Suppression mainly. You get any?" He answered.

Dave shook his head no. "That makes three, plus one wounded. Not bad. Especially considering none of us are hit. Cripes there were a lot of them. Those weren't any damned guerillas. They were Regulars. Wonder why the hell they came back?"

"Maybe it wasn't them that did it." Denny suggested.

"It was them." Aussie and Dave said in Unison. "I asked." Dave explained.

I told them about the woman and child and described her injuries.

Bro looked positively pissed. "They went way overboard with that village. Shit wasn't right."

"What about that little girl though?" This was bugging me, and I was worried about her.

"Not much we can do right now. Maybe later. Going back to that village would be suicide." Aussie said.

"But she won't live without help!" I argued. I was starting to choke up. Emotions were running wild within me.

"Keep quiet." Dave warned.

"She's probably already dead, Joe. Not a damn thing you can do. Sucking chest wounds are a bitch, and if it exited out the back, not much chance without a dust off..." Bro let it hang.

"Well we aren't letting them get away with it." I said firmly, although I said it with a lot more conviction than I felt.

Everyone one looked at me. "What the ell do you suggest Joe? That we attack *them*?"

I looked at Dave. "Could we attack them? They wouldn't be expecting it. Could we pull it off, with a good plan?"

Aussie raised his eyebrows, with what appeared to be, maybe, just the tiniest bit of sadness, while Bro's mouth dropped open and his eyes got big. Looking at Dave, I saw nothing but coldness in his eyes. "No Joe, we can't. If we had artillery and air support, which we don't, the odds would still be stacked against us. The odds are five to one. That means every one of us, would have to kill five of them, not three, not four, but five *each,* and not get any of us killed. Do you think you can kill five of them by yourself, while we're each trying to kill our five?"

"He's positively off his rocker. Banty little rooster though, he is." Aussie said to no one in particular.

"Well how about we just slip in behind them and pick a couple off from aways out? Just even the score a little bit." I suggested.

Dave snorted. He had had enough and didn't want to discuss it any further.

"Well Joe, feel free to let them know where we are. Tell you what, you just go right ahead and do that. Knock yourself out. We're getting out of here."

Thinking about being on my own, against all of them didn't sound so good. I knew if I turned and went after them, no way in hell would I come back. Now I was kind of trapped. I didn't know what to do. I knew for damn sure, that I wasn't leaving the safety of the other guys. No sense taking *stupid* chances.

Bro, I think sensing how I felt set me straight. "I understand how you feel, but us being stupid won't make it better. Just get us killed too. If we head back now, maybe we can kill some of them later. What they done, was atrocious. It needs to be dealt with. But we ain't capable of it, not today. And we did put some hurt on them too. Maybe Dave can let his friends across the border know about it."

At the mention of his "friends" Dave looked sharply at Bro. Bro stared back at him, obviously not intimidated in the least.

Looking hard at Dave, Aussie voiced his opinion. "It would be the right thing to do. What they did, cannot be ignored, Davey."

Dave looked pissed. Lifting the butt of his rifle off the ground, he closed the conversation. "Let's move out. I'll take the point. Denny, watch our asses."

Bro and Aussie looked at each other and nodded. Seemingly they had come to some silent assent.

Now what in the hell was that all about? I wondered.

Negotiating the waterfall was a little tricky and took plenty of muscle on all of our parts. Glad to be doing something with all the energy, I stayed behind Dave and watched and listened as we made our way up, what had become a rocky narrow gorge. I was aware that we were slowly circling. We had started following the stream west, it was getting drier as we rose. Now as it crept up the mountain I knew I was heading southeast. Back towards the village, but coming in behind and above it. As we moved out of the ravine and onto the mountain side, Dave called us all up close. Pointing northeast, down the mountain side, he whispered; *"The village is down there, we have to cross this mountain above it. Stay loose and quiet. Twenty meter spread, single file. We need to stay hidden. Aussie take point.*

The forest didn't seem particularly thick here. Thick enough that we couldn't see the village, but easily able to see movement anywhere from one hundred to two hundred yards. It actually looked kind of exposed to me. New adrenaline started to surge through me. *This* could get ugly.

As Aussie started out slow and methodical, I waited and watched, then followed, walking in a crouch, and watching where I placed my feet, I tried to keep an eye on

Aussie while watching for any other movement. Dave followed me, then Bro, with Denny in the rear. Twice I heard Dave's movements and looked back. I caught occasional sight of Bro behind him, never Denny. Aussie was picking a route that lent itself to moving quietly and through low spots that offered us the least exposure from below. Once or twice I noted, that I thought he was better at it than me. Not that I had done this before, but to me, it was like hunting. The idea was to keep from being seen. When I saw what I thought was a better route, I took it.

Rounding a tree slowly, I saw Aussie's left hand come up into a fist signaling a stop. As he froze in place, I held my fist up for a stop and slowly and quietly squatted. Straining to see and hear, adrenaline surged through me and the only sound I could make out was the blood rushing through my ears. Although I had never been in this situation, Aussie, Bro, and Dave had never stopped coaching me on tactics. Hearing about it and taking part in it, was different though. This was scary as hell.

After several seconds that seemed like forever, Aussie turned towards me. Holding his hand way above his head to indicate Bro, he then used his fingers to indicate "look." I slowly turned and gave the same hand signs to Dave who then signaled Bro to come up. Holding my position, Bro went around to my right several yards away from me and came in quietly above and behind Aussie. This took several minutes but was done with almost no sounds made by us. I could see Bro and Aussie whispering to each other, but couldn't hear them. As my legs started to cramp from squatting Bro made his way back to me. Pausing, he leaned over and whispered in my ear; *"I think it's one of the Regulars that me or Aussie hit. He's dead. Can barely see him. Move up."* With that, Bro signaled Dave to come on and I moved up to Aussie, grateful to be out of my squat and moving. When I got to the tree, Aussie pointed to the ground about seventy yards away. I couldn't see anything. Shrugging my shoulders, Aussie leaned in and whispered; *There Joe. See the uniform, just a bit of it."* After a few more seconds of searching, I finally saw it. Without Aussie pointing it out, I am sure I never would have seen it.

"You sure he's dead?" I whispered back.

"That's why I called Bro. Good eyes. He says there's flies on him."

That was good enough for me, and with that I looked ahead and nodded. Aussie moved out, I waited for him to put some distance and then followed. Dave had moved out from Bro, but was pointing out where the dead soldier was so Dave would know. Apparently none of us had a desire to get any closer, at this point. I was wrong.

As Dave moved to the tree, he cut left and started sneaking down towards the dead soldier. Bro looked exasperated. I stopped too, and glanced at Aussie. He was still moving away. I sat down quietly resting my rifle in a firing position across my knees. As Aussie glanced back he saw me and held up. His look said it all; "What in the hell are you doing?"

I indicated Dave, and after a few seconds Aussie saw him creeping down to the dead soldier. Sixty or so yards away I could see Denny looking positively scared out of his mind. I wasn't feeling too damned brave myself.

As Dave got closer, he slowed even more, keeping his M16 pointed directly at the body. A few feet away I could see him visibly relax. Apparently he was satisfied that the soldier was in fact dead. Dave moved closer still I watched him lay down behind the soldier, shielding himself from view below. Searching the dead body as he alternately looked down the mountain. While Dave did whatever the hell he was doing, I could feel the sweat running down the back of my neck and smell my own fear. We needed to move. This was too close for me. After what seemed like an eternity, Dave finally started moving back up towards us. We started to move out. We had all had enough.

Arriving back at the trucks, about thirty minutes later, we were exhausted and relieved. Before leaving earlier in the day, we had stashed the guns, a short distance from the trucks. Dave made the decision to leave them. They were well hidden and it made just as much sense to leave them where they were. Besides, with a regular unit in the area, we didn't want to stick around any longer than we had too.

The other thing I couldn't figure out and was starting to annoy me, for some inexplicable reason, I had a raging hard on.

When we arrived back at the house, Aussie and Bro immediately took their boots off. I wasn't sure why but I followed suit. Peeling my socks off that had been soaked from the stream earlier in the day, I was somewhat surprised by what I saw. My feet were clammy and looked like prunes. Closer inspection made me think my feet were soggy. Bro and Aussie were both wiping their feet off, drying them, then applying powder. Dave and Denny seeing our feet, sat down to do the same thing. Bro explained it would help prevent jungle rot. I didn't know what jungle rot was, but it didn't sound like anything I wanted to catch.

Bro looked around at all of us. Something was up. "Dave…" he started. I knew he was going to bring up the reference to Dave's "friends" mentioned in the gully, earlier.

"It's a closed subject. I will take care of it. Joe, is staying until tomorrow a problem?"

It wasn't, but even if it had been, I would've said "No." I had to see this to the end. The little girl was still fresh in my mind. I couldn't stop thinking about it, and said as much. Besides, I wanted to meet Dave's "friends." This was intriguing to me, to say the least.

"Fine. I'll fly over and back tonight. We'll leave in the morning."

"You could just stop by on your way out, Davey." Aussie suggested.

Dave exploded. *"I am not, repeat, I am not going to take Joe and Denny to a place that no one is supposed to know about, or be at. Are we fucking clear?"*

Aussie fixed Dave with those cold gray eyes and answered him in a low voice that sounded as serious as death itself.

"I don't care how you handle it, so long as it gets handled. Are *we* clear on that?" As Aussie spoke, Bro turned to face Dave and with equal coldness fixed Dave with his own eyes and waited for an answer. Denny decided he didn't want to be a part of any of it and walked out of the room and into the hallway. I had been lacing up one of my boots and paused to watch.

Dave looking back and forth between Bro and Aussie finally answered, in a more normal tone of voice. "I said I would handle it, and I will. I still have to maintain cover and operational security though. You know that." With that everybody seemed to relax. I finished tying my boots. Dave may have been the boss, but he knew when he was outmatched.

This left a whole lot for me to consider and try to figure out. But did I want to figure it out, I wondered.

Dave left within the hour. Aussie and I sat around the kitchen table and talked with Bro as he fixed dinner. Denny went to a bedroom, and keeping to himself, crashed out and left us alone. Even with Denny removed and Dave gone, there was a tension in the air. I wasn't sure I should broach it or not. Finally Bro reached into the fridge and pulled out three beers. On the second one, we started to relax.

"Should I ask what's going on?" I said.

As Bro said "No." in unison Aussie said "Probably not."

"Oh. Ok." I answered dumbly.

"We gotta tell him something, Aussie. Cain't just leave him hanging." Bro said.

"Why the ell not? Mate doesn't need to know, except what we tell'em." Aussie replied with a twinkle in his eye.

Bro laughed out loud. "Truth be known Joe. You don't want to know."

"Yes I do." I said excitedly.

"No, you don't." They both said again in unison, chuckling as they did so.

"It's not that you're not trusted." Bro started to explain.

"You really don't want to know." Aussie continued.

"Look, if you get caught, what do you *really* know? You know an Australian, a black guy, an old fat white guy, and a whacked out vet. If you're ever picked up by the authorities, you are guilty of smuggling. That's it. No international incidents, no government conspiracies, no intelligence breeches of national security issues. You do your time, and you're out. If you get caught knowing all that other stuff, well, let's just say you're subject to a different set of rules. Not any you want to play by, either. Even me and Aussie don't like playing by them. That's why we just keep our mouths shut and take the money. Information you don't know, you can't let slip and come back to haunt you or us. Does that make sense, Joe?" Bro asked as he set three plates of steak and potatoes on the table.

"Yeah. I guess it does." I answered, as I realized once again just how far above my head I was involved with this. My appetite started to wane. I didn't want to go to prison.

Picking up where Bro left off, Aussie started talking. "Thing is though mate, what's coming we may or may not ever hear about. Just the way it is. Have to live with it."

This was *twice* in a row that the trips had not been problem free. Things really were getting hotter down here. I had gotten into the habit of evaluating my personal performance after any trip, problem free or not. This one, I really didn't care how I had done. All I could think about was the little girl and her Mother. I couldn't begin to imagine this happening to me or any of my family. The idea of my Mother going through that sickened me. What Mother wouldn't watch over and try to protect their young?

Thinking about my Mom watching over me, depressed me. Thinking about killing those murderous bastards, excited me. And as far as I was concerned, they deserved to die, every last, lowlife one of them. Send them to hell on a rocket sled, and let me be the one to light the fuse. It was the *right* thing to do. Aussie had mentioned that we might not even know about any action taken, and deep down inside this is what I think I wished for. I wanted to know, and I wanted to have a hand in it. But first, I had to get through the next trip. Two trips in a row I had seen action. I guessed that could happen, but not three times. I had no idea how many trips I had been on, but trouble had only occurred three times altogether. So with that rationalization in my mind the next trip would be a cake walk. I had seemed to forget about Dave's other incident with Denny. We would just be a little high strung next time around was all. That wasn't necessarily a bad thing.

Another life lesson here. *Just because it didn't happen to you, doesn't mean it didn't happen."*

14

LOCK AND LOAD

N othing had been said about Dave's "friends" this trip but I somehow I knew it hadn't been forgotten, and nothing had occurred yet. I don't know how I knew, I just knew. I had missed a trip and my guns were sold in my absence, so that was a good thing at least, and there hadn't been any problems. That made me feel much better. I had made some more money. With this trip, if everything went well, it would be even more money for the trip back. Kind of like "two for the price of one."

Dave was in the process of setting up a deal. It would be different this time, as in no agreement had been made yet and we didn't have the guns with us. First we would meet with the buyers and Dave would reach an agreement. Denny, Bro, Aussie and I would go to the meeting to see their people and vice versa. We didn't expect any trouble as we would meet in town and we had nothing with us for them to try and take. Either way, I put my nine millimeter under the front of my shirt. No sense taking any chances.

Dave and I were the last ones to show up for the meeting. Walking across the dirt street, I remembered the woman pulling the machine pistol on Dave. Being with Dave could be dangerous. Adrenaline started to flow, and I became even more aware of my surroundings.

When I walked in, she was the first person I noticed. Flawless, brown, strong legs, and well defined calves came out of a pair of cut offs, with a little bit of ass cheek hanging out. As I raised my head, our eyes locked. Big beautiful green eyes bore into me. Like she was looking at my soul, and looking at me with a hunger that I had never seen in a woman. A hunger that even a boy could recognize. She was peculiarly out of place, but yet belonged there. Young, but older than me, probably in her early twenties but older than her years. Beautiful and dangerous, all at the same time. She looked like a guerrilla fighter, which she probably was. A camouflaged fatigue shirt, tied at the middle of a flat, toned stomach, with her breasts swelling out the top. Her hair was tied back in a ponytail, which she flipped behind her shoulder and used the movement to wink at me. No one else in the room saw her do it. We couldn't stop staring at each other. She was smiling at me. I'm sure I was smiling back. I was as hard as I had ever been in my life. I wanted this chick, and I wanted her bad. I became aware of the silence in the room and slowly looked around. Everyone was staring at us.

Dave broke the silence. "I'm sorry, do the rest of us need to leave while you two go at it right here, or are we bothering you?" The sarcasm just dripped from his voice.

She was still smiling at me. As everyone looked at me for an answer, she mouthed the word "Later."

I could have cum right then and there.

I looked over at Bro and walked over to where he sat, in the corner of the room, with his back against the wall. He pushed a chair out for me with his foot and as I sat down, he smiled quickly and said "Don't get carried away. Think." I couldn't think, except about her, and we were staring at each other again. As I broke eye contact, Bro said "Dude, calm down." In another corner Aussie and Denny sat. If push came to shove, we had the center of the room in a cross fire. With Dave in the middle.

"I'm all right, I gotta handle on it." I said, but I was thinking about how to meet up with her later. I was going to fuck this chick like I had never fucked anybody in my life, and I knew it. I couldn't wait.

Somebody asked me what I wanted to drink, and I ordered a Coke. She hurriedly reached across the bar and brought it over to me. I smiled and said "Thank you." She reached down, smiled and put her hand on my cheek, "No problemo, cute one." The smell of Jasmine wafted around her. It made me feel slightly intoxicated, kind of high. She glanced over her right shoulder and smiled at me as she strolled away, her left hand sliding down the butt of her cut offs as if she were wiping something off her ass cheek.

Bro looked at me and said, "You're fucked."

"I sure as hell hope so, dude. She is fucking hot!" I answered.

Bro just shook his head.

"She's also dangerous. Bitch would cut your heart out in a New York second." He pointed out.

The only danger I could think of was whether or not I could keep her satisfied in bed, and I wasn't going to worry about that for the first few hours with her.

After the meeting, we all met back in Dave's room. I couldn't wait to get this over with. I had things to do.

"Well?" Aussie asked Dave

"They wanted to trade dope for the guns. I told'em we didn't do that. Cash only." Dave answered.

"And.......?" Bro asked.

They said "No problem." Dave continued, "I also asked for 1800.00 for each weapon, across the board."

We all looked at Dave. The price was a little high. That would net me over nine thousand dollars! Sounded great.

"They agreed to it." Dave said.

"Cool, we can call it a night then?" I asked. I was ready to go get cleaned up, and go meet up with *someone.*

"Calm down Valentino, you ain't going nowhere yet." Dave shot me a dirty look as he said it. Me seeing his daughter was definitely going to get in the way of this little meeting, even if her and I were on the outs right now. I was getting frustrated.

Aussie laughed. "Ell Dave, can't say as I wouldn't want to leave either, did ya see the way she looked at the lad, I thought she was going to fock him right there in the pub, I did."

Denny gave me a dirty look, Bro glanced at me and almost imperceptibly, shook his head "No."

I stayed quiet. I wondered if she were still at the bar.

"They want us to meet them in the valley at Tierra Negra. Can't land in there; no strip. The meet is at 1400." Dave said.

"We do need to go get the guns. Joe and I can do that." Dave continued.

I just about blew a gasket right then and there. This just sucked!

"We going to carry all that into the valley?" Bro asked.

"Nope, we'll stash 'em, we can relay it in or just tell'em where they are. They've been real agreeable so far." Dave said. Later, thinking back, he had said that somewhat quietly. I was just so frustrated and pissed, I missed it.

"No pussy for you tonight, mate. Just Rosy Palm and her five sisters." Aussie teased.

Denny ended up coming along also. After taking off, loading up the guns, and taking off again, we flew towards Tierra Negra. Landing on a dirt strip in the middle of the mountains (I don't know how Dave found it) Dave taxied back to the opposite end of the strip and shut the plane down. I was ordered to stay with the plane while Dave and Denny stashed the guns and stuff in the jungle. This suited me fine. I was pissed and I hated being here at night. I had a raging hard on to boot. This place sucked, the whole deal with his daughter sucked, and me not being naked with the hottest woman I had ever seen in this god forsaken place sucked!

I heard some noises, that I couldn't identify, which wasn't unusual in Central America for me, especially at night. I quietly took the safety off the G3, and crept into the tree line. I turned back in the direction of the plane, and crawled into a fern, where I could see the plane. I knew as long as I didn't move, I wouldn't be detected. The noises continued, until the sound of Dave and Denny returning reached my ears. Denny tripped and fell and I heard him curse as Dave chuckled. As they came out of the tree line about 15 yards to my right, I stood up and stepped out. Dave, startled, reached for his gun and apparently recognized me, even in the dark.

"I'm glad to see you finally pulled your head out of your ass." he said to me.

"What do you mean?" I asked.

"Get in, let's get out of here." He replied.

As soon as we were airborne, my hard on returned. I wondered if she were still awake, or thinking about me. I fantasized about her all the way back. I wondered if she were *fantasizing about me.* I would have to ask her when I saw her.

By the time we returned, the town was asleep. The cantina was closed too. "Big fucking zero." I thought. I was seriously bummed. I knew if she were with the group tomorrow we would not stick around long. We would make our exchanges and leave. We always did. No sense sticking around rebels with guns. They might get ideas. But still, I might get to see her, and talk to her a little. That would be something.

Early next morning, after a night of tossing and turning and fantasizing, we were up and on the move. We ate Gallo Pinto for breakfast, "sorted our kit" as Aussie would say, and climbed in for the short flight. I kept wondering what the hell "sorting our kit" meant. Asking would bring a new round of teasing from Aussie, and I didn't feel up to it.

As we flew low over the trees, Dave brought the King Air around a mountain and pointed out the direction of the valley and a pass heading into it. I knew we would probably avoid the pass. I knew I would. While it was the easiest way in, it was also the most obvious. As Dave continued around the mountain, he suddenly chopped the power and I saw a dirt strip coming up, and it was coming up fast. The strip wasn't even level! It was built into the side of a mountain for crying out loud. I liked flying, but Dave could honestly scare the shit out of me. As we "touched" down, Dave got the plane slowed down and we reached the end of the runway, Dave spun the plane around and taxied back to the end we came in from. I wondered if this were the same strip we were at last night, I remember thinking. The terrain looked the same. I think we were on the end we turned around at. As Dave reached the end again, he spun the plane one more time, so we could take off into the wind without having to taxi or turn. He cut the engines.

"Time to lock and load." Dave ordered. I hopped out, taking my G3, and cycling a round into the chamber. I dropped the magazine and took another round and topped it off. Twenty one rounds, ready to go, plus the twenty round mags on my belt. Bro cycled his M60 and threw a bandolier of ammo over his shoulder. He looked like a bandito from "Treasure of the Sierra Madre's." A big black bandito, with a modern machine gun. Bro, at 6'9" and 260lbs, of bone and muscle, was so big that the heavy M60 looked proportionate with him. More so than my little ass carrying a G3 anyway. Aussie looked like he was about to puke. He didn't like flying. Aussie had already cycled his FN and replaced the magazine with two that were duct taped together. He also replaced the round he had taken from his original magazine. As he had told me once before when I saw him do it, "It would be 'ell to need that round mate. I've seen many a dead man with an empty gun that would have loved to have had it."

As Dave and Denny came around to Bro, Aussie and I, he gave more instructions. "Over the peak, 10 meter spread, V formation, when we can't, 5 meter spread, Joe, on point, at least 10 meters ahead of us, if we have to, go single file." Aussie and Bro stared at Dave as he said it. Dave eyes met mine. "Listen and look, *hard.*" Of course I would. I was a little proud that I was on point, even if I was a little scared. He had confidence in me, I thought. Nothing would happen anyway. We just had to walk a long way, it would be awhile. As the sun climbed, so did we. When we reached the peak, I led us up the side away from the pass and stopped and opened my canteen. I drained it. We were all sweating profusely. It wasn't even 10:00am yet and it was hot. I realized then that we were going to be real early for the meet. This was good. Maybe I would see her. Dave went around to look down at the pass and came back in a few minutes. We all looked at him. "I couldn't see anything." He said. Starting down into the valley about halfway down, the forest started to open up. We spread out. Dave was on my left rear with Bro further left and a little further back. Denny was on my right and a little to the rear, and Aussie on the far right, even further back, opposite Bro.

About 20 minutes later as we got lower, I looked at Dave, he pointed in the direction of the village and motioned that I should swing left first for awhile and then cut right to come in above it, that way we would be able to see it from above. After about 10 minutes of traversing over and down, I heard something below. I held my hand up and kneeled down. As I listened, I heard a clang of metal against rock and a woman's voice….then kids voices. We were above the village. I stood up and pointed in the direction of the village and gave Dave an "ok" sign. He nodded and we started down.

Coming out of the tree line, I could see the village pretty clearly about 150 yards away. As I looked across it and up the opposite hill, what I saw shocked me to a standstill, literally. There were men, a lot of them, directly across from us, they were spread out about 5 to 10 meters each, and they had guns!

They had been walking down into the village from the opposite direction, and they had not expected us to be there, *yet*.

Everything fell into place, all at once. Dave telling me to pull my head out of my ass, and quietly saying how "agreeable" they had been. Bro telling me to be careful. Us arriving so early. Everyone had been suspicious all along, except me. I had been too busy thinking about *something* else.

As I froze in place, one of them did too. He pointed and yelled. Guns came up. All hell broke loose.

I never considered firing, I never thought of what I should do, or be doing.

I turned and I ran.

As I started to sprint up the hill towards the pass that we had so laboriously avoided, I could see Denny, Bro, Aussie and Dave also running up the hill. We were still in formation, only now, I was in the rear.

I had barely gone twenty yards, when something kicked me in the left side of my ass and knocked me down. I landed on my rifle, barely touching the ground and I was back up and running again.

In my head, I remember thinking. "I'm not shot, I'm not shot, I'm not shot." Deeper down in my sub consciousness, another voice, a little quieter, with a little more authority said to me; "You just got shot, Motherfucker."

I could hear rounds coming past me, whistling and cracking. Ahead of me, about 15 yards, was a tree, with a fallen log, next to it. I headed for it, and with a somersault and twist that would have made a gymnast proud (although it was far from graceful), I landed behind the log, facing the direction that I had come from. The dirt was soft, and I started scrunching down into it.

The reason the dirt was so soft, much to my horror, was because it was an anthill. People can say all they want about lions being king of the jungle and all that bullshit. Ants *rule* and I hate them, or bugs of any kind for that matter. Give me snakes, horses (which I still don't care for) fish, lizards, I don't care, but I hate bugs. Also, in Central and South America, they seem to have lots of ants we don't have. Red ants, black ants, red and black ants, fire ants, flying ants, army ants, ants that are big enough that when you step on them you can hear them crunch. I don't know what species of ants these were, but I did know one thing. They were stinging the shit out of me, and they were the least of my problems. Now that the opposition had seen me "go down," I was catching fire. A *lot* of fire.

Aside from being scared out of my mind, and being stung, I had started to piss. I told myself it was to drown the ants, as I threw the barrel of my G3 over the log and emptied the entire clip in one long, wild burst. Trying to reload, through the tears and pain of being stung, and the embarrassment of pissing myself, I *felt* the shock wave of a bullet pass by my hand! I was in deep shit. I was going to die here.

As I readied myself to waste some more ammo in my blind panic, I heard a sound that drowned out all others, well, almost, anyway.

*BABABABABABABABABABABABABOP, BABABABABABAB
ABABABABAOP.* Bro was firing his M 60 and he had the
opposition's undivided attention. I saw Bro's bursts slam
into two men that were almost next to each other. His machine gun, ripping one almost in half and catching the
other in the upper torso and head, resulting in a grue-
some display of blood, brains, and guts that sent men for
cover. Another burst, from Bro, killed a man that was too
slow finding cover.

I found myself suddenly exposed as I was lifted into
the air by my collar. I turned and looked at Dave, who had
his rifle in one hand and my collar in the other. *RUN!!!* He
yelled at me. I didn't need to be told twice.

As I started sprinting up the hill, I saw Bro, on my right,
wreaking havoc with his M60. Denny was standing behind
a tree, picking his shots, firing on semi-auto. Aussie was
knelt down on one knee behind a tree, reloading and getting ready to turn and bug out too. Aussie glanced at me
with a look of shock on his face as I ran past.

Reaching the top of the hill at the pass we had avoided,
I realized this would be a good place for us to be ambushed.
Looking around quickly, I saw no one. No one at all. Panic
started to set in. Where the hell were the rest of the guys? I
trotted back towards the downhill side of where I had just
come from. One hundred meters below me, was the rest of
the team. Running, although pretty slowly I thought.

"COME ON!" I yelled at them. Why the hell were they
taking so long?

Sporadic firing could be heard much farther down, towards the village.

As Aussie came up the hill within a few yards, I said to him, "Let's go, we need to get outta here!" As if this were information he didn't possess.

"Hold up, we need to bloody well wait for them. Don't be charging off." He answered.

Aussie looked at me and asked "How bad are you hit?"

"I'm not hit, I just pissed myself." I replied, looking down at my wet pants, embarrassingly.

Denny, Bro and Dave trotted over, panting hard and gasping for air. Dave looked done in.

"We've all pissed ourselves a time or two mate, but your pants are covered in blood. How bad are you hit?" Aussie was pressing the issue I didn't want to talk about.

Dave stepped around behind me. "Drop your pants." he ordered.

"Not now! Let's fucking go!" I hissed. This was getting out of hand, panic was starting to return. I didn't want to be shot. Not awhile ago or now either, for that matter.

Aussie stepped in, "Come on, mate, drop your pants, we need to look it over and be on our way."

As I undid my pants, Dave said to no one in particular, "We need to be cautious approaching the plane. Look it over, first."

"Yeah, we do." Denny said.

While I held my pants with one hand, Bro and Aussie examined my butt. "You'll hold." Aussie said.

"Small caliber probably, or it came off the ground and got him." Bro offered.

I pulled up my pants.

"Did you see that collection of weapons?" Aussie asked Bro.

Bro nodded his head up and down. "Yeah, Uzis, M1 carbines, Nagants, M-16s, Carcanos they had it all. What a rag tag looking outfit. Only thing that saved our ass. I bet it was a nine or a carbine round that got him."

"Let's go." I was in a hurry to be gone.

I led the way down the hill as the team followed, heading towards the airstrip. I was now very aware that my pants were starting to stiffen up in places and my left foot squished with every step. I kept telling myself that I must have peed a whole bunch.

The trip down was considerably quicker than the trip up had been earlier.

When I saw the trees starting to thin out, I waited for the rest of them to catch up. I had come in closer to the airstrip's center than I had planned. I had also almost forgotten what Dave had said about looking the plane over.

Brush and weeds had grown along the side of the strip, away from the forest. We all got down on our hands and knees, and then our stomachs as we crawled closer to the edge of the brush line.

Dave saw them first. Holding a hand up to stop, he pointed towards the plane and held up three fingers, and motioned us to him.

As we gathered around him, Dave quietly said, "There's three of them, we can't hit the plane. They're just standing around. We need to shoot all three at once. Aussie you take one shot, I'm too exhausted, I can't hit right now. You get the furthest to the left. Denny, you take the woman and Joe you shoot the one on the right."

"What the fuck? There's a woman?" I thought.

"Woman? I don't want to shoot a woman" Denny quietly whined.

"Ell, I don't give a bloody fock, I'll shoot'er." Aussie whispered.

"Fine then." Dave hissed. "We all got it?"

I flipped my selector to semi-auto and took a deep breath.

We scooted around and took up positions. One did look to be a woman. It was just too far to tell for sure. Dave said, "We'll fire on my count of three. Everyone got their target? Denny?"

"Yeah." Denny answered.

"Aussie?"

"Got it." he replied.

"Joe?"

"Like fast one, two, three or slow one, two, three?" I asked.

Dave gave me a pissed look and said "Like this. One…..two….three." Making a trigger motion with his finger on the "three" count.

"Ok, I got it." I said as rested my elbows on the ground and took up a sight picture, dialing the sight drum to 300 meters as I did so.

Dave started. "One…."

I started taking up the slack in the trigger and adjusting my sight picture.

"Two…." Dave continued.

As Dave started to say "Three" my trigger reached the end of its stroke and Denny and I fired simultaneously. Aussie's shot was a split second behind ours.

As the rifle recoiled, I saw the guerilla I had shot fall, as the round took him high in his chest, flailing his arm out and kicking as he hit the ground. In my peripheral vision, I knew the other two were down also.

Without thinking about it or why, I was on my feet and moving fast towards the plane, my rifle at a high ready. Nothing was going to stop me from getting to that airplane. Right now it represented everything good, safe and secure. The rest followed.

After covering about a hundred meters, one of the guerillas started to rise up. As I slowed from a trot, bringing my gun to bear, everything started to happen in slow motion. It was the guerilla Aussie had shot, and *it was a woman.* *"Damn!"* I thought to myself. Aussie had hit low and struck her on her right side. The bullet had traveled through the right side of her stomach and exited out the left side, opening a gaping hole and spilling her intestines out halfway down her thigh. On her knees, holding her eviscerated stomach contents in her left hand, trying to gather them up, she was making the most god awful noise I had ever heard. She was dying. Her right hand was on the pistol grip of an AK 47. As she lifted it slightly and slapped the gun down flat on the ground, she scooted herself forward on her knees, closer to her weapon. Still on her knees, she howled and started to try and raise the gun again. I was on one knee by this time and as I brought the front sight post onto her chest, I finished taking up the slack out of the trigger, and fired. I saw the muzzle flash of my rifle, but I didn't hear the shot. "What the hell happened? Did my gun malfunction?" I thought. But then the bullet slammed into her chest and pitched her over backwards, her body sprawling between her own legs underneath her.

Back on my feet and moving I ran around the opposite side of the plane, purposely avoiding the carnage that I had just taken part in. I didn't want to see any of it. The coppery smell of blood and entrails filled my senses as I swept the tree line for any sign of more guerillas. Aussie, Denny, Bro and Dave climbed into the plane.

"Let's get the hell out of here!" Dave said.

As I climbed in and turned to shut the door, brought to my nose by the breeze, was the distinct scent of Jasmine. *"Aw, dude."* I thought to myself.

Dave had us airborne quick. As he cleared the trees and started to climb, he looked over his shoulder at me and asked, "How are you doing?"

"Ok." As I answered, I remembered that I had a little problem, and immediately switched subjects in my mind.

Twisting to my left, I looked down at my left butt cheek. It was bleeding.

Bro said "Let's get a better look at it, take your pants down." Still slightly embarrassed, I pulled my pants down and tried to twist around again to see. There was a lot of blood. The back of my leg was covered in it. I looked at Bro and Aussie, trying to read their faces. I looked back at my leg and got a little nauseous as Dave pulled the plane up a little higher. I was shaking and couldn't seem to control it. The fear and emotions were running through me like fire.

"I think I'm going to be sick." I said to no one in particular.

Aussie smiled at me and said "No you're not, mate. You're fine." Aussie being as straight forward and honest as he was, made me feel much better. I knew that if I had been dying, he would have told me that too. My stomach settled down and as Bro handed me some bandages, I pressed them against my butt and continued to bleed all over the seat. This was kind of embarrassing.

"I'm sorry I ran." I said. Bro and Aussie looked at me.

"If you hadn't run, you'd be dead." Bro said flatly.

"Yeah, you would be. You did the right thing, spot on, I would say." Aussie looked straight ahead as he said it.

"I thought you and four or five friends, in Africa fought down thirty people, one time, Aussie?" I asked.

"Rhodesia, and we did mate, but to begin with, we had no choice. The little rocky peak, where we stopped for a break, where Dave looked over the pass. That place was defendable. We could stand four to one odds there and maybe make a go of it. But we would have taken losses, and we took casualties in Rhodesia. The thing is Joe, in Rhodesia, we had the water, they had no choice but to try and take it and we had no choice but to stay and fight.

You're lucky, thought we might have lost you mate, and that would leave me nobody to tease except Bro, and he's too focking big, don't you think?"

"You did look surprised that I was alive, when I ran by you." I told him.

Aussie looked at me curiously, as he started giggling. "I wasn't surprised you were alive. I've neve'r seen anyone run that bloody fast! Scared the ell out of me you did."

Vigorously nodding his head up and down, Bro started laughing as he told me; "Dude, you were fucking moving! You do realize that you started out behind us, but made it to the pass over 150 meters ahead of us? You were running like Walter Fucking Peyton!"

I had never experienced that kind of adrenalin dump before and as the laughter spread through us it was almost as if it were contagious.

Aussie was mimicking me now with his eyes big and his legs and arms pumping furiously and had everyone, including Dave (who hardly ever laughed) in stitches. The plane leaned to one side a little as Dave rocked back and forth in the seat, begging Aussie to stop because he needed to piss.

Denny even chimed in. "Have Joe piss for you, he can do it on the run!" The laugher was so loud and uncontrolled it nearly drowned out the sound of the twin engines of the airplane.

Dave couldn't contain himself any longer and had to get in on the fun. "Piss like fast, one, two, three, or slow like one…two….three?" This just blindsided me and I started laughing harder. Watching Aussie and Bro, with tears in their eyes, as they lost control and giggled liked school boys. I was happy to be alive.

"That just scared the shit out of me." I said to no one in particular.

"More like scared the piss out of you, I'd say." Dave howled some more.

As the laughter subsided and we started to quiet down, I started thinking about our return to the plane. I looked down at my seat. I was still bleeding. Although I was looking over my wound, I was aware of Aussie watching me out of the corner of his eye. He knew I was aware of it. Breaking the silence of the drone of the engines, Aussie leaned over and quietly told me. "You had no choice, if you hadn't done it, one of us would have, only difference is one of us would probably be dead too, or you. Don't think about that shit. No good will come of it. Ancient focking history, you sure wouldn't want to fock her now, would you?"

"Geez, Aussie. That's harsh…." I said as my stomach turned. Aussie could be hard. Real hard.

Aussie continued. "Well, if that's how you have to think about it to keep your mind clear, then that's the way it is. *Do not carry that around in your head.* You understand me? Let it go."

"Ok, dude." I didn't want to continue this conversation. I decided to change the subject.

"This seems like a lot of blood to me. I'm not going to bleed out?"

Bro explained. "Blood spreads like gasoline does. A little looks like a lot. I would say you've lost less than half a pint. But you sure as hell have made a mess of this plane."

"Fuck it, *I'm alive!*" I announced.

"Exactly." Someone answered.

Dave, after gaining some altitude, set a course to somewhere. I wasn't sure where and didn't care at the moment. After flying about an hour and a half, I felt us losing altitude. Dave brought us in on another dirt strip, outside of a decent size town. Looking out the window it looked like high desert area to me. Very much like my childhood home in New Mexico.

Children had come out to see the airplane. Dave spoke to some of them in Spanish. After telling Denny to stay with the plane, Dave stuffed a pistol underneath his shirt as well as Bro, and Aussie. I reached for mine but Dave indicated to leave it. Walking into town, Dave gave one of the boys some money as he continued with us......leading us somewhere.

My ass didn't hurt too badly, but my left boot had inches of blood in it, and positively squished with every step.

We drew some looks from the townspeople, but not as much as you would think. They had seen years of civil war, refugees and strife. Four men walking down a dusty street, with one leaking blood was not that big of a deal to them. We didn't appear armed, therefore we didn't seem to be a threat. Surviving the day and making a living went back to the top of their lists of things to do.

As the boy led us into the center of some shacks, he hollered out in Spanish in front of one. A woman, probably in her late fifties, came to the door. She was wearing a dirty white polyester pantsuit that looked like what a school nurse would wear.

As she nodded at us, Dave and her spoke back and forth in Spanish. I caught the words "Medicina" and "Bruja." Medicina was obviously "medicine" I couldn't remember what "Bruja" meant. At any rate, I decided her being a nurse was a good sign. She motioned us in. She looked up approvingly at Bro, as she greeted him and cackled in Spanish, she reached up and patted his chest with her hand, as if to make sure he was real. Being only about five feet tall, she actually had to reach up to do this.

"Bro, I think she's positively smitten with you." Dave grinned at him. Bro rolled his eyes.

Leading us into another room, she motioned for me to lie down on a padded table. As I climbed up on the table, she indicated my belt knife. I opened up the sheath and handed it to her. My Dad had given me that knife and sharpened it himself, and it was *sharp*. I had cleaned my first deer with it, and Bro and Aussie constantly borrowed it from me, which was a source of pride for me. They couldn't get theirs as sharp as my Dad could sharpen one. I guess they didn't want me wearing any weapons. Made sense to me. After all, no sense them taking any chances.

Bro, Aussie, and Dave stood around, looking at the walls.

As I lay down, I wondered how long it would take for the Doctor to arrive. The nurse was getting things ready. She went to a cabinet, pulled out sutures, and a needle. She shuffled back to me, examined my butt and went back to the cabinet, as she spoke to Dave.

Dave translated, "Bullet holes can't be stitched. You can't pull a round hole together. A larger cut, across it, has to be made to allow the stitches to pull both sides together somewhat evenly. Also, she doesn't have anything to get the slug out with, so room has to be made to get to it."

"Okay." I answered. It didn't mean shit to me. I figured a good shot of anesthesia and I could care less.

The nurse then took a piece of cloth out of the cabinet and left the room for a moment. When she returned, the cloth was obviously wet. Setting it down in front of me, I could smell the Mescal. "What in the hell is this all about?" I wondered.

As there was no running water in the building, what passed for a sink (as in most places) was a large metal bowl. I watched the nurse take isopropyl alcohol out of the cabinet and poor it into the bowl. "Well thank God for that, at least the place was sterile." I remember thinking.

Then she did what I thought to be a most unusual thing. Picking my knife up off the counter, she opened it, and lightly pulled her thumb across the blade, in several places, checking the sharpness of it. Nodding her head up and down in approval, she smiled. Putting my knife in the bowl and rinsing it in alcohol, she spoke to Dave in

Spanish. She shuffled over towards me, still carrying my knife. As Aussie, Bro, and Dave stepped closer to me, my world started to close in very suddenly.

"Whoa! Wait a minute!" I said as I started to get up. "What the hell is this all about? What's going on?"

"Calm down Joe." Dave said.

"What the hell is she doing with *my* knife?" I wanted to know.

"Probably doesn't have any proper instruments mate. You wouldn't want something duller used would you?" Aussie answered.

"Well, no. I guess not. But where's the Doctor?" I wasn't liking this one damned bit.

"She is the Doctor, Joe." Dave said.

"Oh…..ok." I didn't know what else to say. I laid back down.

After saying something in Spanish, Aussie, and Bro stepped closer to me. Dave, put a hand on each of my calves.

"What the hell, guys?" Butterflies were coming on now.

Dave answered. "It's going to hurt, Joe. Put the rag in your mouth, and bite down on it."

"I'm not John Wayne. Biting a rag ain't gonna help. Is it?" I asked.

"Probably not, but what the hell, it's an option. Hold him down." Dave said.

Dave laid across the back of my legs, Bro and Aussie each grabbed one of my arms and pinned them flat to the table.

I decided I could tough this out. I braced myself, and nodded my head yes, like a bull rider giving the signal to open the gate.

The "nurse" made her first cut across my ass cheek. A feeling of liquid fire burned into my butt. I hunched my butt down and tried to rise as I screamed.

"HOLD HIM, DAMMIT!" Dave yelled.

"ARRRRGH.STOP!" I yelled as she made another cut. As soon as that cut was done, I felt her insert two fingers into the cuts. I only *thought* the knife had hurt. I couldn't take this, I had to get up. I started to fight.

"LET ME GO YOU FUCKERS! LET ME UP, NOW!"

The nurse made another two cuts, and probed again.

I screamed the entire time. I had heard that pain can overcome a person until they pass out. Surely this would happen to me any second. Another cut was made, and another probe. My throat started to hurt from the screaming. As if on cue, Bro grabbed the rag soaked in Mescal and shoved it in my mouth. I knew this was my chance and started to fight like hell.

"He's a wiry little fucker." Bro said.

"Just hold him down!" Dave ordered.

I felt the nurse probing the cuts again and this time she pulled. I screamed some more. That REALLY hurt! Bad!

She cut and pulled some more. I sucked on the rag between screams. I felt a sharp sting as she inserted the needle and began to stitch. Pulling the cut together she had made, I had to wonder how much less painful it would have been to just leave it be.

As I lay there whimpering, my throat hoarse from screaming, I thought about how I could pay everyone back for this. I couldn't remember anything in my life being this painful. Everyone let go of me and I was free, at last. All I could do was lie there.

"Seven stitches Joe, looks like a bang up good job to me, Mate." Aussie informed me.

As someone helped me up, I started limping to the door, pulling up my pants as I went. I didn't want to talk to anyone. Walking out, I suddenly remembered what "bruja" meant. *"Witch!"* The fuckers had taken me to a witch doctor! I couldn't think anymore. Physically and emotionally, I was toast. I wanted a joint and some down time. Sleep called to me like no other time in my life.

Reaching the plane, Denny looked at me and smiled. I realized just how little I liked Denny, then. As Aussie and Bro helped me in, I decided I would smoke first and then lie down. I was still thinking about it, as I lay down on the floor of the plane. Before the door was shut or anyone else climbed in, I was asleep.

When I awoke, Dave was shaking me. I was groggy and my entire body seemed to hurt. "We need to eat, fuel, and piss before we head home."

"I'll wait here." I informed him. "No. Get up. You need to eat. It's a long flight." Dave answered.

I took the first step out of the plane and as my right foot touched down, pain rocketed through my foot and into my leg. Forgetting about my butt momentarily, I quickly placed my left foot down. Pain shot into it as well. My feet hurt, they were on fire and throbbing. I tentatively took a step. *PAIN!* "Oh God, what now?" I thought. Dave and Aussie looked at me strangely.

"What's wrong?" Aussie asked.

"I don't know, my feet hurt, it's like they're broke and on fire or something."

"It was that *run*." Dave said.

"Probably collapsed his arches." Aussie said. "Can you walk, Joe?"

"I think so." I took another step, more pain, another step….still more pain.

Hobbling along, I followed Dave, Aussie, Denny and Bro. Food was set in front of me. I don't remember where, or what other than at an airport. Eating a few bites, I got up and slowly started to the plane, taking my time and walking as gingerly as I could. After taking what seemed like forever to get to the plane, I crawled in and laid back down. Sleep seemed like the way to escape thoughts and pain. Blackness washed over me as I fell back asleep.

I didn't wake again until we touched down in El Paso.

15

When we arrived back in El Paso, I said my brief goodbyes to Dave and Denny and limped to my truck. Still groggy from the long sleep, I tried not to limp. I gave up on it after about three steps. By the time I had gotten on the interstate, I still didn't feel awake enough to drive home. I had X-rock 80 blasting on my truck stereo and Jackson Browne was playing running on empty. Wow, did that hit a note with me. I swung by Rob's house only to find he wasn't home.

I felt depressed and with nowhere else to go I just drove home. Pulling into the driveway, I was overcome by an ominous feeling. Drawing my 9mm, I held it under my jacket with my left hand and unlocked the door with my right. The first thing I thought as I entered was that maybe I smelled jasmine. I limped in slowly and as quietly as I could, I found the house all quiet and normal, in spite of the adrenalin dump I was on the verge of. As my heart rate returned to normal and I got a hold of myself, I knew I needed down time. I felt strung out. Setting my 9mm down, I sat down on the couch as carefully as I could. My ass still hurt. I needed to think. I felt like crying but I was too damn exhausted. I couldn't seem to get woke up even after all the sleep I had. Instead I laid back down on the couch and slept another couple of hours. When I woke, I felt much more rested, but my ass hurt like hell. Stripping my clothes off, and starting a shower, I held a mirror to my butt. What I saw turned my stomach a little. The wound was red, ugly and had pus oozing from it. The stitches however, did look good. The witch bitch *had* done a good job, at least on the stitches. With that reminder, I took one of the penicillin capsules Bro had given me.

I tried calling Rob but he wasn't home. Billy and Brad weren't home either. I was kind of out of the loop, and had no idea where anybody could be. I felt a little lonely and wanted company. I headed into town and picked up a couple of chile verde burritos. Eating seemed to restore my energy quite a bit. Feeling better and nothing else to do, I started driving the back roads and pretty soon, found myself at Dana's house. I just wanted to see her and talk. She may have been crazy, but I had known her for years, and though we hadn't dated in awhile, we were still friends. She was just a little too emotional and moody for me to date was all. Her brother-in-law Ben and I were still friends and I stay in touch with him to this day.

Knocking on the door, Dana answered. Seeing me, she looked a little shocked and then she smiled. Her smile was always warm.

"Joe! How in the world are you? I haven't seen you in forever."

"Yeah, I've been busy. Working. I was just in the neighborhood and thought I would drop by. I hope you don't mind?"

"No, of course not. You're always welcome here, you know that."

Dana closed the door behind her and sat down on the porch. I wanted to sit down but remembered my sore ass wouldn't let me. I stood with my hands in my jacket pockets.

"Are you seeing anybody now? I wouldn't want to cause you any problems." I asked.

"No. Men and I don't seem to get along. They always want to go drinking and hit on my friends. I needed a break." Suddenly as if a thought had occurred to her, she looked at me strangely, and asked "Are you cold, Joe?"

"Uh, no. Not really." Realizing it was a little warm for a jacket. I didn't know what to say. I couldn't tell her "It covers up my gun, Dana. You understand, right?"

Dana waited for an answer. I didn't have one. So I kept talking.

"What have you been doing?" I asked.

"Not much. Going to school. My Dad's been real sick. Trying to help Mom take care of him. I'm worried about him." Standing there politely I listened to her talk, telling me here worries and latest drama. Which Dana usually had plenty of.

After a bit, running out of things to talk about, she looked at me and seemed to study me before asking.

"Joe, are you okay? Is there anything you need to talk about or tell me? You seem really distant. Like something's wrong. You didn't knock up that girl you've been seeing, did you?" Referring to Jenn.

Chuckling dryly, I replied. "No. No I didn't. Not even seeing her anymore. Haven't been for awhile."

Standing there on Dana's sidewalk, I realized I couldn't tell her a damn thing. I had changed. I didn't belong here, and I had no business or reason to sit here and talk to Dana.

"I've got to go Dana. You take care."

Rising up, she gave me a hug. "You take care, Joe. Call me if you want to talk. I hope you get worked out whatever is bugging you."

As I turned and tried to walk without limping, back to my truck, I answered her. "I will. Don't worry about it." I could feel Dana watching me as I walked away. I didn't see her again for almost five years. When I did, she asked me "if I ever got that problem worked out?"

That night I found myself in Juarez, with a pocket full of money and a bottle of Tequila in front of me. I stayed for three nights, and lost count and memory of about everything I did. Also for some inexplicable reason, now and then I thought I could smell jasmine. It was disturbing.

One other thing that was very apparent by the time I returned home, was the fact that I had forgotten to take the penicillin Bro had given me, and the infection was getting worse.

After taking the penicillin and stuffing the bottle in my pocket so I wouldn't forget, I called Dad.

"How ya doin, Pard'ner?" He asked.

"Fine Dad. How's work going?"

"Well I was just getting ready to call you about that. My boss knows I won't work my long weekend, but we have a man out on vacation and another out hurt. I could make a little extra money. Don't really need it, but thought I better check with you. You holding out ok?"

"I'm fine Dad. Go ahead and work if you want."

"You got enough money?" He was concerned I could tell.

"Yep. Only spent twenty of the hundred you gave me."

"Well are you getting enough to eat?"

"Yeah. I've been eating at home a lot. Trying to eat up these tamales." (That was another story in itself, Dad and I ended up with one hundred and twenty *dozen* tamales)

"Well ok, but if you need something, call me. You could come to here, or I could meet you half way. If you need something."

"I will Dad, but I'll be fine."

"I know you will Pard'ner. Love you. Talk to you later."

"Bye Dad."

As soon as I sat the phone down, it rang again. Hmm? Too fast to be Dad. I let it ring one more time. It was Dave. I couldn't ever remember him calling me.

"Can you stop by the house later?" He asked me.

"Yeah. What time?" I answered.

"The earlier the better."

"I'll see you in an hour, then." I told him.

Arriving at Dave's I was met at the door by Jenn. She seemed really happy to see me.

Smiling at me she spoke, taking me completely by surprise. "Good to see you. I'm glad you came by Joe. Will you stay for dinner?"

I just couldn't figure women out. I had just spent the better part of three nights whoring my way across Juarez and *now* she's interested? What the hell was that all about? It was like she *knew* something, but she didn't know what the "something" was.

Dave rescued me. "Jenn, why don't you and your Mom go pick up some steaks for dinner. Joe and I will fire up the BBQ grill." With that he reached into his pocket and pulling out a twenty dollar bill handed it to Karen. Karen wasn't one to look a gift horse in the mouth and was taking the money with one hand and shouldering her purse with the other, as she called out for Jenn to hurry up.

Watching them leave, Dave fixed his eyes on me. "How's your ass?" He asked with a touch of smile.

"It's healing." I lied. With that I reached into my pocket and took another penicillin capsule.

"Could you be ready to head back out tomorrow, if necessary?" He asked.

This didn't feel right. We hadn't sold the guns from the last fiasco, and had nothing to take down. Was I being setup? Why would he set me up though? Plenty of chances to do it before now.

"Why? We didn't sell the last ones, and we've got nothing to take?"

"I went ahead and picked some up for you. I've driven by your house three times and you haven't been home."

Images of Juarez, and tequila bottles flashed through my mind. Then Tierra Negra, and the conversation with Dad, that he wouldn't be home.

"Yeah, I can go. Something up that I should know about?"

"No. Not really." I got the impression he was lying to me, and said as much. I almost over stepped my bounds.

"I will *not* be called a fucking liar by you or anyone else. You want the money or not?" Dave sneered. He was most definitely pissed.

"Dave calm down. You know this isn't usual, and you know it's not about the money either." Dave was a little scary when he was mad. He very seldom got that way and it was rare for him to cuss, except in the most extreme circumstances. I seemed to be around a lot whenever those incidents came around. He had also diverted my attention away from the question. Had he lied to me?

"I want to be out of here at 0100. Can you make that?" He asked me.

"In the morning? Yeah, I'll be ready." I answered.

By the time Karen and Jenn returned we had the grill going. Jenn kept motioning for me to come into the kitchen and talk to her. Dave, now that he was pissed at me didn't seem very talkative, so I drifted into the kitchen.

Jenn and I had several long conversations in the kitchen when we were seeing each other, and it seemed the natural place to be.

Telling me she had broken up with her new boyfriend, she wanted to know if I was dating anyone. I told her no and she promptly made it clear she didn't believe me. What the hell was I supposed to do? Make something up? As Dave announced the steaks were ready, Jenn changed the subject and asked me if I wanted to go to a movie after dinner. Knowing I needed to be ready, and that this definitely wasn't going anywhere, I declined. That really pissed her off. "I even went out and bought a new perfume, Joe. Don't you like it?" She pouted.

"It's nice. Is it jasmine?" I asked.

"No. It's not." She glared at me. Well it smelled like it had *some* jasmine in it to me. "Since when do you like jasmine so much?" Jenn asked as we drifted into the dining room and took our seats.

"I don't. Just thought that's what it was is all. Not a big deal Jenn."

Before dinner was over, Jenn had brought all this out in the open and got Karen to side with her too. Why didn't I want to go out after dinner? Was I seeing someone else? Where have I been? How come I haven't been by? Or called?

It suddenly occurred to me, that I had the entire family mad at me. Why was I even here? Looking at Dave at the far end of the table, he looked at me with a mirthful smirk as he cut into his steak. He was enjoying this. The rotten bastard.

"Fine, we'll go to a movie." I gave in. Dave shot me a cautious look.

"Well why didn't you want to go Joe?" Karen pressed.

"One, I'm just tired, but I'll go. Two, I didn't really realize I was supposed too. I thought we were through. I didn't quite realize I was back in the fold. After all, Jenn broke up with me."

Dave almost laughed out loud.

After dinner, Jenn did the dishes and I helped dry them. Not because I wanted to, but because she wouldn't let me out of the kitchen. She couldn't make up her mind to interrogate me or kiss my ass. This was going to be a long night. I wasn't sure what she wanted. Maybe, I thought to myself, I should just tell her about the countless whores I had been with the last three days and be done with it. A smile crossed my face as I thought about how *that* would go over. Dave stepped into the kitchen to hand off a dirty glass and saw me smiling.

"Whatever you're thinking about saying. Don't." He warned. I almost started giggling. Jenn looked at me strangely.

"What *were* you going to say?" She asked.

Dave answered for me in a stern voice. "Leave it be, Jenn."

"Yes Sir." Jenn replied. Dave could certainly read people. At least me anyway. I know there was no way Dave could have known what I was going to say, but he knew it wasn't going to go over very well. That was Dave's gift that I will always remember him for. Like him or not, he could read a situation and a person quite well. It was like he was trained to do it.

It turned out Jenn didn't want to go to a movie at all. She wanted to go to a motel, drink wine, "make love" and me take her home when she was good and ready and to hell with what her Dad thought.

Double checking to see if I had this in my mind right. My *ex* girlfriend, wanted me to take her to a motel, get her drunk, bang her, and bring her home blasted, just before I flew with her father to a foreign country with a civil war going on. How could this possibly turn out bad? Of all the stupid things I had let myself do, this one would be way over the line, even for me. This didn't even sound like fun, and I didn't really feel like it now either. In the end, it turned into a screaming match about who lied to who, and who had been seeing someone else. It was her on both counts. Dropping her off, she stormed to the front of the house, about as pissed as I had ever seen her. I didn't really care. I had already decided she was not in it for the long haul. In the past year or so, I had matured beyond her though, and I didn't see that turning around anytime soon, if ever. Putting the truck into gear I thought; *mental note to myself: If you don't like your daughter's boyfriend, get him into a gunfight. If he survives, it'll probably ruin the relationship anyway.* Besides, I had more important things to think about.

As far as I knew though, this was the *first* time in my life I had ever passed up a piece of ass. It would be a longed damned time before I ever passed up another one. I mean, you never know when your last one might be. You shouldn't take chances like that.

16

BAD COMPANY

At 0015 hours, I arrived at the hangar and helped Denny load the plane, while Dave went through his preflight inspection. Denny wouldn't be coming but did bring crates for us to load. At 0100 we took off, and started to climb. These flights had become absolute drudgery to me. I hated them now. I climbed in the back and went to sleep as soon as Dave got to cruising altitude.

Waking up before dawn, I climbed in the seat next to Dave and watched the sun come up.

"Do you still shoot a lot, I mean for fun or practice?" He asked.

"Yeah, whenever I can." I answered truthfully.

"Are you getting any better? I don't mean that like you're not good, I just wondered if you're better now than you were like a year ago?" He pressed.

"Yeah, not as good as I would like to be. I'm accurate enough. Wished I was faster though."

With a puzzled glance, Dave asked, "You don't think you're fast? How fast do you want to be?"

That was a stupid question I thought but answered him anyway. "Faster than anyone else."

Dave laughed. "Faster than *anyone* else. Quite a goal Joe. I don't think you'll ever reach it though. There's always someone faster."

"True. But like Aussie and Bro say; *Train for the professional and hope you come up against an amateur.*"

Dave seemed to study me a little harder now before asking. "Do you think you could take three men with a pistol, Joe?"

I was somewhat taken aback and considered my response before answering. "I sure as hell wouldn't want to try. You mean like old gunfighter style, standing in the street? Sounds like a good way to die fast."

"No, not like that. But let's say, three guys. One with a pistol, flap holster, and a couple more with let's say rifles, but the rifles are slung. On their shoulders, all close range. In the same room. Could you handle that?"

I wasn't sure what Dave was getting at, if anything. I thought carefully, I damn sure didn't want to inadvertently volunteer for some nonsense.

A flap holster would put that guy way behind the curve of the action. He could also move the easiest and fastest, considering all else being equal. The rifles in confined quarters would be just about certain death if allowed to be deployed. One of the rifle guys would have to be the first one dropped from extremely close range, with maybe some diversion or concealment of your intentions until things were started. Then the one with the pistol, before he could draw, and be closing on the second rifleman, before he could get into action. That would be really tight.

"I guess it's possible. I think it would be really touch and go. Lots of ways for things to go bad. I sure as hell wouldn't want to try it." I added, just in case he was considering something I didn't know about.

Dave looked at me and nodded as he thought about my answer.

Staring out the window, I thought about Bro and Aussie. How much they had taught me and how much I liked being around them. Although we had been gone less than a week it only seemed like a day or two. Apparently I had lost track and sense of time during my Juarez foray. I reached into my pocket and took another penicillin capsule as I thought about the wound in my ass. It wasn't hurting very much anymore. I think the infection was coming down, but the stitches weren't ready to come out yet.

Arriving almost midday, we fueled and tied the plane down. Dave explained we would come get the cargo later. It was a risk but we didn't want to draw any attention unloading in daylight. Things had been touchy and the Sandinistas were edgy. Firing up an old Ford truck that I had not seen yet we headed to the house. It coughed and sputtered and died as we pulled into the house. I pushed it the last little bit to get it into the backyard and out of our way. As I pushed and Dave steered, I looked up and saw there was a Jeep already there that Dave pulled past. Bro was wiping it down as if he had just finished waxing it. Aussie sat on the back step with a bottle of beer, watching Bro and giving instructions or pestering him, maybe both. I had watched this many times, and Bro seemed to totally ignore Aussie and sometimes I wondered if Aussie wasn't talking just to hear himself talk. For at least the hundredth time, I wondered where the hell all the vehicles came from. I hadn't seen the truck or this jeep before today. Surely they weren't stolen. Were they? I couldn't really see taking the added risk.

Aussie stood up and walked over, greeting Dave but coming over to me, smiling as he clamped a big hand on my shoulder. "Ello mate. How's the backside healing up?"

"Good Aussie. Thanks. It's not quite healed but almost, if I can remember to take the damned antibiotics Bro gave me."

"Good to 'ear it mate. I think this round will go quite well. Shouldn't be any problems. Davey seems to 'ave it all squared up."

"I hope so. Last time was enough to last me forever." I answered seriously.

After saying "Hello" to Dave and I, Bro asked what happened to the pickup. Dave said he thought the timing was off, and Bro replied that he would take a look at it later.

In the house, I retrieved my H&K from the bedroom, after checking it, I leaned it against a wall in the kitchen. I still had my pistol underneath my shirt too.

Bro couldn't resist teasing me a little, "Just being prepared, Joe?"

Smiling back I replied, "Damned straight."

Dave was standing by the sink already on his second glass of water. Informing us he would be leaving shortly and be back in time for the meet tomorrow, we would have dinner without his wonderful presence. He had to fly out to confer with some friends of his, after a nap.

I caught the sharp looks from Bro and Aussie and decided to leave it be. I didn't want to know, anymore. I had decided I would never see any retribution for the little girl and I would just have to live with it.

Dave headed to the back of the house, to get some sleep. After grabbing a soda from the fridge, Bro, Aussie and I drifted outside and raised the hood on the Ford. With a little bit of help from Aussie and me, Bro had the truck running fairly good after awhile.

With the hood closed on the truck Bro told me to turn it off. I did. Nodding his head to go in the house I climbed out and shut the door. Aussie stood up from the back step and stepped into the kitchen.

"Dave asked me, on the way down, if I thought I was good enough with a pistol to take down three guys."

Bro looked back over his shoulder and down at me as he stepped up onto the porch, screen door in hand. He seemed puzzled like he hadn't heard me right, and continued into the kitchen.

"Aussie, Dave asked Joe if he thought he could take down three guys with a pistol." Apparently he had heard me just fine.

"I eard it mate. I hope you told him no, Joe?"

I explained the conversation on the way down. Bro and Aussie listened intently. When I was done, Bro said, "You should've told him, no. You couldn't."

"I don't think I follow you. Is he asking me to do something or going to ask me to do something?"

Bro and Aussie gave each other a long look before answering me. Finally they spoke.

"Not sure, but anytime someone asks your skill level, downplay it. Or you might have to prove it."

"Good advice he's givin, mate. No sense anyone knowing how good you are. You wouldn't tell them your weaknesses would you? Of course not."

"The thing is Joe, appearing harmless isn't always a bad thing. But if Dave is asking you to do something to that effect, pass on it. I'm telling you, it cain't be good. Even if you got'em, whoever *they* are, how would you guarantee getting out? It ain't worth it."

"Bro, you don't think Davey, would be thinking about one of the Sandinista commanders do you? Play on Joe's sympathy over the little girl."

Bro locked eyes with me as he replied. "It crossed my mind. Thing is, Joe, *No one* could you get you away from a

MISADVENTURES OF A TEENAGE GUNRUNNER

company of regulars that were close by. Which they would be. It would be suicide."

"Then again, mates, it could ave just been a bullshit question." Aussie said as he shrugged his shoulders.

Bro started fixing dinner and Aussie and I sat at the table and quietly drank a beer. Not being much of a beer drinker, this one tasted especially good. Why? I couldn't tell you.

As Bro finished making dinner Dave came out of the bedroom rubbing his eyes.

"Did the truck get fixed?" He asked

"Worked on it, didn't I?" Bro answered grinning.

Bro set the table and handed out our plates of steak, fried potatoes, and green beans. Mine didn't have any green beans, as they all knew, I absolutely hated them. Dave sitting down laced up his boots and issued instructions.

"Bro and Joe can take me back to the plane in the pickup. It should be dark by the time we finish dinner and get there. We'll off load the plane and you two can head back here. Aussie can hold down the place here. He's a little too pale to be out and about at night, might get noticed as nervous as this place has been."

"What about the guns from the last trip, Dave?" I asked.

"They've been delivered. Bro and Aussie took care of it. We've been paid in full and all we have left to do is deliver the other half." Dave grinned back at me.

"How the hell did you get them back? We had flown them in, near Tierra Negra." I asked incredulously.

"We only flew in because it was faster, not that far of a jeep ride mate. We only brought ours back though. Left yours we did. Didn't think you would ever be back after being shot in the back side." Aussie teased.

After supper Aussie volunteered to do the dishes as Dave, Bro, and myself made ready for the airport ride. I slid my H&K into the front of the pickup and stuck five full magazines into the front seat crevice where they would hopefully stay put. I thought it might be a little much, but after the last incident, I wasn't taking any chances.

Dropping a semi folded blanket on my H&K, I covered the magazines also and climbed in. Bro started the truck and as Dave pulled out in the Jeep, followed him. Dusk was approaching, but Bro had on a set of teardrop shaped sunglasses.

"What's with the shades, Bro?"

"Cause I look cool. Gotta look cool when you're a man on a mission. That way you don't look like a man on a mission. My eyes are free to roam. Nobody sees me watching them. I'm alert though, watching everything. Acting like I ain't watchin nuthin."

Laughing, I answered, "You do look cool, for a 6'9" Mississippi farmer."

"Cools *cool*." Bro answered smiling as we followed Dave through the city.

It only took about five minutes to move the merchandise from the plane to the pickup. Covering it with a tarp, we loaded up and Dave said he would be back by daylight for the meet, and told us to be careful. Bro nodded affirmative and we headed back at a fast clip. Not fast enough to draw attention but not slow enough for anyone to look us over for any length of time.

Back at the house Aussies helped us unload the pickup and we brought everything into the living room in a matter of minutes. Aussie had left his FN FAL by the door the entire time. When everything was in, I grabbed my H&K and the magazines and brought them in too. We were done for the night.

Next morning I woke early. Looking over at Aussie, I saw he was still fast asleep in his bed. I went into the kitchen and started the coffee, being as quiet as I could, not wanting to wake anybody. As it brewed I slipped out the back door and pissed off the porch. The temperature was perfect. Just a touch cool, but the sun wasn't quite up. I noticed the Jeep was back and remembered that Dave had returned during the night. Knocking once, pausing and then knocking twice more before entering. Not that it mattered, I'm sure we had all been awake anyway the second he pulled in.

Shuddering from relieving myself I zipped up my jeans, and turned around to step back in the house. As I let the door shut quietly behind me I looked up in time to see a large dark shadow closing fast from the hallway.

My stomach turned and I instinctively crouched, "Bro!" I said just in time to keep him from launching himself at me. Bro's momentum was up though, as I ducked and prayed he didn't run over me he raised his arms to stop himself and slammed into the doorjamb, arms stiff in front of him. By this time I had squatted to his waist level, bumping me just enough to knock me off balance. Behind him, down the hallway, I heard a safety on a weapon click off and at least one set of feet hit the floor.

"You scared the shit out of me, Bro." I said loud enough for everyone to hear.

"Why you up this time of day?" Bro asked as he unlimbered himself from the awkward position he had got himself into while keeping from creaming me.

"I don't know, I just woke up. I started the coffee, and went out to piss. Jesus." I said shakily.

"You about met him." Bro grinned in the dark as laid down a large Ka-Bar knife on the table.

"I about met who?" I asked still feeling the butterflies in my stomach.

"Jesus. You about met Jesus you dumb ass." Dave said as he leaned around the corner of the hallway, flipping the safety back up on his .45. Turning back around he walked back down the hallway and into the bathroom. God I wanted a cup of coffee.

Sitting at the table, I waited for the coffee to be ready as Bro cracked eggs into a skillet.

"Nobody ever beats Bro up in the morning." Aussie announced as he came out of the hallway and walked over to the coffee pot. It was ready.

"Trust me. I won't again. Next time I'll just piss in my bed." I answered earnestly, as I stood up and followed him to the coffee pot.

Bro chuckled. "Sorry Joe."

Aussie sitting at the table looked ready for the day, except for the fact he had blond hair sticking everywhere. He looked like he could have just come off a surfboard. As I sat down, and took my first sip of coffee, Dave walked back in and poured himself a cup. Quietness filled the room as everyone tried to get woke up.

Aussie studied me as he drank. He seemed to be in deep thought, as I looked back at him waiting for what would obviously be a very serious question. Finally he spoke

"You didn't hurt Bro did you, Joe?"

Dave choked on his coffee and started coughing.

"Not unless Bro can't stand the smell of shit, cause I'm pretty sure, I did." I replied with a smile.

"Yes sir, there I was. Just me, my ba'r hands and the baddest little motherfucker on the planet. Thought I was done for shore." Bro teased.

This was getting out of hand I had to defend myself.

"After the first hit, I would've been in the game." I said.

Bro looked over his shoulder at me as he flipped eggs. "That's the spirit Joe. Never give up." He smiled.

Dave rolled his eyes, and stated coughing again, still dealing with the coffee he had choked on. Aussie saw way too many openings and attacked immediately.

"What were you going to do mate? Piss all over him to make yourself slippery, perhaps? Or maybe throw him off the top of you, broken ribs and all and choke him out?"

"Actually the thing that came to mind was to roll up in a ball and hopefully get away from his big ass." I replied.

I wasn't going to win this. I had nothing, except left over adrenalin.

"Yeah, that might of worked. Or keep digging the hole he had made with your body, and tried to bury yourself faster." Dave said. He had barely quit coughing from Aussie's first comment.

"Never a dull moment, around here. Unh Unh. Not with Joe around. No Sir." Bro said.

These were good times. Some of the best in my life, and it was all about to come crashing down.

17

WHEN THE LEVEE BREAKS

After breakfast, Dave outlined the day's events. We would load the guns into the back of the truck. Dave would run interference for us in the jeep, to keep us appraised of any road blocks etc. that the Sandinistas had taken to throwing up. Bro, Aussie and myself would follow in the pickup. Bro would drive, Aussie would ride shotgun, and I would ride in the back.

While loading up the truck, I realized, this was kind of like a double payday for us. Except that I didn't get paid last time. We had sold the guns from our last trip and this one to a new group. Dave assured us these were definitely rebels and a fairly large group with some organization. These guys were out to end the Sandinista regime. It would be awhile, but groups like this had a habit of forming up and coming together, given enough time.

As I climbed into the bed of the truck I sat cross legged with my back against the forward part of the bed with the rear sliding window open. My pistol was digging into my hip, so I slid it around behind my hip and to the rear more. Better. It was comfortable again. I had crates on either side of me and some stacked sideways in front of me. I had cover, this was nice. Placing three of my extra mags on the floor of the bed, they really had no place to slide off to, that I couldn't reach them. Also with the crates being lower than the top of the bed, from a distance, it didn't even look suspicious.

Dave started the jeep, and swung out of the driveway. We followed, dropping back farther as we got further out of town. Heading south the sun was warm and I watched our rear and left the front to the rest of the guys. Passing the occasional truck we wound out of town and into the forest and hills. As the roads turned into dirt, they became narrower and less traveled. We had taken so many turns now, I wasn't sure that I remembered them all. The sun had disappeared and it had started to rain lightly. From inside the cab, Steve Winwood was singing "I'm so glad you made it" on a cassette tape, Bro had him outmatched for volume, and I actually think Bro sounded a little better. He really could carry a tune. Any time I tried, Bro had a look on his face like I was causing him pain. I wasn't a good singer, I guess. Aussie in spite of the drizzle had his window down and was keeping time on the inside of the door panel, with his head bobbing to the music, constantly scanning his surroundings as he did so. The man was born to be a warrior, and I felt very lucky to have them both as mentors. I only hoped I could be half the men they were.

We turned up an old road, Dave, in the jeep ahead climbed up a hill into the trees. Bro followed, spinning tires and fishtailing occasionally in the mud. Dave slowed and spoke to someone standing out of my line of sight, as we passed the same spot, I could see a Nicaraguan who stood holding an M-16 with magazines strapped to his chest. I felt the butterflies start to flutter in my stomach as I remembered how serious the situation was. We continued up and topped out into a bowl, or a "holler" as Bro called it. Dave brought the Jeep to a stop, Bro looped the pickup around him and that faced me towards the encampment and backed up. *"Thanks, Bro."* I thought to myself. Dave was out of the jeep, shaking hands with an older man that was obviously a leader. Already I could see about twenty fighting men. More were coming, everyone seemed relaxed. There were bound to be some women and children too, with this many men around. One young rebel probably about my age, perhaps out to prove himself or just being cautious, drifted off from the rest towards us and to our left. Although he kept his rifle low, I watched him plant his feet, and slightly shift his weight, setting himself and staking his lanes of fire in his head, towards our pickup. Casually unlimbering, I stood and faced him with my H&K pointed down. Our eyes met and locked. I don't know if mine were as cold as his or not, but he had to know I had him if push came to shove. Apparently I wasn't the only that noticed. The man speaking with Dave called out a name I didn't catch. The rebel broke eye contact with me and looked at his commander.

"These are going to be friends of ours. We want to welcome them." Said the man in charge. The rebel understanding his meaning, broke from where he was and slung his rifle after he nodded at me, and then walked over and to Aussie and Bro and shook hands. Rifle still in my hand, I jumped out of the truck. I had won in my mind, but saw no reason to push the issue. Little victories or losses of pride could mean an awful lot to these people. Machismo abounded. Way too much as far as I was concerned.

I dropped the tailgate bed and Dave indicated to the rebels to help themselves. As they pulled the crates out, they pried them open and looked inside. Their leader and Dave drifted over and watched. The leader leaned against the pickup bed and seemed to examine it as he spoke to Dave in broken English.

"We heard about some bandits who were killed. They say a giant negro killed many, and the bandits killed some of them too. I hope all your people are they safe." He barely glanced at Bro.

Dave answered with a smile. "I wouldn't believe everything you hear, but all my people are good."

"Bueno, I'm happy to know that. You know some of those bandits, want better. Some come to me later. They don't always know who to let lead them. Is this ok for you?" He asked.

"Your decision. I won't tell you how to run your people." Dave answered casually.

Shit! Some of the people from last week were with this group now? I felt the butterflies take flight in my stomach again, as I looked around nervously trying to recognize people from the cantina or ridge where they shot us up.

"Easy Joe" Aussie whispered. He still seemed relaxed.

Seeing my nervousness much as he had seen it in his own man, the "Capit'an" as I had come to think of him, glanced at me and spoke to us as much to Dave said, "But I not let them be here today. I want us to be friends. No how you say, misunderstanding?"

Dave chuckled. "I'm sure my people appreciate it." He glanced at me too.

Now it was the "Capit'ans" turn to smile as he looked at me and said. "These young ones. Always ready for the fight."

I was beginning to like this guy. He was pretty cool. He damn sure understood the dynamics of a fight. I sure wouldn't want to go up against him. He was cunning, and he had survived this long.

Slapping the bed of the truck with a calloused hand, the "Capit'an" continued. "This is good pickup. We could use it. How much would you sell it for to me?"

"It's yours. No charge." Dave said.

The "Capit'an" looked at Dave with surprise and graciousness in his eyes before choosing his words, carefully.

"They say you a good man. It's true."

Dave turned and shook his hand. "To help you and your people, anything I can do to help, I will."

"Thank you, Senor. The bastards put up road blocks at night going into Managua every night for three times in a row now. So don't go back by big roads. We ambush them soon though."

"Okay, thanks for the information. Keep the truck now. We can all fit in the jeep. Stay safe my friend." Dave said as he climbed in the jeep.

Aussie sprung into the jeep and sat down behind Dave on the wheel well, there were no rear seats. Then Bro, climbed in and sat across from Aussie. That left the front passenger seat for me.

"Bro you want to sit up front? I can sit in the back with Aussie." I offered.

"Nope Joe. My knees bang the dash. Sides that, you rode in the back on the way down. I'd rather my knees bang Aussie than the dash, anyhow."

"Thanks a lot you big lug." Aussie smirked.

I climbed in the passenger seat and Dave started the jeep and swung around and we headed back down the hill the way we had come in, waving at the sentry as we left. Turning down the canyon we had come up, the sun suddenly came out, and it started to get warm. My pistol was now digging into my back. I moved my H&K to the side and set it between the seats still muzzle down. As I tried to slide my pistol around, I noticed Aussie and Bro had their guns muzzle up so as not to inadvertently point them at one another. Wasn't very inconspicuous either.

"Do you two want to put those up here, next to mine?" I offered.

"I thought you would never ask Joe." As Aussie slid his on top of mine and then Bro's on top of both. Now I was damn crowded. My pistol was really digging into me also. I reached under my shirt, drew my pistol out and stuck the muzzle underneath my right thigh. Now it was pinned there. I could reach it if it was needed and it was certainly more comfortable. Turned out, I was wrong about that. That little act, taught me a life lesson I carry with me to this day. If something is loose in a vehicle, it's a missile waiting to launch. If you think you can grab it or hold it, you're wrong. I then rearranged the rifles, with mine and Aussie's on top and Bro's on the bottom as it was by far the heaviest.

We drove another thirty minutes in silence, alone with our own thoughts. I watched Dave negotiate the hills and twists and turns in the jeep.

Finally Aussie broke the silence.

"I thought Joe was going to positively take a squat and empty his magazine, when that rebel said some of the guys from last week had joined him."

"Yeah, I could sure feel the tension come up about 500% in him, when he heard that." Dave said. He had a big shit eating grin on his face.

"Never a dull moment with Joe around, No suh!" It was becoming one of Bro's favorite sayings apparently.

"I still can't get over that some of the group from last week had joined them." I said.

"Quite common actually. It's not that their loyalties are misplaced, it's just the fact they don't have regular, structured leadership. Yet. It's getting there, though." Dave explained.

"That jefe there, he's been around the block a few times I would say. Had a good base there. Relaxed but lot's of discipline." Bro offered.

"You would know relaxed, wouldn't you? You big lug." Aussie interjected.

"He's got some background and experience, that's for sure. Used to be a Sandinista. Switched sides after they came into power." Dave told us.

"No shit? Wow!" I was stunned but really shouldn't have been. I was still young to the ways of the world.

"Man sounds like a true patriot to me, mates. Hell, I like him already. If he's got a daughter though, we should probably keep Joe away. That could wreck everything." Aussie said.

"I ain't shore *who* that was pointed at. Dave or Joe." Bro teased.

"No shit. Little bastard's trying to breed himself across two continents." Dave said dryly, as he down shifted for a hill.

"How the hell does this always get around to pick on Joe, anyway?" I asked to no one in particular.

We came over a small hill as Dave down shifted again to negotiate a hard right up a small steep hill, as he started up the hill he looked at me and started to answer. "Well Joe, it's like this…"

As we crested the hill my heart dropped into my stomach.

Sandinistas!

At the bottom of the hill was a hard left turn and a clearing used for a pull off. In the pull off area were two pickup trucks. They were Sandinista military and there were perhaps ten soldiers standing around it. To me, it looked like fifty.

Seeing the look on my face Dave whipped his head around, eyes front and saw what I was already seeing. Instinctively Dave slammed on the brakes launching my pistol out from under my leg into the floor board. Great, I had lost my gun. Realizing it was too late to stop and back up, Dave hammered the throttle down. I bent at the waist and tried to retrieve my pistol as we accelerated toward the Sandinistas. After a couple of attempts I finally got my hand on the grip of my 9mm as everything went into slow motion for me. I heard glass break and an angry buzzing bee passed above me and thwacked itself into a slab of meat. Rising up to the sound of a weapon on full auto I pointed my gun out the side of the jeep and started pulling the trigger as Dave shot past the mostly startled soldiers. I couldn't hold the gun still enough in the crazily bouncing jeep to aim at anything in particular. I just kept pulling the trigger as fast as I could. Only one or two seemed to have any desire to use their guns. The rest were scattering for cover like flushed quail.

"Bro's hit!" Aussie screamed.

As Dave topped the next hill about 60 yards away he slammed the jeep to a stop, just a few yards past the crest. Was he crazy? We needed to get out of here. Now!

Dave slid out of the jeep yelling, "I've got Bro. Aussie take Joe. Do NOT let those fuckers call this in. Take the 60."

I grabbed my H&K and I bailed out. Bro was crumpled in the back of the Jeep. The bullet had hit him somewhere under his right armpit and came out the right side of his chest. He was reaching up trying to stop the lake of blood that was coming from his wound. He looked bad. Aussie leaned forward and retrieved his weapon and the 60, following me out as I spun out of the jeep with my H&K. As I started towards the crest of the hill, Aussie passed me in two long strides carrying a gun in each hand and issuing orders. "Take out the trucks and radios first, mate."

I cut left a little and put about five yards between me and Aussie. Flopping down on my stomach as I reached the crest, I sighted in on the pickup and put three rounds into the radiator, then two rounds on each side where I thought the batteries would be. A Sandinista picked up a radio as he slid behind the wheel of the other pickup. Aussie let go with a burst from the sixty, shattering the front window and spraying blood and brains inside the cab. It was graphic, even from where we were.

Hearing a burst from an automatic weapon, I saw a Sandinista had reached the mounted machine gun in the back of the pickup. Almost simultaneously Aussie fired also hitting the machine gun itself and then let out a painful yelp. I glanced right and saw blood pouring from Aussie's left hand. He wiped blood splatter from his face with his right, sliding back a little as he did so. This was getting worse by the second. I scrambled backwards, my stomach churning in fear, momentarily forgetting everything except Aussie. Reaching him, I could see his left ring finger was only about half of its normal length as blood poured from it, and I could see meat from his middle finger as well. Looking at his hand then the 60, Aussie dropped the weapon and reached for his Galil.

"The sixty's focked! Time to kill the bastards Joe. You work to the left, I'll work to the right! Get with it mate, we can't let them get organized or call for help. I'll meet with you on the other side."

We crawled back up to almost our same positions on the crest as we were before. We could see one man, probably an officer or Sergeant starting to rally his men. Standing in the open he waved his arm to follow him. Aussie shot the man in the chest. As they started to shout to each other, Aussie shot the dead leader about five more times. On one hand I thought it was waste of ammo, on the other hand, it couldn't have been easy on them watching that be done to someone they knew. Aussie's message was clear.

Attack us, you die.

Taking all this in, I came to the realization that I was going to die. Here, today. Not a lot later, not after all this. Death was coming in the next few minutes or the next few seconds. *Was the bullet already on its way, I wondered?* We were outnumbered three or four to one and now we had two men hit, and we were separated, and Aussie only had me to help him.

Aussie started screaming. I stole a quick glance over at him, fearful of what I might see. Knowing this was it, Aussie yelled as he rolled across the ground to his right. "Get to killing, Joe." He wasn't hit again and neither was I, yet.

"Fuck this!" I thought. Deep down inside of me, I could feel something coming up. It felt ugly and powerful, as if my soul were releasing itself. It was building, and boiling. I had never experienced anything like it before. Coming from deep inside of my brain and my guts it overtook me. Fear, it had to be. Fear fueled by rage and doubt and anger and acceptance that I was going to die. It pissed me off! I let it come and yelled at the top of my lungs in rage. In my peripheral vision, I saw Aussie's head jerk towards me in wide eyed surprise, thinking I was hit. "That's it Joe. Give it to the bastards!" He yelled.

Rising to my knees I fired into the other pickups radiator as I saw someone going into the cab despite the gore, surely going for the radio. Raising my barrel up, I fired into the cab as Aussie had done before, with no way of telling whether I had hit anything or not. I dropped and rolled to my left and looked the scene over again. Two Sandinistas were yelling at one standing in the pickup bed that was trying to get the damaged machine gun to work. Sighting on his chest, I squeezed off the round. As the bullet took him, the rest dropped from sight. Three down, or was it four? Wiggling backwards, I stood up and bolted to the left, being careful not to skyline myself. After about 35 or 40 yards, I came back to the crest. I could hear Aussie firing and I could see one Sandinista crouched behind the pickup and another just beyond him. He looked over and saw me and started to rise up to either run or shoot me. I fired. The bullet hit him in the stomach. He dropped his weapon clutching his stomach and sat down hard on his ass, then fell over screaming. I didn't really give a damn anymore. If I was going to die, I would make them pay. Resisting a stupid urge to run down into the middle of them and kill all I could, I backed up and continued circling. Cresting over and firing, a foot sticking out here, an arm there. I circled further around, getting behind them. When I had come almost half circle, I caught a glimpse of movement barely fifteen yards out. Lying behind some brush on his side was a young Sandinista. He had his gun cradled by his body and was looking at me. He was obviously terrified. His eyes wide with fear. How the hell had we gotten so close to each other? As he tried to bring his rifle into a firing position I shot into the top of his head, the hydraulics of the bullet creating a fan of grisly mess from his head. His body went instantly limp. I kept scanning for targets. Time slowed, noise stopped. I felt my final moments would be a series of shooting, moving, and reloading until I was dead.

Eventually circling almost three quarters of the way around the Sandinistas, I came upon the road we had come in on. I hadn't seen or heard Aussie for quite some time that I could remember. I was sure he was alive, just because the Sandinistas had been trying to seek cover and return fire on two fronts at once. The only ones left now, had either made it to cover or were hiding underneath the trucks. Firing a few more rounds, evenly spaced underneath the pickups didn't seem to have any results. I made a decision; Time to leave.

I turned and bolted into the forest as hard and as fast as I could. I ran at least a mile before slowing down and listening. My legs were burning and my chest heaved, as I gasped for air. Finding a shallow divot on the forest floor, I laid down on my back in it, trying to catch my breath. I could hear my heart beating, it was beating so hard it sounded like a helicopter. Or did I in fact hear a helicopter. I strained to listen harder. I couldn't tell what the hell I was hearing.

After a few moments, I sat up and put my back against a tree, staring out at the direction I had come from. No one came. A chill on my sweat covered body made me realize, I was cold and wet. Wet from sweat and now the shadows were growing long. It was going to get dark quick. Taking stock of my situation, left me trembling with fear and doubt. I had no food (but I wasn't hungry either) or water, (I don't think I could've held it down anyway). I had a lighter but I sure as hell wasn't about to start a fire. I had an image of being surrounded and then summarily executed by the Sandinistas and some commander asking me why I started a fire for them to find me. The only answer I had for them was because "I was cold." Then they would laugh at me and take turns shooting me. Yeah, fire tonight was definitely out. I pushed the thought from my head. I also had two twenty dollar bills in my pocket. What the hell good was that going to do for me? Order pizza? The only reason I had it was a habit I picked up from Dad. Never go anywhere without some money, it might be needed. I didn't think that applied in this situation. Turned out I was wrong about that too. Seemed like I had been wrong about a lot of things today.

I pulled out my 9mm, it was digging into my ribs hard enough to hurt. I looked at it stupidly as if I seeing it for the first time in my life. How the hell did it get there? I don't remember what I had done with it after the initial contact. It had a magazine in it. I dropped it out. Empty, but the slide had been down, indicating I had dropped the slide. In my right pocket I had one loaded magazine. I had no recollection of handling the pistol after we bailed out of the jeep. Quietly I inserted the loaded magazine, chambered a round and returned the loaded gun to my holster. The empty magazine was useless to me as I had no ammo for it. I shoved it down into the dirt and covered it up. Aussie had told me many times that empty magazines were useless to me and not to screw with them, unless there was a chance of resupply, which there wasn't. In fact when Aussie used to have me run reload drills if I tried to catch the magazine, he would throw a rock or dirt clod at me as a reminder. Slipping the magazine out of my H&K, I put in a fresh one. That left me with one plus the one that had been in the gun. I knew it wasn't full, but it was getting darker and I didn't want to unload it to count the rounds I had left. So I had forty some odd rounds for the rifle and fifteen for the pistol. It didn't seem like a lot, but in reality there was no way being by myself, that I would ever have a chance to expend it all. That was a depressing thought. I wondered how much I had shot earlier. I could clearly remember reloading once and I thought a second time. I wasn't sure how many magazines I had come out of the jeep with. Some details were really hazy, I just didn't understand why.

I wondered if the Sandinistas would have trackers? Of course they would and I had not tried to hide my trail. Time to move, and move I did. I started slowly, moving straight away from my line of travel, crawling sometimes, walking on rocks others, my goal being not to leave any tracks. After about half a mile I came to the bottom of a steeper hill, with a rock formation at the bottom. Getting behind the first pile, I could see my back trail. I now had large rocks behind and above me so I was protected from the back, with brush to my right. I leaned up against the rock and tried to sort out what to do next.

Dave had left with Bro. That I was sure of. I had heard the jeep start at some point and race away. But where the hell was Aussie? For that matter where the hell was I? Where should I go? I don't think I could find my way back to the Contras camp. Well maybe in the daytime, follow our tracks back to it. No, walking on roads would be out, I couldn't do that. How long before a shitload of Sandinistas started searching for us? That seemed like the big question, and no good answers were coming from asking it. I was probably still too close. Shit! I had to move, but "when" and "where?" Daytime I would move, but not before then.

"Where" was another question entirely. I needed to figure out where I was and where I needed to go. Digging into my thigh, I realized I had the bottle of penicillin Bro had given me. I took one out, worked up some saliva and swallowed it.

I was studying the terrain in front of me as it grew darker. Trying to memorize it, in case I needed to move or shoot later. I strained to hear anything at all. The forest had been very quiet, but as darkness fell the sounds of the forest started to return. Many animal sounds here I was not familiar with and they occasionally freaked me out, but I grew accustomed to some of them quickly the more I heard them.

Straight in front of me something moved. I froze, watching silently. About 60 yards away, moving from right to left was a large animal. I couldn't see any details or colors. Much too big to be a human, it didn't make a sound. I noticed a little breeze in my face so I knew it wouldn't or couldn't smell me. I wasn't really worried now that I knew it wasn't a person or people. I was armed and figured that even a large predatory animal would be scared of human scent much like back home. I should've paid more attention to finding out what large animals did roam here. It was damn big, whatever it was.

I hoped Bro was alive. Dave too for that matter. I should have run into Aussie though. That really worried me. I couldn't picture him leaving me, and I had a strong feeling he wasn't hurt. Well not any more than what he had been when we separated. He did have a finger shot off, but with Aussie, it was like a minor inconvenience. Me personally, I would be real fucked up over getting my finger shot off.

I returned to thinking about getting out of here. The rebel camp was out. I was sure I couldn't find it in the dark, and trying to back track during the day would be suicidal. Note to self; *"Be looking for people looking for me."* And I damn well better see them first. With my not so good eyes, that meant move slow, look hard, and listen harder. My senses of smell and hearing were pretty acute, just my vision sucked.

Trying to figure out where I was and needed to go returned to my thoughts as I replayed the beginning of the day. We had left the city and headed *south,* and then maybe a little west. When we left the contra camp we had headed another direction, *northwest,* to avoid the road blocks. Which is exactly what we probably ran into, or was going to be one. With this in mind, that meant I should be southwest of the city and when I moved I should go *northeast* to head back towards the city. The one problem with that was the battle or "skirmish" as Dave would call it, was northwest of me. I had to go past it, not close to it, but still, I wouldn't be heading away from where it happened. That concerned me. Then again, maybe that's exactly what I needed to do. I couldn't make up my mind on this for quite some time. After weighing the possibilities of going *way* around it, I came to the conclusion that the longer I stayed out here the better the chance of me getting weak or being discovered, or God forbid, get in another "skirmish." Conclusion: get back to the house. I sat with my back to the rock, with my H&K on my lap, and tried to sleep. Howler monkeys announced that daylight was coming, and for once in my favor, the sun was coming up where it was supposed to. That gave me confidence. Maybe I wasn't such a dumb ass after all. I couldn't believe how much I hurt. Every muscle in my body, from my feet, calves, thighs, stomach, back, chest, neck, and hands were really sore. Effects of the massive adrenaline dump, was my guess. I wasn't injured that I could find. I made a mental note to find out the difference between a "battle" and a "skirmish." It sure as hell fell like a battle to me. In fact, it felt more like a war. I wondered who came up with the differences?

I felt so damned tired and sore. Deciding to rest just a little longer I started to close my eyes. Out of the corner of my eye something moved. Close. Not daring to move anything but my eyes I looked hard right. About two feet away in the brush I could make out about two feet of snake. It was about as big around as a fire hose. It moved again. Adrenalin started to come up in me and I realized a snake of this size had to be a boa. I couldn't see the head or tail. After all I had been through, getting excited about a snake seemed stupid. I just didn't give a damn anymore. Over the next couple of minutes it continued to move away. Damn, it was a big snake though.

Standing up slowly, I took stock of my surroundings, stretched out my sore muscles and checked my H&K and 9mm. I also noticed I stunk. Pretty damned bad too. With nothing I could do about it, I started slowly north east. Seeing small game occasionally reminded me that I hadn't eaten, but I wouldn't dare take a chance of shooting and drawing attention to myself. I would just have to do without. Going hungry was not a big deal. It beat dying. The terrain was mountainous but I could tell I was dropping altitude. About midmorning I came across a small stream. Cupping some water in one hand I raised to my lips as I looked around. The water was cold and sweet. Not realizing how cracked my lips were and how thirsty I had gotten, I set down my rifle and lying on my stomach, I drank up. Catching my breath I drank some more. The temperature was nice so I took off my shirt and rinsed it in the stream to get some of the smell out of it. I was going to wash my pants next but as soon as I got my shirt back on, I became chilled. Screw that. That would have to do. As if conspiring against me, it immediately grew dark and started to cloud up. The ever present rain started twenty minutes later.

The country side started to open up and become less forested I grew even more cautious and scared. Clearings were getting too big to skirt and I was spending more and more time watching instead of moving. Early afternoon and I still had not seen or heard any people or vehicles. I had crossed a few dirt roads with some trepidation though. I would crest a ridge and watch, then drop down, start up the next ridge and repeat. Cresting over one small ridge found me looking at a brushy draw, being fairly thick I kept moving. As I crossed over the top of the ridge I heard movement. I stopped and crouched. Listening harder, I could tell whatever it was, was coming towards me, not fast but not slow either. The breeze was from the side of me so I didn't think it had my scent. Half expecting a small deer or other game animal to appear I was startled to see a denim covered arm reach up and move a branch about ten yards away. It stopped. After a few seconds I heard someone urinating. Finishing her business an old woman stood up and looked directly at me. I stared back, trying to determine my situation. If she was startled, she gave no indication, but she knew damn well what she was seeing. A man with a machine gun was crouching just a few yards from her. I could see the concern in her features but not fear or embarrassment. After staring for a few seconds at each other, I tentatively raised my right hand at her as if to wave. She glanced over her shoulder and looking back at me motioned with her right hand for me to "come." I stood up and as I approached her, she looked at me with appraising eyes. Apparently satisfied, she turned and crooked her finger at me to follow her. She was wearing an old denim long sleeve work shirt that had seen better days and old baggy pants that I would have pictured a hobo wearing. On her feet were dirty black sneakers with holes in them. She was about 5'2" tall, skin and bones and looked about fifty years old going on eighty. Her back was no longer straight, and she walked with the gait of an old woman. Glancing back occasionally she continued to motion for me to follow as she checked on my progress. I dutifully followed along about ten yards behind wondering if I should trust her. About two hundred yards later, we came to a small village, sitting on the edge of a dirt road. More like an encampment really. There were no permanent buildings, shacks and tents the order of the day. Probably no more than fifteen people in the whole place and I saw no children. One old woman stoking a campfire watched us and called to someone inside a tent. An old man poked his head out and watched us walk over to what was obviously the old woman's shack. I tried to appear nonchalant as if a man with a machine gun walking amongst them were an everyday occurrence. Hey I could live with it, if they could. I thought.

Ducking into the door way, I let my eyes adjust to the dimness. It was cooler in here. The place was sort of made into two rooms. With the divider "wall" being a blanket that hung from the ceiling that was stretched about three quarters of the way across the room. An old mattress that I wouldn't dare lay on was in the middle of the dirt floor in the left hand room. Old boards sat on blocks as shelves with some cooking utensils sat behind it along the wall.

The old woman and I stared at each other. Not knowing what to do or say, I sat down cross legged on the floor and laid my H&K across my lap. She continued to stare. I made a motion of eating. "Comida?" I asked trying to communicate. She shook her head. "No dinero." Meaning she had no money. Hell I had money. I leaned back and reached into my pocket and pulled out one of the twenty dollar bills and handed it to her. Her face lit up, and smiled a broken toothed grin. Palming the bill she indicated the mattress, and that I was to rest and stay here and not go outside. She would return with food, later. I hoped. Could I trust her? Maybe I should move to the edge of the village and watch for her return. She kept indicating for me to wait here. As she left I again thought about Bro and Aussie. Bro had to be dead, and the feeling filled me with sadness. The bullet that hit him would have got me in the face if I had not lost my pistol in the floorboard. Not that I wanted to be dead, but it seemed like it was my fault.

Aussie might be dead, but I doubted it. I also felt guilty for not looking for him more before leaving. Dave was, well wherever Dave was. I wondered if he had managed to bury Bro. I started to cry, thinking about Bro and all the things that had led to this. I was really screwed here. The only reason I was still alive and walking was because I was armed, and with guys that knew what they were doing. Without them, I was nothing. I was in a foreign country, where I wasn't supposed to be with very little resources. I couldn't even get to a phone to call Dad or Colter, even if I wanted to. The thought of turning myself in even crossed my mind, although not for very long. That would just end this whole episode, which was what I wanted, but the end would be pretty permanent, prison or death. No sense taking any chances.

18

DESPERADO

My heart beat so rapidly I thought it would give me away, surely they will hear it, adrenalin surged through my body, following the fear that was building inside of me uncontrollably. This was not good!

The three Sandinistas were less than 30 feet away, talking to the old woman who had fed me earlier in the day. My conscious brain trying hard to override my subconscious and keep from puking up the food and warm goat milk, as the "fight or flight" reflexes kicked in with the fear coursing through my body.

I had given her a twenty dollar bill for food earlier, (which she had left with and returned two and half hours later) and I let her keep the change of about seventeen dollars. Then and there twenty dollars went a long way. Apparently it went far enough for her to risk her life for me. She had nothing to drink except goats milk from a pail that was covered by a piece of plywood, that had been sitting in the shade. It was horrible, but the only thing wet there was to be had. No water even close by that I was aware of. I could not understand how people lived this way, even though I did realize, they had no choice. It was survival. Period. Nothing else mattered much. I was beginning to understand this concept in my present situation. In fact, I down right appreciated this whole survival concept!

The Sandinistas were looking for me. Well us, actually. They probably had no idea that we were separated, and that I was on my own.

The cold plastic of the H&K G3 assault rifle was wet from my sweat, or was it tears? I don't really know now. The Sandinistas had their M-16s slung on their shoulders, giving me a little edge. Two were on the left of the old woman, one on the right. Could I get them all? I wasn't so sure. Would I hit the old woman? Did I care if I hit her? It would seem simple enough to shoot all three, before they could get me, but could I? Things like that work well in movies, but in reality, I had no damned idea. Pulling the trigger could mean me dying. Top of my list of things not to do today. Die! Screw that, dying sucked! "DO NOT DIE!" I thought. To this day, that thought crosses my mind on a fairly regular basis. All of these questions and a hundred more spun through my mind at once. I needed to answer the important ones. "Be cool." I told myself. Yeah, right! I was way out of my league and I knew it. This was a "Big Zero" as my pot head friend Brad would have said.

Laying on the cool dirt floor, I wondered how many times it had been swept, so many it was almost, well it was almost clean. It felt clean. And cold. It had been swept so much the floor was probably five inches below the outside ground surrounding the little two room shanty. Pine and juniper limbs sticking out of the ground had been used to hold cardboard up against the limbs with bailing wire, forming the walls. Discarded bread ties or anything else that would hold the walls up and provide protection from the elements had been used. I asked myself why these stupid details were running through my head, not really understanding the effects of fear on a person's mind at that time in my life. Too young to comprehend, but old enough to appreciate the fact I was in real trouble. The events that had led me here were a blur and muddled, it didn't matter anyway, I had to deal with this, this here, now. Besides my pistol, I had one, twenty round magazine lying next to my hand in the dirt, one in the gun, one on my belt. The one on my belt was mostly empty. I would not have time to reload anyway.....it would be over before I got that far, I was pretty sure of that.

Back to the problem at hand. Watching through a gap between the cardboard and a limb, I could see one Sandinista keep looking in my direction. He was the most alert, by far. He also appeared to be the youngest. He would be the first one I would shoot. There was little doubt in my mind, that if this went down, he would die a sudden and violent death. Thirty caliber bullets had no mercy, especially at that range. Another was conversing with the old woman in rapid fire Spanish, the third, alternating between being bored, looking at the shack and occasionally joining in the conversation. The woman was apparently lying through her teeth for me. The Sandinistas had driven up a few minutes earlier in a green Chevrolet pickup, with a 30 caliber machine gun mounted in the bed, simple but effective. I wondered if it was the same pickup from yesterday and the same Sandinistas. Maybe some had survived. Looking at the passenger side of the truck I realized that the day before, I had been looking at the driver's side, when we topped the hill in our jeep and all hell broke loose. It could be the same truck, or a different one. As the Sandinistas loaded back up, and got ready to leave, I knew I would see the driver's side as they turned around to return from the same direction they had come from. If the left side of the truck had bullet holes in it, I just might have to open fire. Fear and a little bit of aggression was building in me. Only now, they were mobile and had a 30 caliber belt fed machine gun. I had screwed up! I should have shot them while they were standing around with their heads up their asses. The truck completed its turn, allowing me to see the driver's side. No bullet holes. Besides that I remembered I had shot up the radiator on the pickup yesterday. It couldn't be the same one. I eased the pressure off the trigger. Opening fire would have been a bad mistake. I could not seem to make good decisions. This sucked!

Apparently they had believed the old woman. Another few minutes of precious life. I was still alive. I needed to calm down. I breathed a sigh of relief and dropped my forehead into the cool dirt floor, my arm and hand still on the stock and grip of the G3. The burning in my face was cooled by my tears.

The old woman, ignoring everything, went back to her chores.

19

CARRY ON WAYWARD SON

It was almost dark now. I needed to move. I had not slept much, too worried that the Sandinistas might return. I asked the old woman in my broken Spanish which way to the city. She pointed northeast. I didn't know how to ask her how far. I left the encampment walking down the dirt road and then moved off to the north of it, by a couple hundred yards trying to keep it in view and still allow myself time to get to cover if needed. About two hours later, I knew I was getting closer. A couple of pickups had come by and I could see the lights from the city. I kept walking. Around daylight I was near the edge of the city. Judging by where the air traffic had come in, I needed to go farther east to get to the house. But I couldn't very well walk into town carrying the H&K. I would have to leave it. The thought filled me with dread. It was getting light fast. Stripping the H&K down, I buried the pieces of it, a few yards apart in a sandy wash. My 9mm would have to do. As I got into the outskirts of town I drew some looks and decided the best thing to do was head for the heavier populated areas in order to blend in better. I hitched a ride at one point, walked some more and after hitching another ride jumped out of the back of a farm truck less than half a mile from the house. My feet were hurting like hell, but the old farmer had let me drink from his water bag in the back of his pickup so at least I wasn't as thirsty as I had been. At 10:00 am, I walked through the back door of the house. I was alone.

Someone had been here though. I could tell that. Not one item was lying out in the open. It looked like it had been cleaned. I called out but no one answered. Moving through the house quickly, I was disappointed to find myself alone. I went to the fridge and popped a beer open. Drinking half of it down, I took out a can of beans out of the cabinet to heat up as I chugged the beer. Setting the bottle down momentarily to open the beans, I remembered my spare credentials. Forgetting everything, I went to the bed room, and lifted Aussie's mattress. His stash was gone; mine was still there, with an addition. Lying next to my passport in the name of Joseph Johnson with four hundred dollar bills tucked into it was something else. Ten twenty dollars bills were arranged in an arrow pointing north. On the bill that formed the point, was writing. It said "Go north." *Aussie!* He was alive and made it out. And apparently he thought I might need more money too as he had left me an additional two hundred dollars. I was so happy I started to cry. I wiped my eyes and gathered up the money and passports and pocketed them immediately.

Back in the kitchen I warmed up the can of beans, and after eating and drinking three more beers, I sat down on the edge of Aussie's bed to relax. Leaning back, exhaustion overtook me and I fell asleep in seconds.

I woke up groaning in pain. I had fallen asleep with my legs hanging off the bed and now by back was screaming for relief. Sore enough that I could not just sit straight up, I rolled over and from my knees, I attempted to stand up, staggering a few steps I fell backward until the wall caught me. It took a few seconds to let my blood get pumping and for me to not bust my ass, I decided I needed to piss. I stumbled to the bathroom bouncing off the walls and cussing. After I relieved myself, I trudged back to the bed room and took off my boots, socks, shirt and finally my pants and sprawled face first into bed. It was dark out and I still felt exhausted. An idea had formed in my head while I was in the bathroom and as I considered it, I fell back to sleep.

When I woke it was still dark, but I was awake. I had been asleep since 10:00am the previous morning, except for the one time I got up and relieved myself. I guessed it was about 1:00am. Turned out it was closer to 3:00am. That meant I had slept almost seventeen hours. I still felt tired but knew I couldn't sleep. Picking up my pants, I quickly decided it was time for a fresh change of clothes. Everything stunk, bad. The pants probably could've walked off by themselves. The shirt and socks had been wet and dried so many times they were ready for the trash. I was feeling pretty ripe too. Gathering up my pocket items, holster, pistol, passports and money I put them into the pair of jeans I kept in the closet. I didn't dare leave anything behind. Taking the clothes into the bathroom with me I started a hot bath and examined my face while it ran. Trying to judge how old I looked was hard for me. I didn't look white. I had a full beard, never got carded, but knew I didn't look thirty. Early twenties was my guess. With that, I pulled a pack of disposable razors that Bro used out of a drawer, lathered up and started shaving. I had never attempted to shave my beard before. This hurt. After two razors and a half of can of shave cream, and turning the bath off, I looked like hell, but was almost done. I grabbed one more new razor and lathered up again. When I was done I reappraised myself. Better. Hair was too long, kind of shaggy, I had worn it straight, down to my eyes and to my collar. I could change that and would take care of it later. Climbing into the bath, I scrubbed up, and soaked for a while. When I climbed out the water was filthy, black in fact. After letting go of the water, I saw there was a considerable amount of dirt in the tub. Bro would've had a fit if he saw it.

I considered the house. Aussie had obviously cleaned it and then some. No dishes had been left out. His bed was made and nothing was "left." No trash in the trash can or dirty laundry or empty beer bottles. Maybe I should do the same. After dressing I pulled all the sheets off of the bed, and along with my dirty clothes, put them all into the trash, bagged it and set it outside the front door. The sun was starting to come up and I decided it was time to move. Grabbing a dishrag, I wiped down everything I could think of that I had touched, although I wasn't sure it was necessary. I carried the trash bag about a block before dropping it off by some other trash cans and walked towards the center of the city. I went through a mental checklist at least six times. I had my pistol underneath my shirt, passport and identification. In my left pocket I had one hundred in twenties, another hundred in twenties in my wallet, and the other four hundred in my right jeans pocket. Looking around as I walked, I realized I was ravenous. Seeing an early breakfast place I walked in and took a table at the back, where I could watch the door. I ordered coffee and my last bowl of gallo pinto. I figured it would be awhile if I ever got it again.

After eating, and drinking more than five cups of coffee, I realized it was still too early for a barber shop to be open. By staying here I would draw attention so I paid my bill and started to walk in the general direction of the airport, taking my time and appearing to shop when I could. Finally I found a barber shop. I realized it would be open shortly but wasn't yet. I didn't want to hang around and look suspicious so taking my time, I circled about three blocks and came back to it. The old man had just unlocked the front door and sat down in his chair to wait for customers as I walked in. He appraised me over his newspaper. He didn't like what he saw. Looking around, it looked much like an American barber shop. Red and white striped pole and one chair inside that probably wouldn't move up and down and was covered in duct tape, but it was a barber's chair. I smiled at the man and pointed at my hair and tried to show him I wanted it cut shorter and parted on the left. When he was done, I paid him five dollars, thanked him and stopped at the mirror on the way out. As I was looking at myself in the mirror, the old man opened a drawer and tossed me a comb to take with me. I had overpaid him and he was being nice. I missed the comb and had to pick the damned thing up off the floor. Thanking him again, he watched me leave. I could see written all over his face that he thought I was a dumbass. I felt like it too, but wasn't sure why. I then realized I looked *too* young to be out around here by myself. That was exactly what I had hoped to achieve with the beard gone and haircut. With that in mind, I found a cab and headed for the airport.

As the cab drove me in, I scanned the area. The Queen Air was gone, I knew it would be, but it was still depressing as hell. Getting out of the cab, I spotted several Sandinistas and damned near had a heart attack. They were standing around joking and smoking and watching the crowds. Resigning myself to the fact I was here and locked in, I got out of the cab after paying and walked straight into the airport without looking at them. I had no bags or luggage. With that in mind, I probably looked less like a traveler than someone stopping in to pick someone up or check on a flight. That might work in my favor, if they were even on alert at the airport.

I should look more like a tourist, I had decided earlier. Heading towards the shops, I wished I had done my shopping prior to coming to the airport. I could feel the Sandinistas watching me. Turning into a shop, I picked up shorts, t-shirts (two), and a small workout bag, along with some snacks. Not that I wanted them, I just wanted to blend in. Turning out of the shops I went to see what flights might be arriving or departing. I needed to leave fast, no way could I stick around here and stay under the radar. I was too worked up. I saw that the earliest flight to the U.S. was not until almost 5:00pm and that was to Miami! I couldn't wait it out that long. As I considered going back to the house, I continued to stare, then I saw it. Mexico City. It was scheduled to leave in forty three minutes. I found the Mexicana counter and bought a ticket.

As I headed for customs my heart was beating faster, and breakfast was going through me. I located the bathrooms and headed for it. In a the stall, I pulled my pants down barely in time to avoid shitting myself as I drew my pistol and set it on the new athletic bag. The restroom door banged open and I could see uniform pants walk in and pause. One of the soldiers had apparently followed me into here. Hearing me vacate my bowels, the Sandinista walked to a urinal and relieved himself, then left. I breathed a sigh of relief. A gunfight in an airport armed with nothing but a pistol would be disastrous. I wasn't ready to give up my 9mm quite yet. Getting caught with it would mean big trouble. Getting caught without it wouldn't be too damned good either.

Finishing up, I re-holstered the pistol and made myself ready to walk out. As I exited, carrying my bag in my right hand, I put my left hand on my stomach as if I had an upset stomach, leaving it close to my pistol. I was plenty scared and starting to get shook so it wasn't too hard to pull that off convincingly. As I turned into the main part of the airport I noticed out of the corner of my eye, two Sandinistas. Both were looking at me and one spoke quietly to the other as they laughed. Another tourist with a case of Montezuma's Revenge, they seemed to think. Good for me. If my luck would only hold out a little longer, I thought. Now I just had to get rid of my damned gun. As I drew nearer to customs I spotted a bar, turning to it, I ordered up a Coke. The man hardly looked at me as I laid a dollar on the bar and sat down. He popped open a can of Coke and sat it in front of me, no glass, no ice. Looking around I saw that the bar was set in a little alcove. To my rear and on each side were columns. Just for decoration probably, but it did shield the view from the main corridor somewhat. Next to one of the columns was a trash can. Setting my new athletic bag on the stool next to me I thought it out. I could unzip the bag, and put the gun into the bag, and then as I turned around dump the gun into the trash can. No, that would look like I was emptying my bag of something, like dope. Bad idea. Then it occurred to me, *don't make this hard.* I sat and watched the crowd, as it thinned out, I picked up my bag with my right hand while holding the empty soda can too and turning away from the bar drew my pistol with my left hand, using the bag for cover to push open the trash can, I dropped the pistol in it and then took the can from my right hand and dropped it in also. I heard the can barely clink against the metal of the gun but at least there had been some trash to cushion the sound of the gun going in. To the casual observer I had just thrown away a soda can. Next I had to get through customs. As I approached, a customs agent indicated for me to hand over my bag. The bastards searched it. What the hell did they think I was? Some damned drug smuggler! I watched closely as if they were going to steal something. The one handling my passport barely looked at me as he stamped it. They didn't even ask me if I had enjoyed my visit. I was through in less than two minutes. Another plane from Mexico City to Juarez had me in El Paso by sundown. A cab ride from downtown to the airport had me in my truck and walking in the front door by 8:00 that night. I was certain I would never see any of Central America again. We were done. At least I was. Of all the things I had experienced on my trips, this had scared me the worst. I still wasn't sure if it was the firefight or the being lost with no resources. I was shook to my core and I knew it. I had a feeling we were all done.

Not wanting to deal with it right this minute, I knew I needed to call Dad. My sister answered the phone, and told me "Dad's been trying to get ahold of you, hang on, I'll get him."

As Dad came to the phone I could hear my sister in the background. "It's Josey, I told you he was fine."

"Hey pard, I been trying to get ahold of you. Where ya been?" Dad asked, I could hear the concern in his voice.

"I've been around Dad. Been having dinner with Jenn a lot."

"I thought you and her weren't seeing each other anymore?"

"Well apparently we're not, *now*. I don't know what the hell she wants Dad, I can't figure her out."

"Watch your mouth. I don't know either. You're too young to get serious anyway." Dad was already bored with this conversation, I could tell.

"What are you doing the next few days?" he asked.

"I was thinking about going up to Colter's. What about you, Dad?"

"Sounds good. I'll meet ya up there. I may have to work, might not. Let me know when you head up, so I won't worry."

Worry? Worry about a 90 mile drive? Easy here. "Okay, Dad. I sure will.

We said our goodbyes and hung up.

I thought about calling Jenn, but what if Dave hadn't made it back it yet. Didn't matter, I supposed. She didn't know that I had left with him. I decided I really didn't want to talk to her. I drove by the house, to see if Dave's truck was back. It wasn't but from the vehicle out front I would guess that Jenn had company. It didn't surprise me in the least and I even surprised myself by not caring to damn much about it either.

I picked up a couple of burritos on the way home, and fell asleep before I could finish the second one. The next morning I woke up thinking about Bro and cried for awhile. After taking a bath, I swung by Dave's (still not home), then went back to the house and called Dad to tell him I was heading to Colter's. Dad was going to have to work after all and couldn't make it. I headed up anyway, and used the time to think.

I found Colter and Samantha at the bar. After working all week, Colter had decided to start playing guitar in the local bar on weekends. He had just started his break when I walked in. "Where the hell ya been? You look good without that scraggly damned beard." He added without waiting for me to answer.

"Colter said you were probably in a Mexican jail somewhere. Were you?" Samantha asked.

I promptly made up a bullshit story about Billy and I being thrown in a Juarez jail. And it sounded like bullshit too. Colter immediately lost interest in the story and bought me a shot of tequila, which is exactly what I wanted on both counts. I didn't feel like playing twenty questions on what I had been doing. I stayed drunk through Saturday and headed home on Sunday.

I got home around noon and I couldn't stand it any longer, I called Dave. Fortunately he answered and I didn't have to deal with Jenn. "Hey, how are you, Dave?"

"I'm fine. How are you?" He sounded happy and relieved. Not waiting for me to answer, Dave continued, always cool. "Do you have time to run me to El Paso sometime today?"

"Yeah, I can do that. What time?"

"An hour's good. Pick me up at 1:30."

"Ok, see you then." We hung up.

I actually had about an hour and fifteen minutes before picking him up, so I used the time to clean up and change clothes. On the way out the door, I reached into the hall closest and took my .380 with me. After all, no sense taking chances.

Arriving at Dave's he walked out just as I pulled up. In the pickup, Dave paused as he looked at me, as if seeing me for the first time. He had never seen me clean shaven before. We headed towards El Paso. The first few minutes were in silence. "When did you get back?" I asked. He answered by asking me when I got back. I told him what had transpired and about me trying to find him, while making my way back to the States, and then about spending the weekend at my brothers.

"Take the exit after next." Was Dave's only response. The first stop was at a bank. Dave went in and came back out with a manila envelope, and handed it to me as he got in. I opened it, and looked inside. It was money. "Count it, if you want." Dave said. "It's all there."

"I'm sure it is. So are we all done?" I asked.

Dave sighed heavily. "Yeah, we're done. But I've got a little surprise for you, and indicated for me to jump back onto the freeway. I had to admit, I felt relieved about it being done. While I might not have been able to stop myself from going down there, all that had transpired could. Plus it gave me a good reason not to look at the fact I may have suddenly become a cowardly chicken shit. Which is exactly how I felt.

I suddenly remembered to tell Dave about getting back to the house, and how I found it. As Dave gave me directions, he informed me that Aussie had in fact gotten out, back to the house, and left. He had been in touch with Dave and had pulled out of the country. Pulled out of the whole damn North and South American Continent, in fact. "You did very well, Joe."

"Aussie said, you two had pretty much finished up. He was out of ammo and tending his wound when you ran by headed south at top speed. He lost some of his finger. Said you passed within fifty yards of him, but he couldn't holler out. Said it was the last he had seen of you."

That sucked. I could've been with Aussie the entire time!

The next bit of information floored me and lifted my spirits, all at once.

"I got Bro out. He's alive too." Dave stated matter of factly.

As Dave gave me more directions, we entered into a lower middle class neighborhood until Dave had me stop in front of a house. Getting out, he indicated for me to follow. I wanted to ask about Bro, but Dave had deflected the question at each turn. Now he had something else going on. This was growing frustrating. Walking up to the door, Dave knocked.

I heard movement and then a dead bolt sliding back, the door cracked open and a large black female stuck her face out, glanced at me and then stared disdainfully at Dave. She looked like she was thinking about killing him. When she spoke it was with a soprano voice that I just knew had to have grown up singing gospel music. "Legardis, (coming out Lee-guide-es) Davey is here with some skinny little white boy. You want's to see them?"

"Bring em on in Sugar Pie." *Bro!*

I positively beamed as the woman opened the door as I rudely walked past her and into the house hurrying towards Bro's voice. Remembering my manners I brought myself up short as the woman shut the door behind Dave, and walked past me giving me a most curious smile. She could tell I was eager. Taking the time to look around the rest of the house I saw that it did not fit with the rest of the neighborhood. It was furnished exquisitely. Leather couches and chairs with oak accents. African relics adorned the walls. They looked authentic. We were led into a bedroom off the main room.

Sitting in a regular hospital bed was Bro. He had a sheet over the lower half of his body and bandages across his huge chest. He had tubes and an i.v. in him, but was sitting up in bed holding a remote control for a television that was sitting on a dresser. Aside from the dresser and the t.v. it looked like a regular hospital room, except for the wood floor. I had to keep myself from running over and hugging him. He smiled and spoke. "Joe! Glad to see you. I see you met my wife, Dolores."

I stuck my hand out for Dolores to shake. "So this is Joe. You said he was little Legardis, but I thought you just meant smaller than you. He is a little bitty thing. Young too. Your Mama know what you're doing, boy? Running 'round with bad men and my Legardis?" I was somewhat taken aback about Dave and Aussie being bad (maybe they were, or one of them anyway) and Bro not being bad, and me being neither, just "little."

The comment made me suddenly realize how young I must've looked without my beard. Now I looked my age, like a teenager, not the young man I usually passed as.

"I expect she does. She's dead Ma'am. Lost her a few years ago."

"How about your Daddy? You got a daddy or any folks, or is they dead too?" I had a feeling I was about to get adopted.

"No, they're alive. They don't know."

"How old are you? Can you even *vote?*" Holy shit, this woman was hell on wheels and now she was looking at me and then at Dave. She seemed concerned for me, I was concerned about Dave. He might not survive her. Dolores was staring at Dave as if she were considering torture prior to killing him. I elected not to answer her and kept quiet for the time being.

I stood there sheepishly. "How ya doin, Bro?" I asked, breaking the silence.

Dolores started in on Dave simultaneously, she had her finger in his face and was backing him out the door while informing him he would burn in hell for the things he had done.

"Good now. Dolores is a nurse by trade. She's taking good care of me. Dave said you and Aussie stayed behind so he could get me out. I got to thank you for that."

I didn't know what to say. *He* was thanking *me?*

"You don't need to thank me, Bro. I should be thanking you. That round would've caught me in the face, if I hadn't dropped my gun in the floorboard."

Bro looked me hard in the eye before answering. "If you hadn't dropped it Joe, you would be dead and I still would've had a sucking chest wound. That bullet would have exploded you're skull and still hit me with some bits of you in me too. Absolutely none of this was your doing, except that you and Aussie fought a rear guard while Dave patched me up and got me out."

In the next room, I could hear Dolores telling Dave *"do not interrupt me"* as she continued to chew him out. I glanced at the door. Bro eyes flicked to the door and back to me. "Don't worry, she's always like this with Dave. She can hold her own."

"I'm sure she can. It's Dave I'm wondering about. She sounds really pissed." I replied.

Bro grinned. "Don't make me laugh, it hurts."

"How did you get out anyway?" I asked.

Bro nodded towards the door. "He called in some friends, after sealing off my lung. Took a little longer than a regular dust off, but it made it. Got me stabilized in El Salvador, then got me to a doctor he knows here, stateside, and Dolores is nursing me back to health. Ain't the first time she's done it." *I had heard a chopper.*

"How about you? Dave said you wasn't with Aussie. How'd you find your way back?"

I gave him a brief run down, skipping most of the bad parts, and about ditching my gun, and Aussie leaving me some extra money.

"What next, Bro?"

"I'm done Joe. At least for now. Dolores ain't putting up with much more of this, and things are too hot down there now. The political climate has changed as Dave would say."

I nodded my head. "You going to be ok, Bro?"

"Hell yes. I didn't do all this just for the excitement. I have money saved, Dolores is an RN. We'll be fine. You I'm worried about. You can't keep this up Joe." I stared at the floor ashamed.

"Look Joe, it's not what you think. You've got the heart, the skills. But this ain't a good kind of life for a young man or an old man for that matter. You got brains, you got your whole life ahead of you, boy. Go get an education. Be a doctor or lawyer, or something like that. You smart enough for it."

I nodded my head. He was right about one thing. I needed a break.

Kind of tired now Joe, I need to get some sleep."

I stepped forward and shook his huge hand, as I choked back a tear. "You take care of yourself, Bro."

Bro looked amused as he said "You too, Joe. Go save Dave from Dolores now. That's one woman that *can* kill him, and I mean that."

Walking out to the truck, Dave said "I never worried about a woman trying to kill me here. Maybe I should."

"Might be a good idea, Dave. You do seem to have a way of pissing people off."

20

OH WELL

The next few months found me without a job, no school to attend and a shitload of money, that I was trying to hide. I didn't really want anything material wise. I didn't want a new car or my own home. I acted like I did just to preserve the appearance of not having a lot of money. It worked.

Internally I was still dealing with the things I had seen and the things I had done. No other boys my age were anywhere close to me emotionally or psychologically. I was fucked up and would be for some time to come. I could be absolutely crazy one day, driving over 100 mph, and have such a dark sense of humor the next, that people would go quiet around me and stare. I knew I wasn't right, but I had no damned idea what to do about it. I bottled it up and shut up. Or I tried to anyway.

Everybody told me to get off my ass and go to work or get a job. I spent some time hard rock mining with Colter. I decided from that experience that I did not want to be a geologist, or a miner. He also got me so drunk one night I had alcohol poisoning so damned bad that I was sick for two days. I had never been that drunk before and haven't since either. I spent some time working road construction. (That didn't work out, in a big way.) Computers were the up and coming thing with something called FORTRAN being all the rage. It wasn't. I fell in and out of love, or so I thought. After losing a job, staying drunk, acquiring a roommate, I finally decided I had some decisions to make. I hadn't been able to decide shit right, forever it seemed. One day while sitting at Colter's I decided it was time to actually make some decisions.

I told Colter I was going for a walk and I started off up the mountain near his house. Topping over the ridge, I sat down in a chunk of bear grass and watched the clouds like a little kid. Thirty minutes later a lone fighter jet screamed up the canyon below me, startling the hell out of me and giving me a good look at the top side of the jet.

Another hour, I had come to the realization, that I wasn't getting married anytime soon, partly due to my lack of maturity. I needed a skill but didn't really know what I wanted to do. I decided I would go over to the college prior to next semester and see what they had to offer. I was leaning towards computers, although I didn't know a thing about them. With that in mind, I headed back to Colter's. I found him in the backyard, looking up the mountain yelling my name.

"Where the hell've ya been?" He asked.

"Just went for a walk."

"Why" he wanted to know.

"I just wanted to." It struck me as funny that I had to justify a walk in the hills. I guess that just wasn't something you did without a reason. Hunting, working, traveling, were reasons. Just because you felt like it was not.

"I was worried about you." Colter said.

Really! Oh, I knew he was telling the truth, I just found it laughable as all get out. I wanted to bust out laughing.

"What's with the shit eating grin?" Colter wanted to know.

"Nothing. Just a nice day, and I'm fine."

Come spring, I went down to the college. Stopping for breakfast, I walked into a small diner. A sassy little red haired waitress with her hair in a perm took my order. She wasn't bad looking by any stretch of the imagination, but her attitude seemed like trouble to me. I ate my breakfast, and went to the college campus.

When I got to the sign up room, it was packed. I got into the back of the line for computer science. A few minutes later a mid-thirties male, with blond hair walked up to me from the front of the room.

"You here to sign up for classes? He asked.

"Yeah." *Why the hell else would I be here.* I thought.

"What subject?" he pressed

"I was thinking about computer science."

"That's the line you're in. It'll take you about three hours. That's my line over there. Criminal Justice Majors. Police Academy. I can have you signed up and out of here in thirty minutes, if you're interested."

I switched lines. This could certainly improve my current skill set as well as give me a heads up on not getting caught in the future. After all, no sense taking chances. I headed back to Colter's. Things would come together soon, I hoped.

I made another trip over to Silver City and found an apartment and had another round with the annoying red head in the diner. She was starting to piss me off with her smart mouth. All I wanted was decent service and a good meal. A date wouldn't have hurt either, but with her attitude, I didn't think that was going to happen.

I started college/police academy training in January. I made squad leader for my second semester. It came easy to me. Tactics were something I had been thinking about for some time and in real world applications. To me it was just common sense.

The red headed waitress continued to be a pain in the ass, even after I married her in November. With her, came a little one year old blonde girl. This turned out to be one of the better decisions of my life.

Dave I haven't seen to this day. Denny's dead. I'm not going into it here. He left behind a good wife and children. Bro and Dolores, I saw one more time. Bro indicated he was moving down south like to Georgia or Mississippi and that was that. I did thank him for all he had taught me and wished him well. Bro seemed to want no reminder of his past life. He just wanted to carry on.

Sometime later, I'm not sure when, I was watching a news cast of the Russians in Afghanistan. In the background according to the newscaster were the simple people who were fighting against the Russians for their homeland. The Mujahideen. Some were on horseback. One with blond hair, towered above the others. With his back to the camera he was walking towards the riders on horseback. I would know that walk anywhere. It was the walk of a warrior. A man with confidence in what he's done and what he's about to do. He swung onto the horses back with ease. His face was covered by a shemagh, and although I couldn't see them, I knew there was a pair of grey eyes, looking out. I didn't even know he had ever seen a horse, much less knew how to ride one. Aussie if you're out there somewhere reading this, well dude, I guess one thing to say is, I owe you two hundred dollars, and would be all too glad to see you again to pay it back and get "pissed." You and Bro both were the best friends a man (or kid) could ever ask for.

After graduating from the police academy, I was still too young to go to work as a cop. I had a family to support and concentrated on that. As time went by, I healed a little and grew as a person. Before too long, the craving for adventure was welling up inside of me. It had never totally gone away, just backed off for awhile. I knew it would have to be satisfied, but that's another story.

AUTHOR BIOGRAPHY

Joseph Johnson survived his teen years (somehow). He's still married to "the Redhead," and they have three daughters. He is an accomplished competitive shooter and firearms instructor.

Made in the USA
San Bernardino, CA
18 March 2015